THE LOS ANGELES PRIVATE SCHOOL GUIDE

BY
FIONA WHITNEY

www.thewhitneyguide.com

9TH EDITION

THE WHITNEY GUIDE

THE LOS ANGELES PRIVATE SCHOOL GUIDE

9th Edition
by
Fiona Whitney

ISBN 978-0-9714677-9-8

Published by:
Tree House Press, Los Angeles, California

Cover Design:
Pam Fitch, Fitch Creative, New York

THE WHITNEY GUIDE
Los Angeles, California

Email: FionaWhitney@me.com
www.thewhitneyguide.com

THIS EDITION IS DEDICATED
WITH LOVE AND THANKS TO THE FOLLOWING PEOPLE:

To my Mum and Dad, who gave me the gift of a wonderful
private school education and who continue to be
my biggest supporters.

To my children, Bevan and Charlotte, who inspire me with their love of
learning and continue to impress me with everything they do.

To Pam Fitch for her creative help.

To Marnie and her kids.

TABLE OF CONTENTS

the
whitney
guide

Dear Parents,

The idea for this Private School Guide began as what seemed like a simple project undertaken by parents every year: the quest for the 'right school' for my child. Like many parents, I was armed with numerous private school directories and brochures and LOTS of opinions from parents who all told me what were the most 'popular schools,' but I wanted to make my own informed decisions. So, I took the parent tours, went on classroom visits, reviewed the literature provided by each school, spoke to other parents, ét voila! "The Los Angeles Private School Guide" was born.

I am now in my fifteenth year at the helm. About six years ago, I published my second book in the Whitney Guide series, "The Whitney Guide: The Los Angeles Preschool Guide", and two years ago I published a third book, this time on public elementary schools, "The Whitney Guide: The Los Angeles Public School Guide".

The more research I did, the more I understood the variety of reasons for parents' school choices (financial, educational, geographical, religious, single, co-ed, etc.), and that all schools are not created equal. Some of our kids need the challenge of a rigorous, college preparatory curriculum which will admit them into the Ivy League colleges, while others will do just as well in a less-structured, creative environment which will prepare them for a smaller, artistic school or an Ivy League college as well. When all is said and done, every child should be in the environment where their talents and strengths can be nurtured. As parents we know this all too well. In my case, I had one child in a private school and the other in a public gifted magnet program. Both kids were very happy and I was only paying one private school tuition!

I wrote this guide in the hope that it would help you focus in on the school(s) that will be the best fit for both you and your child. I have given you an idea of each school's physical setting and philosophy, as well as a more in-depth understanding of its teaching methods and programs. Although no two families will end up with the same short list of schools, I do believe that this guide will save you:

Time – It will help you narrow down the number of places that you visit.

Money – By compiling your own 'short list,' you won't need to apply to nine or more schools at up to a $150 per application, and most importantly:

Frustration – You will find just about everything you've ever wanted to ask someone about a school all in a single book and if there is more you need to know, I am here to help!

Remember, do not feel pressured into selecting the school that others say will 'guarantee' admission to that prestigious university or college. No school can guarantee that. Also, don't be too concerned about getting your child into the most 'popular school' or even the school that is the 'most difficult' to get into (these can change from year to year). Keep an open mind and select the school that best fits your child's needs.

I thought it important to include information about some different types of public schools which include Magnets, Charter Schools, School for Advanced Studies (SAS), Gifted Schools, and Highly-Gifted Schools. I wanted to share some of my findings with you because perhaps, like me, there are parents reading this book who cannot afford to send all their children to tuition-charging ones. I hope this is helpful. I also have written a guide.

Please forgive me if I have left out a school that one of your children attended, or a school that you've heard good things about. I would love to know about it for a future edition.

I have tried to keep the information current. Each year I do my best to update information in the body of each review, but this is not always possible, so feel free to e-mail me at: **fionawhitney@me.com** with any comments, suggestions or information that you feel would make this a more useful guide for you as parents.

You can also find information about my School Guide Consultation Service, which I offer to parents, by visiting **www.thewhitneyguide.com**

Best of luck in your search!

Fiona Whitney

Note: The reviews given are based solely on my opinions and the information given to me by the schools. Tuition was fact-checked at the time of publication.

STARTING FROM SCRATCH

First, answer these questions:

1. How much are you willing/able to spend on a private school?
2. How far are you willing to drive to and from school?
3. What method of teaching best fits your family philosophy?
4. Are you looking for a school that offers scholarships? Financial aid?
5. How much research are you going to be able to do yourself on each school versus listening to what other parents tell you?
6. How many schools do you feel you need to apply to in order to find the right one?
7. How much homework do you want given to your child each night?
8. What are your social/academic expectations?
9. Religious beliefs?
10. Co-ed versus single-sex education?
11. Diverse ethnic population?

This should narrow the choices considerably for most families. I saw many schools in my travels that I was crazy about, but when it came down to that 45 minute drive in the morning, I was not willing to be on the road for an hour and a half per day (not to mention how tedious the drive would be for our children).

Make a list of the schools in your desired area and price range. The next thing to ask yourself is, "What is our family's educational philosophy?"

There are traditional, progressive, and developmental approaches to education, and more recently you will find a blend. Defining your preferred philosophy is a very important step because when you aren't in sync with the way a school is instructing your child, you will be engaging in a tug of war that can drive both you and the school crazy. Also, when children pick up on your dissatisfaction, it is likely to negatively affect their feelings about the school.

If you're well versed in the different approaches to teaching, you're in luck! You will find most of what you need to know in the school brochure about the philosophy of the school, and you can skip the next section.

If not, read these brief overviews to see how they sound to you. Use the handy worksheet that I've provided for you to keep track of all the schools that feel right for your child. Then visit as many of the schools on your list as possible. First impressions are usually going to help you make your final decision.

TRADITIONAL

Many parents feel comfortable with traditional schools because it is what they know. Most parents with school-age children went to traditional schools because there were no other alternatives at the time. In addition, they are more confident with a no-nonsense approach. The traditional approach is structured and teacher centered rather than child centered. Children will be expected to sit at desks; there will be times for all activities such as reading, math, art and science; and each week will follow the same schedule.

Academics are stressed in a traditional school, and children are often graded for their work (although there has been a trend recently to hold off grading until fifth or sixth grade). Parents choosing a traditional educational approach will often remark that they feel comfortable knowing their child will have a strong foundation in the three R's: reading, writing and arithmetic. They enjoy seeing a steady flow of papers and homework assignments from which they can chart their child's progress.

Although children from all different types of school go on to college, parents that choose a traditional school feel confident that their child will be as prepared as they can possibly be when making the transition from high school to college.

Progressive and Developmental approaches advocates passionately disagree and believe that students from traditional schools are so burned out from years of academic pressure, tests, and deadlines that they can barely face four years of college.

We all must judge for ourselves and try to pick the teaching method that we think will best fit our child.

DEVELOPMENTAL

This philosophy of education is based on the work and teachings of (among others) Stanley Hall, Arnold Gesell, and Jean Piaget, who studied the process of human growth and identified its stages and norms for those stages. They gave credence to the "reading readiness" notion that maintained that a child would not learn to read until the appropriate stage in development had been reached. They believe that each child develops at a different rate, and one would no more expect a child to read before he's ready than to try to make a six-month old baby walk when its body is simply not developed enough for the task.

In a developmental school, the environment is more flexible, and more emphasis is put on developing social skills. Children are often taught in multi-age groups such as:

- Group 1: 5-7 year olds
- Group 2: 7-9 year olds
- Group 3: 9-11 year olds

In this way, a child not quite ready to move to the next group can stay with the same class for an extra year. This allows each child the experience of being both the youngest in a class of older children that he can learn from and also give him the chance to be a leader when he becomes the oldest in the class.

The developmental system makes allowances for the individual. The multi-age structure mirrors the kinds of relationships found in a family where one child is the leader, one the peacemaker, another the baby. This structure allows children to move through all these stages and play the various roles as they move from group to group. They learn to get along with others and to work together in a non-competitive way. Things you will hear (and probably see) at a developmental school are that the kids love coming to school, they work out their problems with words and logic, and they don't burn out. Instead, they develop a great love of learning.

PROGRESSIVE

The progressive approach is often confused with the developmental philosophy because they share some of the same beliefs. The progressive approach to education however, is a very specific one, quite different from any other. It is based on the philosophies of John Dewey, who believed that the educational process must begin with, and build upon, the interests of the child. The child's education must provide an opportunity for the interplay of thinking and doing in the child's classroom experience, and the school should be organized as a miniature community. In a progressive education, the teacher should be a guide and co-worker with the pupils, rather than a taskmaster assigning a fixed set of lessons and recitations. The goal of education is the growth of the child in all aspects of his/her being. Dewey has written extensively on the subject of education. If this approach sounds right for your family, it would be advisable to read more of his teachings on your own.

Children in a progressive school are taught about the world around them in a practical and hands on way. They study the community. They go out and visit the kinds of places they are learning about such as the county court system, the grocery store or the Department of Water and Power. They come back to the classroom and discuss what's going on in the world and they get wood and tools and construct a scaled-down version of what they have seen. Usually the structure will take up the entire room. If it's a grocery store, then one person will be the manager, another the cashier, another the supplier of produce to the store and of course customers! They will find out through creative discussion and play what possible problems they can run into operating a grocery store and will work together to solve those problems.

In a progressive education, there is a focus on treating children with respect: students are expected to be responsible for themselves. They make their own lunches at home, they are expected to remember to bring items from home for various projects without depending on parents to remind them, and they are encouraged to work on areas where they are weak, rather than areas where they already excel. For example, a student who has a natural talent for math will not be given extra attention and advanced instruction in that subject. Instead the teacher might say, "You seem to have this mastered, so how about working on this painting for our restaurant, or on these buildings for the earthquake preparedness project." The idea is that we should be well-rounded people, that we should fit into our environment in a practical way, working together to solve problems rather than focusing on the individual as a separate entity.

Children are divided into multi-age groups and in the case of developmental schools, often stay with one teacher for several years before moving to the next group. There is a major emphasis on building with blocks. Many skills are learned in constructing block projects by working together, problem solving, and understanding basic math in practical settings (such as a grocery store) where things have to be budgeted, bought, and sold.

Field trips are an important part of the progressive program. Students don't work out of text books. They learn to read when they feel ready, some as young as three or four, others at eight-years-old. Parents should not expect to see graded papers coming home or a log book of homework assignments. What they will see (hopefully) are self-assured, independent children who ask a lot of questions, take responsibility for themselves, are excited about learning, and work well with others.

THE MONTESSORI METHOD

The Montessori Method is a developmental approach to learning devised by Dr. Maria Montessori. She was Italy's first female physician who developed educational materials and methods based on her belief that children learn best by doing and not passively accepting other people's ideas and preexisting knowledge.

The main points of the Montessori Method are:

- Learning should occur in a multi-age classroom where children can learn from each other.
- The teacher is a 'guide' to help the student develop into an autonomous individual, competent in all areas of life and not merely someone with the 'correct' answers.
- Children are allowed to work at their own pace. I asked one twelve-year-old what he thought the biggest difference was between the gifted magnet he had been attending and the Montessori school he was at now and he said, without hesitation, "I don't have to wait for everyone else to finish." If your child tends to work at either an accelerated or a slower pace, this way of teaching could be very helpful.
- The class should be set up according to subject areas and children are allowed to move around the room freely.

Personally, I've found the Montessori Method extremely beneficial for many children I know. There is however a common criticism that some Montessori students 'don't test well' and might not be prepared for more traditional schools. I haven't found this to be the case at all.

THE WALDORF SCHOOLS

These schools are based on the philosophy of Rudolph Steiner, who believed that "man once participated more fully in spiritual processes of the world through a dreamlike consciousness but has since become restricted by his attachment to material things. The renewed perception of spiritual things required training the human consciousness to rise above attention to matter. The ability to achieve this goal by an exercise of the intellect is theoretically innate in everyone."

At a Waldorf school no textbooks are used. Children 'write' their own books on various subjects through teacher dictation, and thus they learn to write and edit as they go. When a child starts out in kindergarten it is a non-academic program, they will not be learning letters or numbers or anything of the kind. In the first grade, your child will meet the teacher who will 'graduate' with the student from grade to grade. The school that I visited went up to the sixth grade. The teacher spends six years teaching the same group of students, then takes a year off. The following year, the teacher will start with a new group of first graders, and continue with them for six years. The theory believes that it is more comfortable for the child to have the same teacher throughout his primary school training. In September, the class simply picks up where it left off in June with all relationships already established.

Art instruction is offered using a dictation method. The teacher will stand in the front of the room and step-by-step instruct the children on how and what to draw. Watercolor is a predominant form of art expression in a Waldorf school. The rooms are filled with the works of the children, all paintings addressing the same subject and looking like the same picture done in slightly different styles.

Math is taught using dance and clapping rhythms. The Waldorf method incorporates art, dance, and music in teaching all subjects.

THE CARDEN METHOD

Mae Carden believed that, "The purpose of education is to teach individuals to think and to develop good judgment. The acquisition of these skills relies on a thorough curriculum that interrelates all subject matter in a sequential manner and is continued from grade-to-grade." Here is an excerpt from a pamphlet handed out during my tour of a Carden School:

> Miss Carden's phonetic approach begins in kindergarten with the alphabet, teaching consonants, vowels, and their sounds. Beginners read by turning letters into sounds and spell by converting sounds into letters. They become sure footed as this method becomes automatic, free, and easy.

> Comprehension, the intellectual character of learning, is emphasized in keyword and outlining training, constant vocabulary study, and grammatical sentence analysis. The Carden system enables the child to read rhythmically, with proper phrasing and to write satisfactory compositions at each grade level. The Carden arithmetic workbooks follow the same successful approach: thorough analysis and steady practice.

Even after visiting the school, I was a bit confused. One teacher tried to explain the method to me. She picked up a Carden book and showed me that it had no pictures, explaining that the children must learn to recognize letters and words without using a picture as a crutch.

The teacher tried to be helpful but explained that to understand the Carden method, one really had to experience it. The teachers are trained at a special Carden school. The method is not something you can pick up a book about in a library, it is exclusive to the Carden program. The best advice I can offer is to visit a Carden school, sit in on a class, and ask a lot of questions.

WHICH METHOD SUITS MY CHILD?

This is a question I heard from many puzzled parents. To answer it, simply think about your child and try to imagine him/her in the atmosphere of the school or schools you are considering.

Does your child thrive in a structured environment, and like to be singled out for his/her efforts? If so, he/she would probably do well in a more traditional setting. A child who cannot take confinement (as in sitting at a desk for varying periods of time) and needs more freedom in his/her daily work would probably do well in a more developmental program. Of course, it is impossible to give an exact formula for picking an approach for your child. These suggestions are offered to give you an idea of the kinds of questions to ask yourself.

Picking the right environment for your child takes time and consideration. Don't worry if the right answer does not come to you immediately. Visit a few places, and use your instinct and intuition about whether or not it is a place in which he/she would do well in. Ultimately, most children will thrive in a well-run school with interested, involved, well-trained teachers, no matter what the method.

Last, but not least, decide which teaching approach you as parents are most comfortable with. It is very important for parents to be in sync with the philosophy of the school. If not, you'll spend too much time in the school office asking them to explain why they are teaching in a particular way.

VISITING THE SCHOOL

Once you have narrowed down the choices, make a list of the schools you would like to visit. Most schools start offering parent tours in September for those interested in admission for the following year.

Schools that are smaller or less in demand will often be willing to give you a tour at any time of the school year. A school that doesn't have a line of applicants waiting to get in sometimes makes people wary. If you encounter this situation, please try to keep an open mind. Just because a school is not 'in vogue' does not mean that it won't offer an excellent education.

The best time to call is mid-morning after everyone has had his or her coffee and is ready to get down to business. Try not to call the admissions office from 2:00 PM because the school staff is usually dealing with dismissal at that time. Sit down with your calendar in hand and make those calls. Ask to speak with someone in Admissions and write down the names of the people you speak to along the way. Take good notes, even the little things that don't seem important enough to write down. You may think you'll remember minor details, but if you forget you don't want to have to call back repeatedly.

These days nearly all the admission steps are done online. Some schools allow you to tour before you submit an application, others want the application first. If they want the application first, make sure it's a school you really are interested in as these application fees can really add up!

Tours usually start between 8:00am and 10:00 am. Some are very simple and straightforward, while others go on for hours as parents stretch the question and answer time with questions like, "What if my six-year-old feels more comfortable sucking on his pacifier in class?"

Tours for the upper schools usually take place on weekends in the afternoon and are well organized and finish promptly on time. Sometimes schools will have Open Houses on the same day and that's when it's important to find out if there is more than one Open House for a particular school so you can see all the ones you are interested in.

QUESTIONS FOR THE SCHOOL VISIT

There are many questions here that you may not have thought to ask and many that may or may not be important to you. Many of the questions will be answered in the school literature. Here is a list of questions that we have collected in our travels. It might be helpful to circle the ones that you feel are important and take the list with you to the school Open House tour.

SCHOOL PHILOSOPHY
1. How would you describe your school's philosophy?
2. Is the school affiliated with any religion or religious institution?
3. Do the children attend church, chapel, or temple?
4. What kind of service is it?
5. What holidays does the school observe?
6. Does the school have a community service program?
7. What is the school discipline procedure/policy?

ACCREDITATION
1. Is the school accredited by The California Association of Independent Schools and/or The Western Association of Independent Schools?
2. If not, why?
3. Does the school have any special memberships and/or affiliations?

SCHOOL BOARD
1. Is the school run by a Board of Directors?
2. How many of the Board Members are parents?
3. What kind of roles do parents play in the running of and decision-making process of the school?
4. How much involvement does the school want?
5. How does one become a board member?

HEADMASTER/PRINCIPAL
1. How long has the current headmaster been at the school?
2. Does the school have any plans to change headmaster in the next two years?
3. Questions for the headmaster:
   - Please describe your educational background.
   - Please describe your employment history.
   - What are your hopes/plans for the future of the school?
   - How would you describe the ethnic/socio-economic diversity of the school?
   - If the school is not ethnically diverse, do you have any plans to make it more so?

TEACHERS
1. What is the teacher-to-student ratio?
2. What credentials are your teachers required to have?
3. How many of the teachers have been with the school for more than ten years? Five years?
4. What percentage of the teaching staff is Male? Female?
5. Does the school require/encourage teachers to take part in ongoing educational seminars/workshops?
6. Are the teachers allowed to create their own curriculum, or do they strictly follow the curriculum set up by the school?
7. Are the teachers trained to work with children who have learning differences such as Attention Deficit Disorder (ADD), Attention Deficit Hyperactivity Disorder (ADHD), Asperger's, or Dyslexia?

PHYSICAL ENVIRONMENT

1. How long has the school been at its present site?
2. Does the school own or lease the buildings?
3. If leased: how long is the lease, and does the school have a renewal option?
4. Does the school have plans to expand or renovate the campus in the next five years?
5. If so, how much of the financial burden will be on the parents?
6. Does the school have a bus program?
7. Are the rooms air conditioned?
8. Is there a nurse on duty?
9. How many books are in the school library?
10. Does the campus have a gym, theater, athletic field, computer lab, science lab, kitchen, swimming pool?
11. How often do the children work with Laptops/Personal Tablets/Computers.

GRADING/CONFERENCES

1. How are the children graded?
2. How many times per year are reports sent home?
3. How many parent-teacher conferences are scheduled per year?
4. Is it possible to schedule extra conferences with the teacher as needed?

BEFORE AND AFTER-SCHOOL CARE

1. Does the school offer before-and-after school care?
2. What are the hours?
3. How much does it cost?
4. Are there any after-school programs available, such as gymnastics, dance, karate?
5. Is the library open and staffed before and after school?

THE SCHOOL DAY

1. What are the school hours?
2. Is there a hot lunch program?
4. How is the school day structured?
5. Do specialist teachers come to the classroom, or do the children go to them?
6. Are foreign languages taught?
7. How many times per week will my child have: art, computer, music, foreign language, library, physical education?
8. At what age is reading taught?
9. Does the school use the phonetic or whole language approach?
10. How much homework will my child have each day?

THE ARTS

1. Does the classroom have a separate studio for art, or is it done in the classroom?
2. Describe the music program.
3. Does the school have a chorus?
4. What instruments are available/taught?
5. Does the school have an orchestra?
6. Describe the school art program.
7. What portion of the art program is dedicated to art theory?

GIFTED CHILDREN & CHILDREN WITH SPECIAL NEEDS

1. Is the school open to children with physical handicaps?
2. Does the school have programs for gifted children?

3. If a child is gifted in a particular area such as math or reading, are there accelerated programs to offer him/her?

SPORTS PROGRAMS
1. Describe the physical education program.
2. What sports programs are available at the school?
3. How many times per week?
4. Does the school host team sports that compete with other schools?

FIELD TRIPS
1. How often do students take field trips?
2. Where are some of the places that students have gone in the past?
3. If buses are used, are they always equipped with seat belts for each child?
4. What is the average cost per family for an overnight field trip (ask for an example from a prior year)?

YEARLY EVENTS
1. Please describe the yearly events/festivals hosted by the school. For example: School Fair, theatrical productions, student concerts, Halloween parade, Christmas pageant, parents' ball and/or a dinner dance fundraiser.

PARENT INVOLVEMENT
1. How much parent participation is required?
2. How many parent-run fundraisers take place each year?
3. Are parents welcome in the classroom to assist, i.e., on a daily basis, for special projects?

SCHOOL HISTORY
1. How long has the school been operating?
2. Is the school a for-profit or a non-profit organization?
3. Please give a brief history of the school.

EARTHQUAKE/FIRE PREPAREDNESS
1. Does the school use a phone tree for emergencies?
2. Please describe the school's Earthquake Preparedness Plan.
3. Have the school buildings been bolted?
4. Are the windows upgraded with shatterproof glass?
5. Do the students practice earthquake/fire drills regularly? How often?
6. What supplies does the school have on hand in the event that the children have to remain on campus?

SECURITY
1. How does the school maintain campus security?
2. Is there a security guard at the school?
3. If so, during what hours?
4. How do you screen people entering the campus?
5. Describe the drop-off and pick-up procedure.

APPLICATION PROCESS
1. What is the deadline to submit an application?
2. What is the Date of Birth (DOB) cutoff for kindergarten applicants?
3. Are there any nursery schools that feed into this school?
4. How many applications in the grade you are applying for did you accept last year?

5. How many openings in that grade were there last year?
6. Of those openings, how many were taken by siblings of children currently attending the school?
7. What is the school policy regarding sibling acceptance?
8. What is a child required to know to be prepared for kindergarten?
9. How does the school decide which children to admit?
10. If a family is wait-listed, what are the odds of acceptance for the Fall school year?
11. Are there scholarships or financial aid available?
12. Most independent schools require applicants for grade 6 on up to take the ISEE (Independent School Entrance Examination). Does yours?
13. Are teacher recommendations and student transcripts required for my child?

WHERE DO THEY GO?
1. What schools do your graduates attend: Junior High School, High School?
2. Last year how many students applied to (pick or fill in your favorite): Harvard Westlake, Brentwood, Marlborough, Oakwood, Crossroads, Campbell Hall, Buckley, etc.?
3. Of those applicants, how many were accepted?
4. Do you have a list of colleges that your graduates have attended in the past five years?

QUESTIONS OFTEN ASKED AT DEVELOPMENTAL/PROGRESSIVE SCHOOLS
1. Since my child won't be bringing home papers, how will I chart his/her progress?
2. We may have to move in a few years, how will my child make the transition if there is only a traditional school available?
3. Do you ever use textbooks?
4. It sounds like my child will be having a lot of fun here, but will she/he actually be learning reading, writing, arithmetic?
5. How do children get along in a multi-age classroom?
6. Aren't the older kids bored?
7. When do you start giving tests?
8. What secondary schools do your students get into?
9. What high schools do your students go to after they graduate?
10. How do your students do in high school with its strenuous study requirements?
11. Do your students have trouble making the transition?

The question and answer portion at some schools is long and thorough, but it varies from school to school. Make sure you get answers to the questions that are important to you.

Usually administrators are happy to explain all aspects of the school to you, but not always. I have heard them get defensive when asked about things like teachers' salaries, their educational backgrounds and why huge, school-financed homes are being built for the headmaster. Ask anyway!

HOW SCHOOLS EVALUATE YOUR CHILD

LOWER GRADES

TESTING AND 'PLAY DATES'

After an application has been submitted and a family member has toured the school, the admissions department must whittle down the number of children applying to fit the number of spaces available. One of the ways they do this is by testing and observing children in small groups.

Traditional schools like John Thomas Dye and Buckley will test the children's academic knowledge. For instance, they may be asked to write their names, recite the alphabet, and to name individual upper and lower case letters on sight. Many schools use the Stanford Binet IQ tests*, even at the Kindergarten level. They may also use Gesell, a kindergarten readiness test.

The admissions staff will often observe the children in a social setting, and this is usually referred to as a 'play date.' A number of children will be invited to the school to play together in a classroom setting. They may then be observed (without parents present) drawing, using manipulative toys like blocks and Legos, and lining up for snack time. Often they are also observed in an open play yard, running and climbing on outside play equipment.

The school staff will take note of the child's small and large motor skills, the social development of each child, and their particular personality types, (i.e. some are shy, others outgoing, comical, etc.). The goal of most schools is to find a good blend of personalities, diversity and an equal number of boys and girls. Traditional schools often want everyone at around same learning level, although as time goes on they will separate kids into different groups according to their abilities. Developmental and Progressive schools are more open to accepting children learning at different levels right from the beginning as they will often put two grades together to start out.

Here are some suggestions to keep the 'play date' less nerve racking:
1. Relax. If your child senses that you're uptight, then he will get tense and won't be able to be himself.
2. Dress your child casually. Let him wear his old sneakers and his favorite shirt. If you dress your child in brand new duds, he will get the feeling that this is a 'Big Deal,' and it will add to his nervousness.
3. Make sure that your child gets a good night's sleep the night before.
4. Be on time! Allow plenty of extra time to get to the school, especially if it is your first time driving there.
5. Remember, your child is more important than any admissions committee. If your child is clinging to you or you see that he's very uncomfortable, tend to his needs first and don't worry about who's watching or what they might think.

The play date usually takes place in a kindergarten room filled with toys and activities that will captivate most four and five-year-olds. It can last from one to two hours during which time the children are often served a light snack. After everyone has arrived and the children are acclimated, the parents are directed to a waiting area where they are served coffee and pastries while an administrator answers their questions.

Meanwhile the children are being observed for the following kinds of behaviors:
- How well they get along with others.
- Do they share?
- Which ones are "leaders?" Which ones are "followers?"
- Who is the "shy" one? Who is the "friendly" one?
- Do they push to get a seat at the snack table, or do they hang back and wait for an opening?

Your child will usually be asked to draw, cut out, and perhaps write his name while the teachers on hand take note of his small motor development. The play date will often include some outside play activities so that your child's large motor skills can be evaluated, i.e. running, jumping, swinging. There may be a private interview where your child is asked a series of questions to evaluate developmental level.

It is often intimidating and upsetting to know that our small children are being evaluated with an IQ test just to gain acceptance to kindergarten. Often the schools will let you sit quietly in the corner while it's going on. A trained specialist will take out some props such as shapes and pictures and ask your child questions like:

"Which one of the dogs on this page is different?" or
"Can you fit these two triangles together to make a square?"

It can go on for fifteen or twenty minutes during which time you'll have to resist the urge to whisper "You know THAT one!" from your folding chair across the room.

Below is an example of a test used to evaluate children at the pre-K and kindergarten level.

SAMPLE INTERVIEW QUESTIONS

1. What has wings?

2. What has wheels?

3. Tell me the color of:
   • an apple
   • a banana
   • grass

4. Which is bigger?
   • A dog or a cat?
   • A cow or a pig?
   • A man or a boy?

5. What time of the year do we go swimming?

6. What time of the year does it snow?

7. What is ice when it melts?

8. What makes a cloudy day bright?

9. If today is Monday, what day will tomorrow be?

10. What makes day warmer than night?

11. How do we hear?

12. What are your eyes for?

13. Mother is a woman; father is a _____?

14. A fire is hot, an ice cube is _____?

15. An airplane goes fast, a turtle goes _____?

16. How many feet does a dog have?

17. What are these made of:
    - cars
    - chairs
    - shoes

18. What is a key for?

19. Where does meat come from?

20. How many squares do you see?

21. Repeat: 3725 _____ 4531 _____ 8694 _____

22. Define:
    - apple
    - rain
    - to whisper
    - to chase
    - elbow

23. Letter recognition: B   L   Y   D   __ __ __ __
                          d   f   t   e   __ __ __ __

24. Numbers: 5 3 7 4 1   __ __ __ __ __
                8 6 2 9 5   __ __ __ __ __

25. Perception: The child will be shown pictures of items and asked to identify them:
    - chair
    - moon
    - flower
    - table
    - doll
    - box

26. Point to the picture that shows what we use when it rains:
    - umbrella
    - shovel
    - bike

27. Point to the picture that shows what we ride in:
    - car
    - dog
    - chair

In addition, the child may be asked:
    - to follow multiple directions
    - to recognize shapes and colors
    - to count objects pictured on a page
    - to write his/her name
    - to recite his/her address and phone number
    - to demonstrate skills with paper and scissors

Each school is different, some are informal and require only general information, while others are specific about what skills they are looking for.

* The Stanford Binet IQ test is used by schools to measure what is generally considered intelligence. The concept of IQ, or "Intelligence Quotient" was first introduced by French psychologist Alfred Binet in 1904. The "quotient" refers to Binet's definition of IQ (Mental Age) divided by (Chronological Age) or M.A./C.A. This quotient is then multiplied by 100 to make it a whole number.

The Independent School Entrance Exam (ISEE®) is an admissions exam used for entry to many independent, private and boarding schools in the United States. The ISEE® is developed and administered by the Educational Records Bureau (ERB).

The ISEE® has three levels:

    Lower level: for grades 5 & 6 entrance
    Middle level: for grades 7 & 8 entrance
    Upper level: for grades 9, 10, 11 & 12 entrance

All levels consist of five sections: Verbal Reasoning, Quantitative Reasoning, Reading Comprehension, Mathematics Achievement, and an unscored 30-minute essay sent to the applicant's school.

The ISEE® is intended to measure a student's ability to learn as well as assess a student's strengths and weaknesses in mathematics and reading.

Students should begin ISEE® preparation at least 3-5 months before taking the exam since unlike the SSAT®, they can only take the ISEE® once in a six-month period. This means that it is important for a student to test well when they first take the ISEE® since they will not have a second chance during the same admissions period. Schools typically request students take the ISEE® between October through January the school year prior to the intended matriculation year.

For information and to receive a student guide:

Educational Records Bureau
220 E. 42nd St.
New York, NY 10017
(800) 989-3721 x 312
www.iseetest.org

TIP: Make sure your child is familiar with the format and the scoring card (and pencils are well sharpened). It's also important to make sure they have had a proper breakfast and are well-rested and have an appropriate snack (no Twinkies!)

Other schools require a HSPT (High School Placement Test). The HSPT® is a comprehensive placement test for eighth graders for placement in the ninth grade. It provides a maximum of information in only one morning's testing time. The HPST® is published in two forms: the Closed Form and the Open Form.

Each year, STS publishes a new form of the Closed HSPT®. The contents of our tests are based on select items which have been piloted and studied to determine their effectiveness. Piloted test items are later introduced into the rotation of forms to help ensure testing integrity.

For most applications, you need Teacher and Head of School Recommendations. Your child may need to complete an essay, or fill out a questionnaire, so the Admissions Committee can see if your child is a good fit for the school.

PRIVATE SCHOOL COUNSELING

I was born in London and was educated at two of England's finest private schools. I moved to Los Angeles right after college and have never looked back! I have brought a lot of my own personal experience living in the world of private schools in England and have successfully created a business in helping parents find the right school for their children.

I have been offering my Private and Public School Consulting Services for over fifteen years and am the author of three books that are updated regularly. I will personalize my service to fit your family's individual needs. Some families might only need a one-time phone or in-person consultation just to set them in the right direction. Others may wish to retain my services from start to finish or anywhere in between. This may include setting up private tours, helping you with your applications, managing critical dates, interview preparation, and child prep (see P & Q's on page 22).

Often, after having sifted through mountains of materials parents can find themselves even more confused than they were before! There are so many choices, but don't worry I can help. I can also save you many precious hours by doing a lot of the research myself. With my extensive knowledge of the schools here in Los Angeles, I know how best to get your questions answered.

Here are some of the ways that I will be able to help you:

- I will help you understand the various school teaching methods.
- I will help you decide on which method feels right for your family by either talking it through with you or setting up a number of private tours in which I will accompany you.

- I will tell you your best Kindergarten/Elementary/Middle and High School options once I have spent time with you and your child and got to know you all.

- I will discuss public versus private and give you options and advice on how to navigate both.
- I will give you insight into the 'total' cost of a private school as there are many hidden costs that you don't see at first.

- I will tell you the difference between a charter school, a magnet, a gifted magnet, and a school for advanced studies and how to apply to them and have the best possibility of getting in.

- I will talk about the realities of commuting to school in Los Angeles and different ways in getting children to school, as many schools have introduced bus routes.

If you choose to retain me, I will help you get into one of LA's top private schools using my strong sense of instinct and the good relationships I have created with the Admission Heads and Heads of School. My reputation has been built on making good matches.

RELOCATING FAMILIES

I have also become well known for helping families relocate from other parts of Los Angeles, California, The United States, and indeed, the world. If you are a family relocating for business reasons or are not happy at the school you are currently at, don't despair as this has become one of my specialties. Of course I love it when you come to me in a timely fashion but I know how life is and can help place your children in one of Los Angeles' top private schools (sometimes just weeks before school starts!). I will only work with clients and their children who I believes would be an asset to a top notch school.

Consultation Appointments available upon request by contacting Fiona directly at **fionawhitney@me.com**
Or by visiting my website at **www.thewhitneyguide.com**

A MODERN MANNERS COURSE

First there was Cotillion... now there's P's & Q's! The P's & Q's Modern Manners Course was designed to prepare your child (ages 4 and up) for entering a top-notch private school. As we all know these schools are highly competitive and the admissions process is rigorous. Learning to conduct yourself properly and having good manners is a vital skill that can often get your child to the "top of the pile". We are giving your child the tools to make sure they make the best impression possible.

We also spend time working with each child using K-readiness tests that are designed to measure a child's ability to succeed in an academic setting in a variety of ways depending on the school. These include: language, knowledge, memory, mathematics, spatial skills, large and small motor skills, cognitive abilities, and speed of thinking

The course is broken down into ongoing 90-minute sessions. We look for strengths and areas that need improvement. We use specialized lesson plans to develop those areas, which we have found really does help prepare the child for school, depending on their age and what grade they're applying for. During each session we make a point to talk to your child at a more advanced level to encourage conversational skills. We really take the time to explain new concepts and words, and generally try to surround them with language and laughter. All our children leave happy!

We relate the materials in our worksheets to objects and events in your child's life to help them practice real life applications. There are a lot of 'what' and 'why' questions. Last but certainly not least, we really focus on their listening skills and how they respond.

Welcome Manners
Generally we start the lessons with an informal conversation held in the sitting room that covers all manner of topics to see how well they engage. It is here that they learn how to sit properly and make a meaningful connection using eye contact and their words.

Class Is in Session
We then move into more of a classroom setting where we work on personalized lesson plans. We are always looking to see how the child can hold their focus, behave and where they are intellectually. Hand writing is an important part of the work we do with them, recognizing letters and numbers and helping decode words and phonics.

Snack Time 'Mind Your P's & Q's'
We then have snack time in the kitchen where we are able to teach them their "table manners" and how to have an interesting conversation, always encouraging them to step outside their comfort zone in how they engage.

Play Time
About halfway through the lesson we break for some fun time, usually some outside play. This is a great way to test the kid's motor skills, listening skills and to engage them in team sports.

Back to Class!
We continue on with our lesson plan introducing more stimulating challenges which the children always enjoy. And we always are reminding them to have good posture, keep eye contact, and be polite.

Reporting Back
Parents receive a detailed written report after each session so they can see where the child is improving and we make suggestions on what work they can do with them between sessions.

With all the children who have completed our P's & Q's Modern Manners Course we have seen major improvement. We have placed our graduates in top private schools in and around Los Angeles.

SCHOOL EVALUATION WORKSHEET

School	Distance from home/bus available	Tuition& annual fees/ payment plan	Application Deadline	Financial Aid Deadline	Number of students	Teaching Philosphy	Additional parental involvement (fees, time)	Activities Offered	Afterschool programs/ additional cost

ADAT ARI EL DAY SCHOOL

12020 BURBANK BLVD, VALLEY VILLAGE, CA 91607
TEL: 818.766.4992 FAX: 818.766.1436
www.aaedayschool.org

HEAD OF SCHOOL:	JOHANNAH SOHN
DIRECTOR OF ADMISSIONS:	MARCIE PALLER
GRADES:	K–6
ENROLLMENT: 206	TUITION: $18,540 - 21,630
NEW FAMILY FEE: $600	APPLICATION FEE: $100
ACCREDITATION: BJE/CAIS/SSDSA/WASC	FINANCIAL AID: YES

ADAT ARI EL DAY SCHOOL is an excellent school for those considering a Judaic education for their children. The day school is a Solomon Schechter School, affiliated with the Adat Ari El synagogue. Membership in this temple is not required, but families must belong to some local Jewish congregation, temple, or synagogue in order to qualify for admission.

The two-story facility is modern, and its classrooms are bright and airy. The office was bustling the day I visited, but everyone was friendly and eager to answer my questions. There are two enclosed playgrounds: one of them includes basketball and handball courts for the older children and the other is set in a large courtyard in the center which houses the Kindergarten play yard. This one has a playhouse, hollow climbing blocks, and a grassy area to run around in. The facility has the feel of an office building (albeit a pleasant one).

The kindergarten program, which is developmental rather than traditional, focuses on nurturing social skills first, and placing more academic exercises second. There are two kindergarten classes each with a full-time teacher and an assistant teacher. Children are able to choose activities from a variety of learning centers in the classroom.

The curriculum consists of language arts, social studies, mathematics, computer, music, art, library, and physical education. Teaching specialists are employed for music, reading, computers, art, dance, science, and physical education. All teachers are certified by the Bureau of Jewish Education in Los Angeles. Each year the staff is required to spend many hours expanding their professional capabilities through in-service training sessions in order to learn the most recent strategies of curriculum and instruction.

In the upper grades, the curriculum focuses on the traditional subjects that include math, science, social studies, and English, with specialist teachers in Hebrew, library, music, art, technology, and physical education.

There is a modern computer lab used by all grades for regularly scheduled instruction, as well as for lunchtime activities such as producing the school newspaper, which is written by the students. The school has a large hall for dance and music classes, and a library which includes general reading material as well as Jewish resources.

Field trips are a regular part of the program in general and Judaic studies. They are many outside classroom activities and each one is carefully coordinated with specific units of study at each grade level. For example, the sixth grade students spend a week at an environmental science camp. The fourth grade visits Sacramento and there are also field trips to the Skirball Museum of Judaica, as well as to the County Museum of Art. One of the many activities scheduled for primary students is a visit to a matzah factory.

There are regularly scheduled assemblies, often with guest speakers. The speakers center around the arts, sciences, Jewish and American holidays and celebrations, as well as contemporary issues that affect our children today.

Parent participation in school enrichment activities is encouraged. Many parents lend their expertise to support the specialists in the after-school program. Private and group lessons are offered in choir, orchestra, drama, cooking, creative arts, and sports.

The school takes its role as a community and extended family for the children very seriously. When visiting the campus, I felt the warmth and vibrancy of its community spirit. Adat Ari El is a conservative synagogue and at the day school, traditional Jewish practices such as kashrut (dietary laws), daily prayers, and the celebration of holidays and Shabbat, are included in the program.

While the school reflects conservative Jewish standards, students are taught to respect and understand all forms of Jewish practice.

HISTORY

Founded in 1938 by 15 couples as the Valley Jewish Community Center, Adat Ari El is the oldest congregation in the San Fernando Valley. A lively and egalitarian shul, the Center soon became home to hundreds of families in the growing Jewish community. After a series of temporary homes – including a former "speakeasy" on Chandler Boulevard – the Center moved to its current, permanent location near the corner of Burbank and Laurel Canyon in 1949.

AT A GLANCE

APPLICATION DEADLINE	January 31
DRESS CODE	Yes
BEFORE AND AFTER SCHOOL CARE	Call school for details
SEE MAP	A on page 255

THE ARCHER SCHOOL FOR GIRLS

11725 SUNSET BLVD., LOS ANGELES, CA 90049
TEL: 310.873.7000 FAX: 310.873.7070
www.archer.org

HEAD OF SCHOOL:	**ELIZABETH ENGLISH**
DIRECTOR OF ADMISSIONS:	**FELICIA PAIK**
GRADES:	**6–12**
ENROLLMENT: 490	TUITION: $35,100
NEW FAMILY FEE: $3,500	APPLICATION FEE: $150
ACCREDITATION: CAIS/NAIS/WASC	FINANCIAL AID: YES

THE ARCHER SCHOOL for Girls is located in the heart of Brentwood, a stone's throw from the village and the Brentwood School. You enter from Sunset Boulevard onto a graceful circular driveway, which sweeps you up to the entrance of one of the most beautifully restored examples of an old colonial mission-style building. What was once a retirement home is now home to about 480 lucky girls. It is a fairly young school, founded in 1995, but their name is on the lips of many parents who are looking for a rigorous athletic and academic curriculum in an all-girl school setting. They moved here from a much smaller campus in Pacific Palisades. Their new home is over six acres complete with basketball and tennis courts and a sports field. The seniors have built themselves their own 'secret garden.' Most recently they have enclosed the outside courts with a dome, creating an indoor gymnasium.

I arrived at one of their several open houses on a beautiful Sunday afternoon in the Fall. So many happy smiling faces greeted us that we immediately felt at home. The school went through a lot of trouble to make our visit a pleasant one – tables laden with homemade goodies, and children everywhere making sure that we had everything we needed. We spilled out into the courtyard garden, a beautifully manicured area with lots of carefully tended flowerbeds. Once we had all gathered outside and been given a warm welcome by one of the teachers, we were divided into groups. My daughter was invited to take a separate tour of the school given by the students. There were approximately 20 to 25 of us in our group, and off we went to experience a day in the life of an Archer girl!

First stop was to meet the athletic coaches who squeezed us into a very small space (I think it was the yoga center). Once we were inside, the coaches gave a very impressive video presentation of their Fitness for Life program. It was shown on three TV screens and included softball, soccer, basketball, flag football, field hockey, volleyball, tennis, badminton, yoga, and something called stuntnastics. I got the feeling they invented this before they created a formal gym! No matter, it looked fun and unique. Each student, in the Fitness for Life Program receives one full trimester of dance. The type of dance is based on the grade level of the student and could be ballet at grade seven and jazz at grade eight.

As you can see they are especially involved in sports at Archer, and if your daughter plays on a team, she will be expected to practice nearly every day after school. Of course, lots of hands went up by worried parents wondering how the homework was going to get done. Archer has taken care of this by providing a state-of-the-art study center, complete with full-time teachers on hand to help children at any time of the day with their work. There are even cubicles with headsets for the girls to watch programs assigned to them by their teachers.

We were then taken upstairs and introduced to the science department teachers, who gave us a comprehensive overview of what a child would be learning with them. The lab was immaculate, well laid out, spacious, and full of up to date equipment. It had me wanting to retake chemistry all over again! As I sat there, I couldn't help remembering my old boarding school's science lab with its rusty Bunsen burners, cracked vials and equally 'cracked' professor who made absolutely no sense to me at all! Here I saw teachers that were enthusiastic and smart and knew how to get the information across.

From there we visited a number of other freshly painted classrooms, all of them filled with brand new desks, beautifully laid out, with views out onto the grounds and gardens. The average class size at Archer is 15 students. The teachers were all articulate and informative and welcomed our questions, as did many of the students, who were more than happy to tell us how much they loved the school. I was impressed with their poise and the ease with which they answered a number of fairly difficult questions. They seemed to enjoy the harder ones and would take turns answering them. We also visited several computer labs, the orchestra room, an electronic music studio, and more than one art gallery.

The incoming sixth graders are separated from the rest of the school in a wing all their own. In this wing there are a couple of more homey-looking classrooms, filled with colorful drawings and circular seating, all of which helps them get used to the school. I thought this to be a very inviting intimate environment. The classrooms for older students were very sophisticated-looking, and I could see a sixth grader feeling a little out of water seeing one for the first time. This way the students spend their first year in more comfortable surroundings, which make it a far easier transition into middle school.

The ground floor had more classrooms and a number of faculty offices. There were also a number of delightful library-type rooms where the older students could eat lunch and read. One such room had a collection of china teacups and saucers. As I stood in the room I felt a little like Alice in Wonderland . . . was this really a school? It felt more like a 5-star hotel somewhere in Europe; apparently the food is '5-star' since a fab local restaurant caters lunch. I met up with my daughter who had made friends with one of the students who then offered to take us on our own private tour downstairs to see the theater. This was a wonderful place filled with props, paint, and costumes, and even a beautiful 6,000 square-foot library.

There are a number of art studios (ceramics, drawing, painting, and photography) as well as the fabulous study center and 12th grade common room which looked lived-in and had not been specially cleaned up for our visit, which I liked. I enjoyed this part of the tour the most since it was given by a seventh grader who simply offered; she was not asked by anyone and couldn't have been more charming. I hoped that my daughter would take a little bit of the Archer experience home with her – I could really see her benefiting in so many ways from a school experience like this.

Arrow Week

Every spring, classes are halted for one week and students participate in experimental study, approaching integrated learning beyond the confines of the traditional classroom. Research, hands-on learning, and physical challenges are some of the activities the children experience. All these adventures are designed to incorporate academics, outdoor education, and service learning. Middle school Arrow Week culminates in the traditional eighth grade trip to Washington, D.C.

Service Learning

Archer wants to inspire its students to become more involved, compassionate citizens. They encourage the girls to use their own gifts and abilities to benefit their community. They might travel to a Tijuana orphanage to help celebrate Dia de los Reyes Magos (Three Kings' Day) or deliver lunches to AIDS patients for Project Angel Food.

Community Service

Upper School provides students with the opportunity to challenge themselves in an altruistic way. Students extend themselves beyond their 'comfort zones.' They donate their time and energy to different causes for a specific number of hours to be completed during each year. With the help of the Community Service Board, their families, and the school's resource guide, each individual organizes these hours. Students are required to keep a journal, reflecting on their experiences. Archer School believes that through exploring first-hand the important and difficult issues facing diverse communities, the students will be better prepared to become positive, productive citizens.

The young lady who was showing my daughter and me around told us that they have lockers but there are no locks. Students are expected to respect the property of others, and if a student sees another student with someone else's belongings, it is not considered wrong to tell a teacher. In fact, not only do the teachers encourage it but, more importantly, the students themselves do as well.

Because the school is in a residential neighborhood, the children use buses to get to and from school unless they are playing sports against another school and arrive back at the campus later in the afternoon – then the parents are allowed to pick them up. The bus fee is included in the tuition fee and none of the girls seem to mind this arrangement. I also think that it's better for parents who work. No more 45 minutes on the freeway at 6:30 in the morning. . . and then 45 minutes back again just to get your first cup of coffee!

If you are looking for an all-girls' education for your child and live on the West Side, or indeed anywhere in Los Angeles, please take a look at this school. They have managed to combine an old-world feel with state-of-the-art facilities to give your girl a very well rounded, excellent education. The school also offers a variety of scholarships and financial aid packages if your child seems to be the right fit for the school.

HISTORY

In November 1994, Victoria Shorr, Diana Meehan, and Megan Callaway founded The Archer School for Girls in an outdoor coffee shop in Brentwood. All three were alumnae of single sex schools and wanted the same for their daughters. By September of 1995, the school was open thanks to the great enthusiasm of the public and the determination of the founders. Archer immediately benefitted from the support of founding donors, many of who funded scholarships. In addition, godmothers (leading educators, activists, writers and artists) responded to the school's mission to educate a diverse body of girls who would be the country's future leaders.

APPLICATION DEADLINE	December
OPEN HOUSES	October, November, and January
SCHOOL TOUR	Call school to make reservation
UNIFORMS	Yes
SUMMER SCHOOL	Yes
SEE MAP	D on page 255

BERKELEY HALL SCHOOL

16000 MULHOLLAND DRIVE, LOS ANGELES, CA 90049
TEL: 310.476.5421   FAX: 310.476.5748
www.berkelyhall.org

HEAD OF SCHOOL:	LISLE STALEY, PH.D.
DIRECTOR OF ADMISSIONS:	NATHALIE MILLER
TYPE OF SCHOOL:	CO-ED
GRADES:	PRESCHOOL–8
ENROLLMENT: 260	TUITION: $10,650 - 30,100
NEW FAMILY FEE: $1,500	APPLICATION FEE: $125
ACCREDITATION: NAIS/CAIS/WASC	FINANCIAL AID: YES

BERKELEY HALL sits on over sixty acres on a hilltop off Mulholland Drive amid the natural beauty of the Santa Monica mountains, and the campus is spectacular. The facilities include eight buildings, among them a 300-seat auditorium and a 2,000 square foot library that is roomy and well stocked, with plenty of seating. There's a very impressive woodshop full of great looking tools and a special room for art where the children can make ceramics and sculpt, and learn to develop their own photographs. Outside, the children have a full- sized field for football and track, fields for baseball and soccer, and two tennis courts. If your child loves swimming, there's a 75-foot swimming pool!

Each department (preschool, primary, intermediate, and junior high) is housed separately in a ranch-style building with its own outdoor lunch and restroom areas. So when students first arrive into the school they have their own area, which gives them a sense of home and identity. I would like to say that with all this land it would be lovely if the school would enlarge the outside preschool play area. It really feels very small when you look at all the land they have. I would also love it if they would give some of the classrooms and corridors a new coat of paint. However don't let this deter you as I'm sure it's on their "to do" list and what's going on inside the classrooms is far more important than what the walls look like, but I have to admit as a parent I love seeing bright, newly painted classrooms that are tidy and well-organized.

In the primary division (grades K through 3), there is one teacher and a full-time assistant teacher for each grade, with a maximum of 22 students per class. The classrooms are large and airy, with reading lofts for those wanting to find a quiet place to read. The classrooms open directly to the outdoors, where they have their own grassy playing field.

Intermediate classrooms (grades 4 through 6) are nestled on a hill above the playing fields, across from the Junior High Building. Each classroom has one core teacher with a part-time aide, and seven specialist teachers in science, art, music, computer, physical education, woodshop, and library. There's also a full-time resource teacher who offers enrichment study to help children develop beyond their grade level.

In Junior High, small classes enable teachers to know and address individual interests, abilities, and talents and to help guide the students through the emotional as well as academic transition from junior high-to-high school. The students have the opportunity to write, produce, direct, and edit their own movies through a digital filmmaking elective. Every year, teachers develop/invent their own elective. It changes from year-to-year from art to technology, to acting or music.

Chapel is a weekly event where students gather and discuss whatever 'quality of the week' is currently being featured in the school's character development program. It could be perseverance, charity, and justice or hope, and is led by the different grade levels, faculty, administrators, parents, or outside role models.

Public speaking holds an important place in the life of the school. Junior high school students compete in regional speech competitions and regularly take home honors. Even kindergarten children are encouraged to develop a sense of ease in front of an audience by leading class assemblies, and participating in all-school chapels.

This school is very active in encouraging a family, community environment. The school likes to do outdoor events with their students and families, such as the Gala Dinner and Family Campout.

Nathalie Miller, the wonderful and charming Head of Admissions tells me that this is not a Christian Science school. It is, however, run by faculty and staff who are all Christian Scientists. She also tells me there is no required minimum proportion of Christian Science families, and they do not teach religion in class. I do know this as I have sent many non-Christian Science families there who have been delighted with its' approach to education and how the school helps keep their children more grounded and able to enjoy their childhood without having to grow up too fast.

I do think it's important for prospective families to be sure that they have no conflicts with the Christian Science philosophy. Please familiarize yourself with their beliefs before you begin the admissions process. Remember it's not about their religious practices it's about the incredibly high level of education your child will receive there. It's a beautiful school, run by a passionate headmistress and teachers who are articulate and easy to reach out to.

Berkeley Hall has a tremendous number of extras to offer its students. The tuition is on a par with all the other private schools, but you'll definitely get your money's worth in terms of facilities and education.

HISTORY

Founded in 1911 by sisters Leila and Mabel Cooper, and Mary E. Steven, Berkeley Hall is one of the oldest independent schools in Los Angeles. It is still run and supported by Christian Scientists who want to establish an educational environment in harmony with the teachings of that religion. Religion is not taught in the class- rooms, but a spiritual foundation of fellowship supports all aspects of school life. Berkeley Hall School Foundation is a non-profit corporation governed by a self-perpetuating Board of Trustees.

AT A GLANCE

APPLICATION DEADLINE	January
GRADES 2-4 TAKE A PLACEMENT TEST	At Berkeley Hall
ISEE TEST	Required for grades 5-8
UNIFORMS	Yes
BEFORE AND AFTER-SCHOOL CARE	Yes
SEE MAP	D on page 255

BRAWERMAN ELEMENTARY

WEST CAMPUS
11661 W. OLYMPIC BLVD., LOS ANGELES, CA 90064
TEL: 310.445.1280 FAX: 310.445.1281

EAST CAMPUS
3663 WILSHIRE BLVD., LOS ANGELES, CA 90010
TEL: 213.388.2401 FAX: 310.388.2402

www.brawerman.org

HEAD OF SCHOOL:	**NADINE BREUER**
DIRECTOR OF ADMISSIONS:	**NADINE ZYSMAN (WEST)**
	PEGGY DAVIS (EAST)
GRADES:	**K–6**
ENROLLMENT: 270 (WEST) & 75 (EAST)	TUITION: $26,000 - 28,500
NEW FAMILY FEE: $1,850	APPLICATION FEE: $200
ACCREDITATION: WASC/BJE	FINANCIAL AID: YES

It's impossible to miss the campus of **BRAWERMAN ELEMENTARY WEST**. Located directly on the corner of Olympic and Barrington in West LA, this reform Jewish elementary school is an extraordinarily well run organization, amidst a campus full of clean architectural lines, set amongst grassy and shaded open areas. While this school has extremely high standards, there is a welcoming and warm feel to the place.

Brawerman WEST opened its doors in 1999 with only ten children and is now in its sixteenth year. Head of School Nadine Breuer's strong sense of commitment to education and excellence have made this expansion possible. Both her and Nadine Zysman, Director of Admissions, have made it their business to forge good relationships with both public and private schools.

The curriculum is designed to prepare students to go on to some of the top private schools in Los Angeles. Students are offered a superb art program housed in a well-stocked art center. They are taught math, science, social studies and Judaic studies. There's a technology lab with brand new Macs along with a technology specialist. Their library is ever-growing and is a wonderful place to study and research in. I was particularly impressed with one of their music programs, where fourth, fifth and sixth graders were asked to become proficient in an instrument of their choice that they had never played before. Mine would have been the trumpet!

Brawerman competes in soccer, volleyball, basketball and track through the Coastal Canyon League. There's also Hebrew immersion and a wonderful exchange program in conjunction with the Jewish Federation of Los Angeles, where Brawerman students visited Israel for two weeks.

Parent-docents lead prospective families throughout the campus after a talk given by the Heads of each campus. They look for children from all types of families from various social/economic backgrounds, but most importantly – who are ripe for learning. Their sixth grade graduates are all on their way to the following schools: A.C. Stelle Middle School, Archer, Brentwood, Crossroads, Harvard Westlake, John Adams, Marlborough, Milken, New Roads, Palms, Paul Revere, Willows and Windward. Acceptance into Brawerman is highly competitive, so take a look.

BRAWERMAN ELEMENTARY EAST campus is located on the historic Erika J. Glazer Family Campus of Wilshire Boulevard Temple, a famous Los Angeles landmark since its dedication in 1929 on the corner of Wilshire Boulevard and Hobart. The Temple's iconic Magnin Sanctuary is a Byzantine-revival architectural masterpiece listed on the National Register of Historic Places. Coinciding with the campus's $150 million restoration and redevelopment, Brawerman East features: new state-of-the-art classrooms, library, art studio, playground, auditorium, sanctuary, food pantry, and Tikkun Olam Center.

HISTORY

Opened in 1999, the Brawerman West Campus of Wilshire Boulevard Temple is a Reform Jewish school for grades kindergarten through sixth grade.

As young Jewish families were moving to areas west of the original Temple site, leaders recognized the need to provide for this constituency and purchased property in West Los Angeles. They converted a 30,000 square-foot structure and added 60,000 square feet of new construction to create the beautiful campus that serves the school today.

Brawerman East Campus opened in the Fall of 2011. According to their website, "Joint programming with both Brawerman East and West allows students the opportunity to experience our diverse, multicultural Wilshire Center neighborhood, as well as our historic campus. Children and families will maintain a lifetime connection to our Temple, and pass along that connection to future generations."

AT A GLANCE

APPLICATION DEADLINE	December 18
GRADES 2-4 TAKE A PLACEMENT TEST	September to November (WEST) October to December (EAST)
ISEE TEST	Yes
UNIFORMS	Yes
BEFORE AND AFTER-SCHOOL CARE	Yes
SUMMER SCHOOL	No
SEE MAP	D on page 255

BRENTWOOD SCHOOL

WEST CAMPUS (K-6)
12001 SUNSET BLVD., LOS ANGELES, CA 90049
TEL: 310.471.1041 FAX: 310.440.1989
EAST CAMPUS (7-12)
100 S. BARRINGTON AVE., LOS ANGELES, CA 90049
TEL:310.476.9633 FAX: 310.476.4087
www.bwscampus.com

HEAD OF SCHOOL:	**MICHAEL RIERA, PH.D.**
DIRECTOR OF ADMISSIONS:	**MARY BETH BARRY (WEST)**
	LAUREN ABELL WINDOM (EAST)
GRADES:	**K–12**
ENROLLMENT: K-6: 300, 7-12: 65	TUITION: $31,890 - 37,725
NEW FAMILY FEE: $2,000	APPLICATION FEE: $100
ACCREDITATION: WASC	FINANCIAL AID: YES

BRENTWOOD SCHOOL expanded from a seventh through twelfth grade, one-campus school to a kindergarten through twelfth grade, two-campus school in the fall of 1995. The West Campus enrolls 300 students from kindergarten through grade 6. The East Campus currently accommodates 690 students.

Brentwood's elementary campus is a beautifully landscaped 3.5 acre site located between Saltair and Bundy on Sunset Boulevard. The facilities include a three-story main building with 14 classrooms, a small library, a common meeting area with stage, and a soccer/football field and basketball court. There are also freestanding science and art facilities with their own restrooms and outdoor flagstone patios. Brentwood also boasts a state of the art aquatics center which rivals anything I've seen in all my travels!

The kindergarten has a separate, secured outside area with tables, a grassy play area with swings, and climbing equipment. The entire campus is fenced, and an updated security system is in place.

The campus is large and open, but there is noise from Sunset Blvd. The main building is built into a hillside, thus the lower floors facing the slope have a slightly closed-in feeling. All the walls are bright white, and there are drop-ceilings which even made me (I'm 5'4") feel like I was in munchkin-land. This is where the Kindergartners live so it's perfect for them!

There are 28 teachers, two classes at each grade level, and approximately 21 students per class. Children receive instruction from their core teachers in language arts, social studies, and math. They travel to other classrooms for specialist teachers in art, music, computer and physical education. Health classes begin in first grade, and Spanish is taught starting in kindergarten. In 5th grade Japanese and French are added as language options, and in 6th grade, Latin is offered as well.

Kindergarten

The kindergarten program has a traditional, teacher-centered format for part of the day, but also allows time for children to work alone or in small groups in a more developmental way. Brentwood has a full- day program beginning at 8:15 a.m. and ending at 3:15 p.m. The emphasis in kindergarten is on language arts and mathematics, with a special focus on communication skills: reading, writing, speaking and listening. Both phonics and whole-language recognition are used to teach reading skills. Mathematics is taught using manipulatives and workbooks with skill-building exercises. Each kindergarten class has one master teacher and a full-time assistant. There is an average of 44 new students that enter Kindergarten each year. The class also utilizes staff and faculty from other areas of the West Campus for art, music, drama, library skills, and physical education. A reading specialist is available for those children who need extra help.

Grades 1-6

The curriculum is made up of language arts, mathematics, science, social studies, computer, health, physical education, music, art, and drama. Also included is a library and study skills program. There is an emphasis on children using their communication skills: reading, writing, speaking and listening, with the goal of teaching students to exchange ideas effectively. The social studies program links history, geography, economics, and the study of modern cultures with other areas of the curriculum (literature, writing, math, and science etc.).

The math program teaches students basic facts and skills and tries to guide students to use that foundation to develop mathematical reasoning. Life, physical, and earth sciences are presented in lessons that relate to the students' life experiences. The science program also introduces the use of scientific tools and equipment.

There are computers in each classroom, which are used in conjunction with every subject to enhance and extend the ongoing classroom instruction. The (voluntary) extracurricular program of the West Campus includes leadership organizations and interscholastic athletic teams. They are implementing a more developmental approach to learning grades 1-6.

Grades 7-12

The East Campus of Brentwood is easily one of the most aesthetically pleasing schools I've had the pleasure of visiting. Palm trees, ivy, and colorful bougainvillea surround the attractive Mediterranean-style main building that sits, literally, in the shadow of the new Getty Center. New additions to the campus include an athletic complex and tennis courts.

Brentwood School's academic program is both impressive and extensive as it offers more than 100 courses!

The year long 'Senior Seminar' was of particular interest. In this course, seniors wrestle with age-old social, political, and philosophical questions about human life. They explore issues such as truth and knowledge, freedom and responsibility, and the nature of ethics and happiness. In addition to lectures and discussions, students must complete a thesis on a topic of their choice. Each year a selected thesis is bound and placed permanently in the library.

One was titled, "I Want My MTV: The Contradictions Behind the Cultural Arbiter of Today's Youth."

Admission to Brentwood (7-12) is very competitive. In any given year, Brentwood receives up to 450 applications for the 70 openings in the seventh grade. Technically, there are 105 openings, but the West Campus school students automatically fill 35 to 40 of the openings.

HISTORY

Founded in 1972, the Brentwood School took over the Brentwood Military Academy, which had existed since 1902. The Academy was founded by Miss Mary McDonnell in a remodeled residence at 9th and Beacon in Los Angeles. During the period from 1902 to 1972, the Academy was operated as a for-profit institution. It was primarily a boarding school, enrolling students of all ages and grade levels. The goals and objectives were those of the founder and her family members. The property was sold to a non-profit corporation, which opened in 1972 as the Brentwood School, a coeducational day school serving students in grades 7 to 10. Grade 11 was added in 1973 and 12 soon after. Brentwood graduated its first Senior Class in June, 1975.

AT A GLANCE

APPLICATION DEADLINE	K-6 by December 18, 7-12 by January 8
MAJOR OPENINGS ARE IN	K and Seventh grade, with sporadic openings in other grades. For the three kindergarten classes of 15 students, they anticipate 250 applicants
UNIFORMS	K-6 yes. 7-12 no.
BEFORE AND AFTER-SCHOOL CARE	Yes
SEE MAP	D on page 255

BRIDGES ACADEMY

39212 LAUREL CANYON BLVD., LAUREL CANYON, CA 91604
TEL: 818.506.1091 FAX: 818.506.8094
www.bridges.edu

HEAD OF SCHOOL:	**CARL SABATINO**
DIRECTOR OF ADMISSIONS:	**DOUG LENZINI**
TYPE OF SCHOOL:	**CO-ED**
TEACHING PHILOSOPHY:	**GIFTED, HIGHLY GIFTED**
GRADES:	**5–12**
ENROLLMENT: 155	TUITION: $37,306
NEW FAMILY FEE: $500	APPLICATION FEE: $150
ACCREDITATION: CAIS/WASC	FINANCIAL AID: YES

I heard about **BRIDGES ACADEMY** for the first time while touring another school out in the Valley. Doug Lenzini, Bridges' Director of Admissions (and a very affable chap) was on the same school tour and over a cup of coffee we started talking. I very quickly realized that his school needed to be in my book and you'll see why.

Bridges is located in Studio City on Laurel Canyon Blvd. They purchased their campus in 2011 and originally shared it with Osaka Sangyo University of Los Angeles (OSULA) that offered Japanese and English language classes to the community and to international students who came over for a couple of weeks to learn the language. Sometimes a small number of international students would sign up for a more intense 1-4 month program. In both cases these students would stay in the dorms. It reminded me of a (very) small college campus with young people of all ages outside throwing frisbees and relaxing on the lawns. However they no longer share it with OSULA and now have 12 administrative/support offices and 22 classrooms; a full-size gym, cafeteria, two gardens, and a large 120 bed dormitory. There are plans to include adding a boarding school component, which I think is a wonderful option for parents who need a school like this but don't live close enough to commute each day.

Bridges has become one of the nation's educational leaders in helping bright, complex students overcome educational and emotional challenges that meet both academic and social goals. Or as Doug likes to put it "to help our 'twice-exceptional' (both gifted and challenged) kids." Some of the learning issues they accommodate, are nonverbal learning differences, organizational challenges, attention deficit disorder, audio and visual processing problems, and dysgraphia. Have any of these terms been used to describe your child? Yes? Well read on.

Unlike many other private schools, they can meet the needs of such a diverse student body because they offer a structured learning environment that simultaneously allows for individualized instruction and an awareness of different learning styles within the same classroom. Note, "awareness of different learning styles," which brings me to a story that I'd like to share with you.

In my work as a school consultant I am asked to help find the right school for a child. One such family asked me for help. Their son had been struggling at a very prestigious private school and no matter what they did to help him it just wasn't working. He was a very smart child so that wasn't the problem. After spending some time with the family and learning more about the child, I suggested that they look at Bridges. They did and it felt like a great "fit." They loved it. More importantly their son loved it and is now a wonderful young man living his life in New York. I saw him recently and without any prompting from his mother, he turned to me and thanked me for finding him the school! Sometimes a kid just needs to be understood by a school and given a different way of learning. Bridges does that.

It's difficult sometimes to understand the "jargon" that schools' use in their brochures so I asked Doug to explain in his own words what they are looking for in a student and why that child might do better at Bridges. Here's what he said:

The intellectual profile:

"Bridges offers a stimulating/challenging program for students who have been identified as gifted or highly gifted (we even have a few profoundly gifted students) so we want to feel comfortable that the program is a good match. Our students may not be gifted across the board but are gifted in one or more academic disciplines and usually gifted in other areas such as technology or visual and performing arts."

The learning profile:

"We need to understand the learning style; visual, auditory, sequential, kinesthetic, and the student's learning challenges. The vast majority of Bridges students are struggling with Non Verbal Learning Disabilities--ADD or ADHD, processing issues, mild dyslexia, and weak executive function skills. Some have not been successful in other settings simply because they are quirky and don't fit in or their social skills are delayed".

The social/emotional/behavioral profile:

Bridges students are inherently good kids. They don't present behavioral problems nor do they possess deeper emotional or psychological issues that require a therapeutic environment. However, Bridges students do possess the normal range of challenges that go with adolescence and the teenage years. Some may also exhibit anxiety or depression and frustration, much of it due to not being in the right environment.

Their class size is very small, an average of eight and no more than twelve for the high school core classes. The kids are required to have laptops and bring them to school just like you would a text book. Every classroom has both wireless and hard-wire internet access so the kids can learn how to search for information, but also critically examine quality and relevance. They've found that seminar-style seating, which they have in some of the classrooms, helps to promote discussion and the exchange of ideas – sounds like a mini-college experience to me!

In the Elementary School

They created the Phoenix Program (the Phoenix is the Bridges mascot) for their 5th and 6th grade-age students. The program is also open to accelerated 4th grade learners.

In the Middle School

Bridges has a 7/8 grade "house" for the core classes of social studies. Math, science, art, fitness, drama and computer classes are taught by separate teachers. Parents are provided with progress reports on a regular basis.
Both the Phoenix Program (4, 5, and 6) and the Middle School (grades 7 and 8) have a teacher and teaching assistant in all core academic subjects; and Media Tech, Art, Drama and Fitness are all part of every student's program.

In the High School

Their program meets or exceeds the University of California A-G requirements for high school graduation. They offer honors courses in Biology, Chemistry, Geometry, English and History. Prep for AP exams are available in select subjects. Technology classes include web design, 3D animation, computer programming and audio/video editing.

Could they be educating our next big movie makers and web designers? Sure they could! In addition, visual and performing arts electives are offered. Spanish and Japanese are their foreign language offerings and I'm sure students HAVE been known to practice their Japanese on those poor international students!

They just recently added robotics and sustainability programs, debate, additional technology electives, music composition/production elective, German language elective, 10th and 11th grade Writing Labs; and senior seminars.

The kids compete in California Interscholastic Federation (CIF) in basketball and cross- country. Other school activities include Outdoor Education and other off-campus field trips, Yearbook, Prom, various school clubs and their Service Learning program. All students must complete a minimum of 30 hours of community service in order to graduate.

Now here's what I like: Parents receive school information through email discussion lists. For High School students and parents, homework assignments, tutoring sessions, grades, attendance, and teacher comments can be monitored through their web-based program, Power School. Now that's brilliant! How many times have you pulled out your hair trying to find out what homework has been assigned and when it's due by? Or wished you could ask a teacher how your kid did at school that day.

In addition to the email discussion lists and Power School web program where high school students and parents can access grades, homework assignments, attendance and comments, all faculty now have their own individual Moodle site so parents and students can access much more in-depth academic materials and communicate with each teacher. Fret no more your kids are in great hands!

The school offers good solid college counseling and since their first graduating class of 1996, graduates have been accepted at virtually all Cal State and UC schools, as well as universities and four-year colleges all over the country. So if anything you've read in this review is striking close to home, do give Doug Lenzini a call and take a closer look at this very special school.

HISTORY

Bridges Academy opened in 1994 when the lives of three young international tennis competitors collided with the career of an enterprising educator named Carolyn McWilliams. With their sights set on college as well as tennis, the young men were looking for a study program that would afford them time to play while still preparing them for college. McWilliams developed and oversaw such an independent study program for the aspiring athletes. McWilliams also was busy helping gifted students with organizational deficits. These were students who struggled to achieve decent grades in the traditional college preparatory school or other settings. Within a year, Bridges expanded to serve nearly 30 students and by 2015, 155 were enrolled.

AT A GLANCE

APPLICATION DEADLINE	Prefer March 1 (rolling admissions if available)
OPEN HOUSES	October and January
ENRICHMENT CLASSES	Yes
UNIFORMS	No
ISEE TESTING	No
SEE MAP	C on page 255

THE BUCKLEY SCHOOL
3900 STANSBURY AVE., SHERMAN OAKS, CA 91423
TEL: 818.783.1610 FAX: 818.461.6714
www.buckleyla.org

HEAD OF SCHOOL:	**JAMES BUSBY**
DIRECTOR OF ADMISSIONS:	**STEPHEN MILICH**
TYPE OF SCHOOL:	**COLLEGE PREP CO-ED**
GRADES:	**K–12**
ENROLLMENT: 805	TUITION: $33,430 - 39,320
NEW FAMILY FEE: $2,000	APPLICATION FEE: $125
ACCREDITATION: CAIS/WASC	FINANCIAL AID: YES

BUCKLEY is nestled in a valley surrounded by mountains. The 32-acre campus is so lush that you almost forget that you're in Los Angeles. The buildings are modern, tastefully designed one-story structures set up like a small village with walkways throughout.

There are 51 air-conditioned classrooms, an outside picnic area with aviary, an indoor pool, two libraries, three computer centers, a gymnasium, orchestra and choral rehearsal areas, science labs, sports stadium, field house, green house, health care, and transportation services. All facilities are designed for the appropriate age level. For example, the lower school has a scaled-down 'child-size' library and a theater designed for the younger children.

Buckley is fully accredited, and included in its admission packet is a list of Buckley staff and teachers giving us their very impressive educational history and degree levels. Even at the kindergarten level, in addition to their regular teacher, children see specialists for art, music, physical education and library.

Buckley's educational philosophy encompasses four principles: academic training, creative self-expression through the arts, physical development, and moral education. Dr. Buckley's approach addresses the development of the whole student, enabling each child to become well-rounded, knowledgeable, and independent.

Their educational approach at Buckley is to develop critical reading and thinking skills in an age-appropriate manner including the ability to observe, analyze, synthesize, deduce and make inferences. The school aims to foster a love of learning and develop an appreciation of and proficiency in the visual and performing arts. Students' development should include an awareness of their own abilities, including the value of teamwork and sportsmanship along with a character based on integrity, compassion, and honesty. A sense of responsibility to the community, respect for diversity, and belief in the value of living a life based on these principles are traits fostered at this school. It is intended that Buckley students will view themselves as citizens of the world with their own specific responsibilities, and develop intellectual, emotional and ethical attributes needed to live in a world of diversity and change.

The majority of students are admitted in kindergarten, grade six, grade seven, and grade nine. They enroll approximately 44 students in kindergarten each year. The school enrolls 20 new students for grade six, and approximately 25-30 new students in grades seven and nine.

This is a traditional, academically oriented school geared for students who plan to go on to a four-year college or university. 100% percent do just that. Founder Dr. Buckley believed, "College begins at two." I also heard from several of the applicants that they were happy to find a good private school that had no religious affiliation.

To get a good idea of what the students are like, I strongly suggest reading a copy of the current yearbook. All graduating students get a full page to express themselves, some have used artwork, some poetry, some letters to parents and step-parents, and monologues written to the world in general. You will find the yearbook very illuminating. In addition to a foreign exchange program, there is a department set up solely for college counseling. A full sports program, includes football, basketball, tennis, field hockey and horseback riding. The boys varsity basketball team came in first place in the Liberty League last year and made it to the CIF quarter-finals. In addition, the 6th grade boys basketball team ended their season undefeated, and they were the San Fernando Valley Private School League champions.

At the annual Scholastic Art Awards, Buckley's middle and upper school students competed against nearly 900 entrants from more than 60 public, private, parochial and home schooled applicants. The 14 selected works, seven gold and seven silver award winners, were exhibited at Otis College Bolsky Gallery in Los Angeles. In 1999, Buckley was awarded the prestigious BRAVO award for outstanding educational programs in visual and performing arts. It is the only time in the twenty-year history of the award that a private school has been selected.

If art or sports is not your child's strength, then Buckley's twenty clubs are a great way for your child to get involved in the Buckley community. The clubs include Junior Statesmen of America, Varsity Club, Social Action Team (SAT), International Thespian Society, Pre-Med Club, Ecology Club, and The Buckley Jazz Ensemble. The school puts on two major theatrical productions each year as well as several smaller ones. Recently, Buckley's Junior Statesmen of America delegation (JSA) won nine Best Speaker gavels.

In order to graduate from The Buckley School, a student in grades 9 through 12 must fulfill the following requirements:

- Social Science, English, math: 4 years • Health: 1/3 year
- Computer science: 1 year • Visual or performing arts: 2 years • World language, science, physical education: 3 2/3 years

Buckley delivers all the extras you could want for your child.

HISTORY

Buckley was founded in 1933 by Dr. Isabelle Buckley, based on the schools she observed in Europe and Australia. She believed that young people needed greater structure, more guidance, values training and more discipline in their lives and that it was the school's responsibility to give it to them.

AT A GLANCE

APPLICATION DEADLINE	December (K-5), January (6-12)
OPEN HOUSES	Oct-Nov
UNIFORMS	Yes
BUSING	Yes
SUMMER PROGRAMS	Yes
AFTER-SCHOOL PROGRAMS	Yes
24-HOUR CAMPUS SECURITY	Yes
SEE MAP	A on page 255

CALVARY CHRISTIAN SCHOOL

701 PALISADES DRIVE, PACIFIC PALISADES, CA 90272

TEL: 310.573.0082 FAX: 310.230.9268

www.calvarychristian.org

HEAD OF SCHOOL:	VINCENT DOWNEY
DIRECTOR OF ADMISSIONS:	LESLIE CLARK
TYPE OF SCHOOL:	CHRISTIAN DAY
GRADES:	PRESCHOOL–8

ENROLLMENT: 430

NEW FAMILY FEE: $1,000

ACCREDITATION: CAIS/WASC

TUITION: $9,250 - 19,750

FINANCIAL AID: YES

CALVARY CHRISTIAN SCHOOL is surrounded by hills on a private and stunning property, nestled in Pacific Palisades. Though traditional in approach, the school is exceedingly warm and welcoming to children and their families. The school is run by a board of parents from the non- denominational Calvary Church.

With a total of 430 students, and 20 students per classroom, each with its' own teacher and an assistant teacher, this school has everything needed for a first-class education for your child. There's a good balance of male and female teachers, lovely bright well organized classrooms, massive playing fields, gym, and music rooms. I was impressed by their reading lists and their technical savvy – all the kids know Excel and PowerPoint by fifth grade!! The school develops the whole child by balancing the academic, the physical (athletics), and the spiritual nature of the child. This spiritual nature is developed by bible classes and a strong desire for everyone to have a personal relationship with Jesus. In the admission process, their goal is to accept students and families best served by their mission. Nearly half of the student body does not belong to this church and the school is committed to a policy of non-discrimination on all levels.

Cavalry has another clear vision for their students: they are being prepared for service and leadership. As taken from the school's brochure:

> Students are encouraged to be responsible, creative leaders and to use their academic skills and Christian values to better our world. We achieve this by developing and encouraging our students' faith, critical thinking skills, core academic skill base, and service-oriented leadership.

To help achieve this vision, they work with six separate organizations to provide community service opportunities for the children. On any given day, a Cavalry student might gather supplies and send them to one of these organizations or someone in need, visit a retirement home, send letters to soldiers serving in the military, help the Los Angeles homeless, and many other "good works." They are a very committed bunch!

The School has a state-of-the-art Technology Center, which is surprisingly bright and airy for a computer/media lab! One-third of its' technology equipment is updated each year to keep the software and services current, providing students with up-to-date tools to work with. Along with computer studies the students enjoy weekly classes in a well-stocked art-room where they're exposed to 3-D design, print-making, art history, multi-media art, and ceramics to name a few.

The layout of the Elementary school (K-5) makes for an intimate and interactive environment, with desks that face the center of the room, like a half circle. The Elementary school has an excellent group of teachers who are well versed in their subjects with advanced degrees. Their middle school is chock full of subjects: science, math, social studies, language arts, bible study, physical education, and annual field trips. Cavalry's curriculum is very strong and far exceeds the state standards.

Calvary has a new Arts & Technology Building with a state-of-the-art performing arts center, fine arts annex, and academic resource center. There is also a new elementary science lab and a technology learning center.

A very active Parent Association keeps families involved in their child's education. They provide a link between the parents, faculty and administration by hosting meetings, promoting Calvary School in the local community and fundraising. Through their annual Holiday Boutique, Book Fair, and weekly Pizza Day, the PA raises over $150,000 and some years even more. Most impressive!

For athletics, the school competes in the Delphic League and the Coastal Canyon League, along with many other private schools throughout Los Angeles. Here are some of the sports that Cavalry offers: flag football, volleyball, basketball, soccer, track and golf. The Cougar is Cavalry's mascot, and there's loads of school pride!

Even more impressive is that the students all move into the top high schools throughout Los Angeles including: Archer School for Girls, Brentwood School, Crespi, Harvard Westlake, Loyola, Marlborough, Marymount, Oaks Christian, Pacifica Christian High, Notre Dame, Viewpoint and Windward.

HISTORY

Calvary Christian School began as a small preschool in 1963 in the heart of the town of Pacific Palisades with approximately 20 children. In 1989, Calvary Christian School celebrated its 50th anniversary with the opening of its newly completed administration and classroom complex that included a computer lab and the first location of an on-campus library. These enhancements were made possible by a successful capital campaign supported by the entire school community.

Calvary Christian School finished a second extensive remodeling nine years later. This allowed for an additional class per grade level, a relocated and enlarged library, a new science lab, and a grass playing field.

AT A GLANCE

APPLICATION DEADLINE	January
OPEN HOUSES	October & November
TOURS	Call for personalized campus tours
UNIFORMS	Yes
AFTER-SCHOOL PROGRAMS	Yes
SEE MAP	A on page 255

CAMPBELL HALL

4533 LAUREL CANYON BLVD., NORTH HOLLYWOOD, CA 91607

TEL: 818.505.5338 FAX: 818.505.5319

www.campbellhall.org

HEAD OF SCHOOL:	**REV. CANON JULIAN P. BULL**
DIRECTOR OF ADMISSIONS:	**GEORGE WHITE**
TYPE OF SCHOOL:	**CO-ED EPISCOPAL**
GRADES:	**K–12**
ENROLLMENT: 1,111	TUITION: $31,700 - 37,260
NEW FAMILY FEE: $2,500	APPLICATION FEE: $135
ACCREDITATION: CAIS/WASC/NAIS	FINANCIAL AID: YES

CAMPBELL HALL is the place to go to enjoy all the advantages of a private school education. The lush campus setting provides 14 acres of open space, modern buildings, sports fields, and grassy play areas surrounded by huge, old eucalyptus groves. Campbell Hall's three-story academic center which was designed by architect Louis Liets (formerly of the firm Laffen-Liets). Its architectural beauty reflects Mr. Liets' own style as well as the influence of Frank Lloyd Wright. This extraordinary building uses well-placed windows and skylights to make the outside foliage and open spaces part of the atmosphere within. Touring the school gave me the feeling of what one might experience in a grade school of the fifties. Many of the parents with whom I toured were warmed by the sight and feeling of a place that reminded them of their own school experiences.

One of the first things that impressed me about the school was that everything was incredibly well-organized. The parent tour was scheduled to begin at 10 a.m., and it did! By the time I visited Campbell Hall, I had been on many (large group) tours where starting anywhere from 30 to 45 minutes late was the norm. Punctuality as well as the thorough presentation that was to follow gave me the impression that Campbell Hall was a well-run organization. Indeed, this is the area where it excels most.

The campus has two playgrounds, two gyms, four computer labs, five science labs, a theater, dance studio, weight room, basketball and handball courts, a football field, soccer field, baseball diamond, and a running track. The 35,000-volume library serves the entire school. Elementary classes visit the library every other week. There is a nurse on duty from 8:30 a.m. to 4 p.m.

The high point of the tour is the beautiful Ahmanson Library. It features 35 computer terminals, a special story time room for younger students, and huge windows (all with window seats) letting in the light, with greenery of the lush campus as a backdrop. On the first floor there are three computer application labs (25 computers in each), an elementary science lab, three seminar rooms, a kitchen, an archive studio, and offices for admissions and administration. The top floor of the building houses the executive offices of the headmaster, the development staff, an executive kitchen, and many conference facilities for administrative use.

Campbell Hall is very proud of their Arts & Education Center, a 111,000-square-foot complex that includes three two-story connected buildings, a multilevel subterranean parking garage, twenty-four state-of-the-art classrooms, an art gallery, a television studio, a video production lab, a photography lab and darkroom, a recording studio, a faculty resource center, outdoor learning spaces, terraces, and gardens, with extensive use of multimedia throughout. It was designed by Gensler, an architectural firm renowned for its expertise in education design and innovative sustainability practices, the project is LEED certified.

The teaching approach is traditional, but children are allowed to work at their own developmental pace with an emphasis on creating a nurturing rather than competitive environment. Language arts, mathematics, science, social studies and Spanish (beginning in the third grade) provide the core of classroom work. Specialized study in music, art, and computer skills enriches the academic curriculum. There are two classes at each grade level for Kindergarten thru sixth grade, with 23 students in a class and 46 students per grade. The teachers weave the subjects together in a way that allows one section of the curriculum to relate to another. For example, first-graders exploring a unit on apples spend their English lesson reading "Johnny Appleseed," and their math lesson estimates the number of seeds in an apple. Meanwhile, fifth-graders learn to make paper and ink as part of their discussions about the United States during the 1800s.

The Kindergarten Day consists of reading readiness, story time, mathematics readiness, "Show and Tell," computer skills, music, lunch, snack and playtime, calendar activities, science, drawing and painting, language arts, printing, physical education, building block play, chapel and listening skills.

The upper school offers a challenging, college preparatory curriculum in the traditional disciplines: English, mathematics, science, foreign language, social science, the arts, and physical education. Supporting this core curriculum is a variety of studies and experiences in athletics, visual arts, music, drama, computer science, and environmental education. Many of their highest achieving students earn recognition from the Cum Laude Society, which honors students in the top 20% of the class. These students receive special recognition at a ceremony during their Senior year and at graduation.

The school orchestra gives spring and fall concerts, and children may study violin in kindergarten with more choices added each year. Campbell Hall also offers a ballet program with two performances each year.

The school brochure lists all the teachers and gives their educational backgrounds. Most hold advanced degrees, either in education or in their subject discipline. All are encouraged to continue their education while at Campbell Hall through additional graduate courses, and through attendance at professional conferences and workshops. The school also has a strong professional development program funded in part by gifts to the school's growing endowment.

The school's goal is to provide an environment where students learn the value of working together as a community, and are taught to have respect for themselves and others. These themes are regularly addressed during chapel, which takes place Monday through Thursday from 8:40 a.m. to 9 a.m. in the lower gym. Campbell Hall is committed to encouraging both the intellectual and the spiritual growth of its students. An emphasis on moral and ethical behavior is woven throughout all aspects of school life. Campbell Hall also has a wonderful parent education series, where they bring in a number of professionals to speak to their students, faculty, and parents on a wide-rage of adolescent related topics.

At chapel, the children sing hymns and listen to the Chaplain talk about various themes relating to spiritual and moral growth. All religions are welcome, and many holidays are celebrated such as Christmas, Hanukkah, and holy days of other religions from around the world. One-in-six Campbell Hall students receives financial aid which creates a very diverse school population

There are many fundraising events at Campbell Hall such as the Hot Lunch Program, Ad- Book, PTC Picnic, and the annual Bagpipe Ball. The 21st Century Fund raised huge amounts of money over the years to make possible the construction of their new three-story building. Many donations have been received from the school's families, although much of the funding came from grants from large corporations and charitable donations. Parents are encouraged to give to the school but are never pressured. However, involvement is strongly encouraged and provides the backbone of the school's activities. Parent volunteers play an important role in the daily life of all Campbell Hall students, and enrich the school by sharing their time, energy, and talents. I love schools that encourage parents to do this. The kids see that their parents are interested in what's going on at school and that's a natural boost for them to want to do well. Here is a list of parent-run and parent-volunteered school activities/functions:

Parent-Run: P.T.C. Picnic, the Bagpipe Ball, Faculty/Staff Appreciation, class coordinators, Student Store, Hospitality, Parent Resources Register, Events Boards, Pizza and Pasta Lunches, Hot Dog/Hamburger Lunch,
Parent-Involved: Library, Emergency Preparedness, Fine Arts Guild, Chapel Program, Homecoming, Ad-Book campaign, College Counseling, Developmental Office, High School Athletic Booster Club, Studio Art Class

Campbell Hall supports many different opportunities for students to serve their communities through the chapel program as well as the student council. Elementary student aides assist in the classroom, the office, the chapel, and in the primary grades.

In addition, the Alternative Gift Fair (held during November) teaches children about the needs of people around the world and provides them with ways to help. Each student in the high school is required to complete 50 hours of community service. Three ongoing projects provide support for Hillsides Home in Pasadena an Episcopal home for abused and neglected children, for the Church of the Advent in South Central Los Angeles, and for Holy Innocents, a partner Episcopal school in Port-du-Paix, Haiti. Outreach projects have included work with organizations like Heal the Bay, and The Tree People. This is why I love this school! They don't just talk the talk, they actually walk the walk!

HISTORY

The school was founded by the Reverend Alexander Campbell on February 7, 1944, with a group of 74 students. Incorporated as a non-profit organization since its founding, the school is guided by a Board of Directors. Under its charge the school grew steadily and by 1964 included kindergarten through twelfth grade. In 1971, Dr. Campbell's familiar man- date, "Carry on friends" was taken up by the Reverend Thomas G. Clarke. This former student's appointment as headmaster provided the school with the continuity it needed to flourish and grow to its present student body of 1,000.

AT A GLANCE

APPLICATION DEADLINE	December 17 (6-12), January 16 (K-5)
OPEN HOUSES	Call school for dates
UNIFORMS	Yes
BEFORE/AFTER-SCHOOL PROGRAMS	Yes
SUMMER PROGRAMS	Yes
ISEE	Required after Grade 5
SEE MAP	A on page 255

CARLTHORP SCHOOL

438 SAN VICENTE BLVD., SANTA MONICA, CA 90402
TEL: 310.451.1332 FAX: 310.451.8559
www.carlthorp.org

HEAD OF SCHOOL:	**DEE MENZIES**
DIRECTOR OF ADMISSIONS:	**LYNN WAGMEISTER**
TYPE OF SCHOOL:	**CO-ED DAY**
GRADES:	**K–6**
ENROLLMENT: 280	TUITION: $25,375
NEW FAMILY FEE: $1,000	APPLICATION FEE: $100
ACCREDITATION: CAIS/WASC/NAIS	FINANCIAL AID: YES

CARLTHORP SCHOOL is located in a residential neighborhood in Santa Monica. Years ago, it underwent extensive remodeling and added a new school building. The main building is an attractive, modern, Spanish-style structure, and sits discreetly among the surrounding homes. In Santa Monica, the zoning codes are very strict, luckily the buildings were well thought out and blend nicely into the neighborhood, so keep a careful eye out for it as you might just drive past it!

The school office is comfortable with plush carpeting, draperies, and upholstered chairs. During my visit the school receptionist was attentive and helpful. Then my student tour guide arrived, a very nice sixth-grade boy with an unmistakably famous last name. He gave me the tour in record time, and I found myself hustling after him with raised finger saying ". . . but wait a minute, what about the . . ." He did a great job and at the end of my tour, while I tried to catch my breath, he did answer all my questions!

The campus is small and compact although the last remodeling helped solve the school's space problem. There is a playground behind the school and another building at the back of the lot that houses the lower elementary grades. I found the rooms to be modern, pleasant, bright, and very well stocked with all manner of resources for the children to use. The credentialed teachers are enthusiastic, passionate about their work, and willing to stop and talk when you drop in.

The majority of students entering kindergarten have attended preschool and are ready to begin the academic studies of reading, phonics, arithmetic, and printing letters. There are 40 students in kindergarten, 20 boys and 20 girls. Their sibling numbers change every year, so they are not always taking 50% siblings and 50% new families. Their space availability varies. However, unless you have a child already in the school, it might be difficult to get in.

This is a very academically-oriented school with advanced programs set up for accelerated learners. The boy who showed me around took a certain pride in showing me the 'advanced' classes in math, English, and reading.

Math, reading, phonics, spelling, English, written composition, geography, history, science, and penmanship are introduced at the appropriate grade levels. There are specialists in art, music, and library science weekly. Computer and typing classes have been integrated more fully into all the classrooms. Spanish is taught in grades K through 6, and all students participate in physical education.

To avoid homework battles your child can go to the after-school homework club, where teachers provide support Monday through Thursday from 3:30-5:15 p.m. How nice! I wish I could have put my own children into a homework club.

In the past, Carlthorp School received the National Blue Ribbon Award for Excellence by earning standardized test scores that ranked in the top ten percent of all independent schools in the nation. They were one of two secular independent schools in the nation to receive this award.

Carlthorp provides an academic education in the purest sense and it is well run and serious. Although there are many wealthy and celebrated families here, Carlthorp puts the focus on providing a high-quality academic education, and it does not feel like a 'celebrity kids' school. Ten percent of families receive financial aid. There isn't as much diversity as you would find in other east side schools, but if your philosophy is in accordance with a strong academic education, then this is your school.

HISTORY

While serving as principal of a private school in Los Angeles, Miss Mercedes Thorp met Mrs. Ann Carlson Granstrom. These two educators came to believe they could create a new school by combining their talents. In 1939, they founded Carlthorp School in a small house on Fourth Street in Santa Monica. They had one student when it opened, but enrollment grew to ten before the year was over. Both women believed there was a need in the community for an alternative to public school education: a structured, traditional school that would emphasize a strong and balanced academic program. Their intention was to provide a comprehensive education for each child, enhanced by good study habits, courtesy, self-discipline, and positive self-esteem. These two educators felt confident that a low student-to-teacher ratio was essential for providing a nurturing classroom setting. Their goal was to prepare each child to meet the challenges of higher education and life.

AT A GLANCE

APPLICATION DEADLINE	November 2
OPEN HOUSES	Tuesdays & Thursdays, starting September
UNIFORMS	Yes
BEFORE/AFTER-SCHOOL PROGRAMS	Yes
SUMMER PROGRAMS	Yes
SEE MAP	A on page 255

CENTER FOR EARLY EDUCATION

563 N. ALFRED STREET, WEST HOLLYWOOD, CA 90048
TEL: 323.561.0707 FAX: 323.651.0860
www.centerforearlyeducation.org

HEAD OF SCHOOL:	**MARK BROOKS**
DIRECTOR OF ADMISSIONS:	**DEEDIE HUDNUT**
TYPE OF SCHOOL:	**CO-ED DAY**
GRADES:	**PRESCHOOL–6**
ENROLLMENT: 539	TUITION: $19,050 - 29,100
NEW FAMILY FEE: $1,500	APPLICATION FEE: $100
ACCREDITATION: CAIS/WASC/NAIS/CASE	FINANCIAL AID: YES

THE CENTER FOR EARLY EDUCATION offers a developmental education with all the extras. The building is a glorious architectural achievement with clean, simple lines, and well-planned exterior spaces. The classrooms are large, bright and full of all the modern educational tools money can buy. In the last couple of years, the Center's campus has added a futuristic and extraordinarily flexible Innovation Lab and Maker's Space for use by all students. Science labs for K – 6 students have also been renovated.

The school is located on one and one-quarter acres in West Hollywood, not far from the Beverly Center and across the street from a local Public School. Plans are underway for a comprehensive campus expansion onto adjacent and proximate properties. There are two rooftop playgrounds which provide ample space for the kids to blow off steam at various breaks during the day, along with their P.E. classes.

This preschool is a showcase for preschools. It is wonderful. In fact, I want to go there myself! The rooms are full of toys and musical instruments, and the play structures outside are state-of-the-art. If you detect any bitterness in this accounting, it is no doubt because I was unable (like so many of us with our noses pressed against the double-thick tinted glass) to get my child enrolled.

Each preschool class has 22 students and three teachers, and each elementary class has 30 students and two credentialed master teachers! There are specialists in art, music, science, Innovation/library skills, and physical education. The teaching philosophy there is decidedly developmental. Each child works at his/her own pace, and emphasis is placed on building social skills, self-esteem, character and developing a joy of learning rather than focusing solely on academic achievement.

The style of teaching at The Center is non-traditional, with emphasis on the 'whole-child' philosophy. Elementary classrooms are organized in continuums rather than traditional grade levels. Team- teaching is employed with two teachers giving lessons to different groups in the same physical space. The focus is on whole-child education and resource specialists allow for additional support or enrichments for children to benefit from this rigorous education. The Art Program is spectacular, and the school has spared no expense. All the teachers and the two art specialists have a great deal of training, experience, and enthusiasm. The art rooms are large and airy, well-stocked with materials, and the students' work can be seen gracing the walls of the entire school. Art History is taught in conjunction with the children using watercolors, oils, pastels, sculpture, pen and ink, by cutting and pasting shapes à la Monet! Some of the work the children displayed was breathtaking. If art is important to you, this is a school you will definitely want to check out.

This is one of the few private schools where there is a provision for welcoming young students whose learning style has not yet been determined to gifted children who have a variety of learning styles. Now for the bad news...getting in.

The Director of Admissions, Deedie Hudnut (a charming, gracious lady with a very tough job), is encouraging and candid with prospective applicants about the low rate of attrition, and the number of siblings applying each year.

The school has an enrollment cap of 540 students that it strictly adheres too. Yes, there are many wealthy families here and quite a few celebrity children, but The Center is doing a fine job at continuing to improve its ethnic and social diversity among its student population. The school also has wide ranging community service initiatives which take students into the community and teach them how to help and support others.

The following criteria are used in the selection of new children entering the school:
1. A balance of boys and girls.
2. Families from different racial, ethnic, and socio-economic groups.
3. Integration of children with different personalities, learning styles, and individual needs.
4. Children's birthdays are equally represented.
5. A mix of first, second, and third children.
6. Families from different geographical areas.
7. Special circumstances are: single-parent families, adopted children students on financial aid, families needing daycare.
8. Siblings are not automatically accepted. Sibling families are expected to have demonstrated a level of support, commitment, involvement, and participation within their community.

You are further informed in the application that the $100 fee does not guarantee an interview for your family, but the Center makes every attempt to interview applicant families. You are invited to the Open House (attendance is a mandatory part of the application process. Because of the scarcity of available spaces, definitely have a second and third choice lined up.

HISTORY

The Center For Early Education is a private, nonprofit educational institution. It was founded in 1939 by a group of psychoanalysts and parents who believed a child's emotional and social development was as important as his or her educational growth, and that the early years were critical to both. It started first as a nursery school, then as a college to train teachers and administrators, and in 1971 it became an elementary school. Reveta Bowers has steered the ship for many years. She will be missed sorely, but they are thrilled to welcome Mark Brooks.

AT A GLANCE

APPLICATION DEADLINE	December 1
UNIFORMS	No
BEFORE/AFTER-SCHOOL PROGRAMS	Yes
COMMUNITY OUTREACH PROGRAMS	Yes
SEE MAP	C on page 255

CHADWICK SCHOOL

26800 S. ACADEMY DRIVE, PALOS VERDES PENINSULA, CA 90274

TEL: 310.377.1543 FAX: 310.377.0380

www.chadwickschool.org

HEAD OF UPPER SCHOOL:	TED HILL
HEAD OF LOWER SCHOOL	JOSIE BAHEDRY
DIRECTOR OF ADMISSIONS:	JUDITH WOLSTAN
TYPE OF SCHOOL:	CO-ED DAY
GRADES:	K–12
ENROLLMENT: 825	TUITION: $27,890 - 32,950
NEW FAMILY FEE: $1,200	APPLICATION FEE: $125
ACCREDITATION: CAIS/WASC/NAIS/CASE	FINANCIAL AID: YES

CHADWICK SCHOOL, founded in 1935 by visionary educator Margaret Lee Chadwick, sits atop a peaceful, verdant hilltop on the Palos Verdes Peninsula with sweeping views of the Los Angeles basin. The only K-12 independent, college-preparatory day school in the greater South Bay area, Chadwick currently enrolls approximately 825 students. The 45-acre campus (yes, 45 acres) provides a beautiful setting for all of those lucky children attending this school.

Here is part of Chadwick's Mission Statement as taken from the brochure:

> Chadwick, a K-12 school founded in 1935, is dedicated to the development of academic excellence, exemplary character, and self-discovery through experience. We live in accordance with our core values of respect, responsibility, honesty, fairness, and compassion. Through active participation in a diverse school community, students prepare to contribute meaningfully to their local, national, and global communities. Talented and caring faculty and staff cultivate in each student the joy of learning, self-confidence, well-being, and the individual gifts that each possesses. By living and learning in an atmosphere of integrity and trust, students come to expect the best of themselves and others.

When I take families on private tours of the school I am always lucky to have the Head of Admissions, the fabulous Judy Wolstan looking after us. She is warm, welcoming, and always up for a hike to show off their incredible campus! I have also got to know the new Head of the Village School, Josie Bahedry, formally from John Thomas Dye. She is a fellow Brit so we immediately hit it off and I was delighted to see that she has taken over the most wonderful house on the property that used to serve as a private home on campus. Having moved her offices into such a comfortable environment immediately puts you at ease and the children are encouraged (and do) often stop by to say hello or ask for advice.

The academic facilities include science classrooms, labs and preparation rooms, global language rooms, science buildings and labs, and a botanical garden. The Village School complex has art rooms, music facilities, and playgrounds for younger students. The arts facilities are impressive with a performing arts facility with indoor theaters, classroom space and studios, an art gallery, fine arts studios and a digital photography studio, a technical theater and amphitheater. Leavenworth Library Learning Center includes 25,000 volumes, four classrooms, a telepresence room, reading and periodical lounges, study rooms, and a technology area with desktop computers and wireless connectivity for students. There is a separate library for K-6 students including a research area and a story corner. There is a technology center, as well as computers in all elementary school classrooms. Athletic facilities include a football field, a gym, a pool, and baseball and softball fields.

Chadwick is composed of three educational divisions: the Village School, (Kindergarten through Grade 6), the Middle School (Grades 7 and 8), and the Upper School (Grades 9 through 12). While each division has its own director and distinct area on campus, the curriculum is coordinated for smooth transitions between the divisions.

Chadwick's faculty is recruited from across the nation and more than half of them have advanced degrees. The Admission Office conducts extensive outreach to identify and admit 'the best and brightest' students. In doing so, the student body reflects the school's commitment to both socio-economic and cultural diversity. The school provides more than $3 million annually in student financial aid.

What sets Chadwick apart from nearly all the other schools here in LA is that it has a second campus in Songdo, South Korea. Chadwick International is a PK-12 international school with 860 students. This second campus affords opportunities for exchanges and collaboration for students and faculty. That's where the telepresence room comes into play. Children are able to meet their counterparts in real time and find out what's going on in each others' schools. What a brilliant idea!

New additions to Chadwick include the Margaret Chadwick Center which houses co-curricular programs including outdoor education, community service, and global programs (academic exchanges, service, conferences). Also, the STEM center is open, enabling students to participate in research, internships, and competitions in math, science and robotics. The Senior Apex project allows every senior to work on a culminating research project through their senior English classes. This helps prepare them for similar work in university.

The College Board has selected Chadwick as one of only a few schools worldwide to pilot its Capstone research course. This pilot program is in its third year and is available to students in the 10th grade and above. Also called a capstone experience, culminating project, or senior exhibition (among many other terms), a capstone project is a multifaceted assignment that serves as a culminating academic and intellectual experience for students, typically during their final year of high school or middle school. While similar in some ways to a college thesis, capstone projects may take a wide variety of forms, but most are long-term investigative projects that culminate in a final product, presentation, or performance. For example, students may be asked to select a topic, profession, or social problem that interests them, conduct research on the subject, maintain a portfolio of findings or results, create a final product demonstrating their learning acquisition or conclusions (a paper, short film, or multimedia presentation, for example), and give an oral presentation on the project to a panel of teachers, experts, and community members who collectively evaluate its quality.

This is a fabulous school and well worth the commute if you are one of those families that doesn't live on the wild and far away peninsula of Palos Verdes and are always aghast whenever someone says they are going there! Go on, fill up the car, turn on your navigation device, and take a closer look. Please remember when you hear the words, "Location, location, location…think Carpool, carpool, carpool!" Or you can move to some of the beach communities where they have buses that can bring the kids to school so you can enjoy a run on the beach!

HISTORY

In 1935 Margaret Lee Chadwick founded Chadwick Open-air School in her San Pedro home with four students, two of them her own children. In 1938 the Palos Verdes, California campus of "Chadwick Seaside School" opened. Seventy-five day and boarding students attend. In 1963, Commander and Margaret Lee Chadwick retired after 28 years of service to the school. The Roessler-Chadwick Foundation is created and appoints its first Board of trustees. In 1968 the boarding program is discontinued. The school's endowment fund is established, today valued at approximately $25 million. This fund ensures Chadwick's long-term financial stability. In 1981, Chadwick's first community service program is established. It was recognized in US News and World Report as one of the finest in the United States. Today, more than 90 percent of Upper School students participate in this voluntary program.

AT A GLANCE

APPLICATION DEADLINE	January
OPEN HOUSES	September to January
UNIFORMS	No
BEFORE/AFTER-SCHOOL PROGRAMS	Yes
SUMMER SCHOOL	Yes
SEE MAP	E on page 255

CHAMINADE COLLEGE PREPARATORY

MIDDLE SCHOOL
119800 DEVONSHIRE STREET, CHATSWORTH, CA 91311
TEL: 818.363.8127 FAX: 818.363.1219

HIGH SCHOOL
7500 CHAMINADE AVENUE, WEST HILLS, CA 91304
TEL:818.347.8300 FAX: 818.348.8374

www.chaminade.com

PRINCIPAL:	**MIKE VALENTINE**
DIRECTOR OF ADMISSIONS:	**BARBARA WILLICK (MIDDLE)**
	ESTHER BONINO-BENNETT (HIGH)
GRADES:	**6–12**
ENROLLMENT:800	TUITION: $14,875
NEW FAMILY FEE: $750	APPLICATION FEE: $100
ACCREDITATION: WASC	FINANCIAL AID: YES

CHAMINADE COLLEGE PREPARATORY SCHOOL is in Chatsworth, which is really not so far away, but as you drive along the 118 freeway towards the Tampa exit you really do feel as if you're leaving Los Angeles far behind you!

The Middle School campus is separate from the high school and it is gorgeous. The grounds are enormous with sprawling playing fields that seem to go on for as far as the eye can see. It was such a pleasure to drive into the ample parking area. Everything is spread out and easily accessible. I was shown their baseball, hockey, and soccer fields, the Assembly hall, music rooms, science labs, and classrooms that seemed to go on forever. As we walked around the campus, I was struck by the warmth and genuine pleasure that the kids exuded when I talked to them about their school life. They were very confident and introduced me to some of their teachers along the way. We were all quite out of breath by the time we returned to the main office!

Chaminade works closely with the families enrolled to provide a challenging, coeducational education in the Marianist tradition. This tradition, grounded in the values of Jesus, educates the whole child while emphasizing family spirit in a nurturing, caring environment, attentive to the moral, spiritual and religious development of students. As the school explained, "The school prepares college-bound students throughout their middle and high school years in a rigorous program of academic excellence. Students from a diversity of cultural, religious, and economic backgrounds come together for an active and varied curricular and extra-curricular program. The mission of Chaminade College Preparatory is to form morally aware and academically capable people to be outstanding contributors to the future."

The following is the course of studies that is offered to the students. It is a reflection of California state standards, university requirements, and individualized programs of study. The curriculum is designed to develop academic skills and to foster inquiry, creativity, and a love of learning and to prepare young people for high school and college.

Advanced or honors classes are offered in mathematics, Spanish, band, and computer science in the eighth grade, and in mathematics and band for sixth and seventh grade. Students qualify to be in each advanced class separately. That is, students may be in one or more of these classes for each year. Evaluation is an ongoing process for admitting or releasing students from the program.

Remedial classes are held each year for those students who struggling to keep up with the rigorous curriculum. Students may be required to attend these classes held either concurrently during the school year or during the summer. Required attendance is determined by the classroom teacher, and is indicated through report card comments.

Chaminade believes that athletics play a very important role in the holistic education of their students. In their brochure they point out that their program "encompasses the areas of spiritual, social, emotional, intellectual, creative, and physical growth for the student-athlete, and emphasizes the principles of good sportsmanship." I noticed that after my daughter's school (Immaculate Heart) had played hockey against many different schools, Charlotte and I agreed that the girls at Chaminade to be excellent "sportsmen." If your child is athletic, then take a look at this list of sports this school offers:

Cross Country, Golf, Football, Tennis, Volleyball, Basketball, Wrestling, Lacrosse, Softball, Track, Swimming and don't forget Cheerleading (considered a sport of sorts!) Plus fencing and sailing.

All students are required to take the religious education classes and attend the liturgical celebrations and retreats. The school expects your child to show up for test dates and to turn in homework without fail. A friend of mine, whose daughter attends Chaminde, told me that the school really is tough about not turning in homework assignments. I then spoke to the students and they told me that it's not that bad and there's plenty of wiggle room if you miss a day of school. The homework is posted on the school's website. There is tutoring and after-school make up time if a child is absent. Should you be looking for a school that offers your child a well-rounded school experience do take a closer look. The school expects a lot from your child, but in return gives a lot.

HISTORY

Founded 1956 by Marianist Order of Priests and Brothers. Chaminade was named after Society of Mary founder Blessed William Joseph Chaminade. It is an independent school guided by a Board of Directors and in 1998 was recognized as a National Blue Ribbon School

AT A GLANCE

APPLICATION DEADLINE	January 16
TOURS	Call admissions office to schedule
UNIFORMS	Yes
AFTER-SCHOOL PROGRAMS	Yes
SUMMER PROGRAMS	Yes
SEE MAP	A on page 255

CHANDLER SCHOOL

1005 ARMADA DRIVE, PASADENA, CA 91103
TEL: 626.795.9314 FAX: 626.795.6508
www.chandlerschool.org

HEAD OF SCHOOL:	**JOHN FINCH**
DIRECTOR OF ADMISSIONS:	**GRETCHEN LURIE**
TYPE OF SCHOOL:	**CO-ED DAY**
GRADES:	**K–8**
ENROLLMENT: 445	TUITION: $21,370 - 23,175
NEW FAMILY FEE: $2,250	APPLICATION FEE: $150
ACCREDITATION: CAIS/WASC/NAIS	FINANCIAL AID: YES

CHANDLER SCHOOL is located in a residential neighborhood in northwest Pasadena. The four and a half acre campus overlooks the Arroyo Seco (at the Rosebowl) and the view is spectacular. There are beautiful old pine trees outside the older campus buildings, which houses grades K-5. The school has a great athletic field that sits between the upper and lower school buildings.

The mission of Chandler School as taken from their brochure is:

> To provide each student with the highest quality and most academically challenging education in a nurturing, balanced and diverse environment. We strive to have our students gain a love of learning, a means of thinking independently and an ability to work collaboratively. A Chandler education seeks to develop character, self-reliance and a commitment to community in students as a foundation for academic and personal success.

The entire lower school was renovated with new classrooms in 1999 as was the middle school in 2008. There remains a hexagon-shaped kindergarten room, and all the other rooms are a generous size with lots of light. The two kindergarten classrooms share a patio where the children have juice at recess time, and a dedicated play space for them that includes a dramatic plays area. Classrooms have reading libraries and centers appropriate to the age of the children. All classrooms have computers with each class also visiting the lower school computer lab once a week. This is a traditional, academic school starting right off in kindergarten. There's lots of classwork on display. Parents choosing this educational approach usually feel comfortable when they are given a concrete way to track their children's progress.

Chandler has a Resource Center office with a full-time educational associate on staff to help children with scholastic tutoring. They also have a part-time school counselor. The art studio, which the lower school students visit once a week for 45 minutes, is located in the middle school.

Lower School Curriculum

The Chandler Lower School Curriculum fosters intellectual curiosity and achievement in its students while nurturing their emotional and social development. The lower school program emphasizes basic skill development, and encourages children to become confident learners. The academic programs are challenging, but age appropriate. Composition, mathematics, science, social studies and foreign language are all taught within a structured classroom environment.

The language arts program includes a phonics-based reading program in K through 2. Beginning in 3rd grade, the reading program is literature based with students reading and analyzing novels, poetry, and short stories. Frequent field trips and visiting speakers enhance the academic programs. "Character Counts" is used as a framework for the children to learn and practice the six pillars of character: respect, fairness, citizenship, responsibility, caring, and trustworthiness.

The math curriculum in the lower school sets out to ensure that children have a firm understanding of a variety of basic math concepts. In Kindergarten, there is an emphasis on patterning, sorting, classifying, counting and sequencing numbers. In grades 1 to 4, children work on whole number computation, geometry, measurement, whole number operations, fractions, and decimals. In 5th grade, students review the basics and explore number systems, estimation, computation, probability, and two and three-dimensional geometry.

Chandler offers a science program starting in Kindergarten. Their science lab allows them to provide students with solid science training. K through fifth grades visit the lower school science lab weekly in small groups for a hands-on introduction to basic science concepts and techniques. The students in the lower school cover the basics of science investigation with an emphasis on the physical, Earth and biological sciences.

Physical education classes and athletic activities form a regular part of the daily schedule for all lower school students. The purpose is to develop self-esteem, pride, and an appreciation of teamwork through physical and motor development. More formal activities begin in third grade.

All lower school children participate in the Foreign Language Program. Students meet with their instructors twice weekly for half hour lessons. Children study both French and Spanish in any given year.

Starting in Kindergarten, children begin their exploration of the world through a social studies curriculum that serves to expose children to new ideas, and to widen their knowledge about their community and beyond. They learn geographical locations and concepts throughout the grades.

In weekly computer lessons held in the lab, lower school students learn how to search for information and practice basic skills using software appropriate to their grade level. Each classroom is equipped with computers, where students can work on writing and research skills.

Beginning in Kindergarten, children visit the library once a week. The Chandler lower school library is a warm and inviting place for children to hear stories, read aloud, and develop skills on how to choose appropriate literature for one's reading level. The library is well equipped with computers.

Art classes are held in a separate art studio equipped to provide students with experiences in a variety of media and techniques including: painting, weaving, sculpture and ceramics. Each spring the students present an art exhibit for the entire school community.

In music, kindergarten students develop basic rhythm and movement through the Orff- Schulwerk method. They continue this study through their fifth grade year. Choral instruction, learning basic notation and exposure to diverse music are also components of the music curriculum. There is an after-school program that introduces children to string and wind instruments.

Chandler's community projects are often done in tandem with the Middle school students, which encourage students to look beyond the classroom as a learning opportunity, and help them understand how they can impact someone's life and learn from their community. Past partnerships include Friends-In-Deed, Children's Hospital, Pasadena Senior Center, and The Tree People.

Communicating student progress to parents is a high priority at Chandler. Parent/teacher conferences are held twice a year while written reports are sent home at least three times a year. Both parents and faculty are encouraged to communicate with each other whenever they believe there is a need.

Middle School Curriculum

The curriculum is departmentalized and includes English, history, mathematics, science, and foreign language. Class size is small (from 12 to 20 students) and the student-to-teacher ratio is 9:1.

Advanced classes of math and foreign languages are offered in grades seven and eight. The focus of the upper school level is on developing strong writing, speaking, critical thinking, and problem solving skills. Homework? Expect one to two hours per night.

The English program includes writing, vocabulary, spelling, grammar, and literature. Writing skills are taught with an emphasis on organization of thoughts and ideas first, and later focus on correct writing technique.

The history curriculum offers ancient and medieval history to grade six, world history in grade seven, and US history and government in grade eight. There is a focus on learning research techniques, oral presentations, note taking, and an awareness of current events.

Mathematics in sixth grade offers pre-algebra and teaches computation and conceptual skills. In seventh grade the students have an advanced algebra program.

The three-year science program covers general science, biology, and introduction to physical science. There is also a three-year French and Spanish program, which offers grammar, vocabulary, conversation, and an appreciation of the cultures.

The three-year computer program develops skills in word processing, spreadsheets, and databases. Art classes are offered in drawing, printmaking, ceramics, and watercolor. Grades six and seven study the principles of design and color theory.

Music for upper school students focuses on creating, composing, improvising, and interpreting. Theater works are created by the students who write the text and music and choreograph the dances.

Mini courses are offered (as electives) in art, music, drama, human development, community service, and drug prevention. Advisor-advisee groups consisting of a faculty member and a small group of students meet twice a week to discuss values, teenage issues, and moral and ethical decision-making.

Boys' interscholastic sports teams compete (after school) in flag football, basketball, soccer, track, and baseball. Girls' teams compete in volleyball, basketball, soccer, and track and field. Co-ed competition is offered (off campus) in tennis, swimming, bowling, golf, and cross-country.

The Tower, Chandler's school yearbook, is published each year by upper school students who are responsible for creating, designing, writing, and editing it. The school's newspaper, Charger Express, is issued six times each year by upper school students who oversee its publication.

Parent participation is strongly encouraged. Volunteers serve as class representatives, work in the hot lunch program, staff the school's Shamrock Shoppe, and instruct the Art Docent Program. Community service programs are conducted through organizations such as Friend-In-Deed, Union Station, and Pasadena Head Start.

One of the missions at Chandler is to prepare the students for success at a competitive college preparatory school. There is an Advisory Program for Middle School students. Chandler students have been accepted into Campbell Hall, Flintridge Preparatory School, Harvard Westlake, Polytechnic, and Westridge School for Girls to name a few.

HISTORY

In 1950, Katherine and Thomas Chandler founded Chandler School with a vision to provide students with innovative, inspired academic programs taught by a caring, dedicated faculty. There were fourteen students attending grades four through eight on opening day at the Altadena campus.

With the help of forty parents, a down payment was raised to purchase the school's present site in September of 1958. The school began with only two buildings and an athletic field, but steadily added classrooms and multi-purpose facilities during the next two decades.

By 1979, 366 students were being instructed in grades kindergarten through eight, and most classroom buildings were completed. Current enrollment is 445 students with a faculty of 47.

AT A GLANCE

APPLICATION DEADLINE	February
OPEN HOUSES	October & January
UNIFORMS	Yes
AFTER-SCHOOL PROGRAMS	Yes
SUMMER PROGRAMS	Yes
SEE MAP	A on page 255

CHILDREN'S COMMUNITY SCHOOL

14702 SYLVAN STREET, VAN NUYS, CA 91411

TEL: 818.780.6226 FAX: 818.780.5834

www.ccsteaches.com

HEAD OF SCHOOL:	**NEAL WRIGHTSON**
DIRECTOR OF ADMISSIONS:	**HEATHER MCPHERSON**
TYPE OF SCHOOL:	**CO-ED DAY**
GRADES:	**K–6**
ENROLLMENT: 120	TUITION: $26,992
NEW FAMILY FEE: $500	APPLICATION FEE: $125
ACCREDITATION: NONE	FINANCIAL AID: YES

THE CHILDREN'S COMMUNITY SCHOOL is a gem, a truly authentic example of Progressive education in Los Angeles. There is no other place like it. It's located in a modest residential neighborhood near Victory and Van Nuys Boulevards.

The main building, formerly a church, has been converted to part of the school that houses offices, music room, printing press, and various workspaces. Outside is a warren of modern classrooms, all sharing a common courtyard. The campus maintains its rustic roots but CCS has added three new classrooms and a large multi-purpose room that allows the entire school community to meet together comfortably. A large library is now housed in the former-church sanctuary.

This is not a chi-chi, manicured place, and it doesn't want to be. The school is not about appearances, but method and philosophy. So if you're looking for a classroom with spanking clean desks all lined up in a row, move on!

If you are looking for a genuine Progressive education for your child, then your search is over. The approach at CCS is based on the philosophies of John Dewey, the preeminent educator/philosopher of the 1900's, whose educational ideas earned him the title of Father of American Education. Dewey believed the following:

> The educational process must begin with and build upon the interests of the child; that it must provide opportunity for the interplay of thinking and doing in the child's classroom experience; that the school should be organized as a 'miniature community,'that the teacher should be a guide and co-worker with the pupils, rather than a taskmaster assigning a fixed set of lessons and recitations; and the goal of education is the growth of the child in all aspects of its being.

As a classroom observer, I sensed in the students an openness and mutual respect for one another. There was a feeling of equality and a lack of competition among the group, despite the varying ages. During a group discussion, each student waited for his/her turn, listened attentively and asked thoughtful, specific questions. I never got the feeling that anyone was putting on airs and graces simply because there was a visitor in the room. Compliance with the rules seems to come from a knowledge and respect for them, rather than from fear of what will happen if they don't follow them.

CCS has a social studies core curriculum, with an emphasis on field trips. For example, a second grade study of Southern California might lead to an exploration of who lived here first. So in this case, the Chumash Indian lifestyle would then be delved into and questions would be asked about what they ate, wore, lived in, and valued. Students would also explore the kind of music, dances and games of the Chumash Indians.

Students go on field trips to places like the Southwest and Natural History Museums, Missions, and the Arboretum. Children enriched with new information would then begin to write, paint, dramatize, build with blocks, sculpt with clay, and cook, solidifying for themselves and illustrating for others, what they have learned.

The curriculum places an emphasis on block building. After a field trip, the children will have a chance to reconstruct the place that they visited with blocks. For example, if the trip were to a market, they would work together to figure out how the market was planned and would discuss what jobs would be needed to run the business in the market might even use the site for dramatic play, which would in turn call upon their math and organizational skills. Through situations like these they learn not only math, history, and critical thinking skills, but how to work together, to problem solve, and to see the world beyond the sandbox.

The school has adopted a schedule that allows students more time in cross-age specialty classes (including fitness classes) and integrates the artist specialist even further into the day to day class curriculum.

Kindergartners, because of their social and academic needs, are grouped separately, while children in grades 1 to 6 are divided into five multi-age groups. 'Traditional academics' are introduced in a non-traditional, age-appropriate manner. Children are expected to take responsibility for making their own lunches to bring to school and to remember their homework. The emphasis is on making the child more self-reliant and less dependent on parents.

There are specialists in dance, visual arts, storytelling, music, and for the oldest group, print shop. The average class size is 20 with two full-time teachers in each class. There is homework, which for kindergarten could be to remember an ingredient for cooking, in the first grade to count the number of rooms in their house, while in fifth grade, it might be to go to the library and do research on Greek mythology. There are no report cards. Standardized tests are given at the fifth and sixth grade level, but solely for practice, not to submit for admissions to seventh grade.

HISTORY

Children's Community School was founded in 1981 by Leni Jacksen and Neal Wrightson. Neal and Leni initially rented rooms behind a small church in Van Nuys; they began with a kindergarten and first grade. Having made an indelible mark on the school, Leni retired in 1996. For over 30 years, CCS has remained committed to offering a progressive education to a diverse community with the belief that democracy thrives when practiced in school.

AT A GLANCE

APPLICATION DEADLINE	End of January
OPEN HOUSES	November
SCHOOL TOURS	Wednesday mornings in Fall
UNIFORMS	No
ISEE TEST	No
SUMMER PROGRAMS	Yes
SEE MAP	A on page 255

CHRIST THE KING SCHOOL
617 N. ARDEN BLVD., LOS ANGELES, CA 90004
TEL: 323.462.4753 FAX: 323.462.8475
www.cksla.org

HEAD OF SCHOOL:	**RUTH ANDERSON**
TYPE OF SCHOOL:	**CO-ED CATHOLIC DAY**
GRADES:	**K–6**
ENROLLMENT: 222	TUITION: $3,910 - 4,360
TESTING FEE: $40	APPLICATION FEE: $200
ACCREDITATION: WASC/WCEA	FAMILY DISCOUNT OFFERED

CHRIST THE KING SCHOOL is located in Hancock Park on the corner of Arden about a block down from Melrose. For those who live or work in the neighborhood, this school is certainly an option for those considering a Catholic education for their children who have been unable to get into St. Brendan. St. Brendan suggests the Kindergarten program at Christ the King to parents if their child is under the prescribed entrance age.

I visited the school during the summer break, and I was buzzed into the courtyard where I was met by the school secretary, who gave me a brochure and invited me to walk around. I was a little disappointed by the size of the playground, which seemed rather small and had almost no greenery, but there were shaded areas where the children could eat under, and I am sure that once the playground was full of children it would look a lot more inviting.

The philosophy of Christ the King school is to educate the whole child, including on-going academic excellence, personal growth, as well as moral, social and spiritual development.

They offer a full physical education program and have many extra-curricular activities. Their sports program features football, volleyball, basketball, and track.

I had a long discussion with one of the teachers who told me that their school attracted a large percentage of non-English speaking parents, and that perhaps their curriculum was not quite as aggressive as St. Brendan's. This teacher was a delight, very warm and welcoming. She introduced me to her daughter who had recently graduated and been accepted to U.C. Berkley. She told me that she had loved her time at the school and had made long-lasting friendships. The school offers an academic curriculum comprised of religion, reading, language arts, math, science, social studies, family life, art, music, and computer education. An important part of its religious program is sacramental preparation, which is implemented with the help and guidance of the parish priests. They also have the Instructional Television Program in all the classrooms and integrate it into the whole curriculum.

The two-story facility is clean and compact. As they point out in their brochure, and I quote:

> One characteristic which exemplifies Christ the King School is the small school atmosphere built on family spirit and closeness of the school community. Parents are encouraged to become active in the Parent Organization and to participate in all our fundraisers.

I did look into several classrooms which appeared to be well-stocked and nicely laid out. Conveniently next to the auditorium is a large dining room and kitchen next door.

If you are looking for a Catholic private school education that is far more reasonable than most other private schools, then I would recommend that you visit the campus of Christ The King School.

HISTORY

Christ the King Parish was founded in 1926 on the feast of Christ the King. The ministry of educating children in the faith began almost immediately through the pastor's involvement in the newly founded program of the Confraternity of Christian Doctrine (C.C.D.). It was not until 1954 that the parish was in a financial position to undertake the task of planning to build a parochial school.

Construction of the school began in 1958 and in the same year, classes were held in the church-owned apartment building which was located on what is now the lower school yard. The classes were taught under the direction of Mother Adrian and four sisters of the Sacred Heart of Mary as well as one lay teacher. Initially there were only five grades and an enrollment of 116 students.

Half of the new school building was ready for occupancy in the Spring of 1959. By September of the same year, the school was opened. It would develop into a full eight-grade school in the course of subsequent years. In 1994, a Kindergarten class was added.

Today, Christ the King School comprises of ten classrooms (TK-8). The newest classroom, the Transitional Kindergarten, opened in August 2014.

AT A GLANCE

APPLICATION DEADLINE	Ongoing
UNIFORMS	Yes
AFTER-SCHOOL CARE	Yes
SEE MAP	A on page 255

CLAIRBOURN SCHOOL

8400 HUNTINGTON DRIVE, SAN GABRIEL, CA 91775

TEL: 626.286.3108 FAX: 626.286.1528

www.clairbourn.org

HEAD OF SCHOOL:	**ROBERT W. NAFIE PH.D.**
DIRECTOR OF ADMISSIONS:	**JANNA HAWES**
TYPE OF SCHOOL:	**CO-ED DAY**
GRADES:	**PRESCHOOL–8**
ENROLLMENT: 300	TUITION: $12,925 - 21,050
APPLICATION FEE: $75	FINANCIAL AID: YES
ACCREDITATION: CAIS/WASC/NAIS	

CLAIRBOURN has a beautiful campus: eleven acres of rolling lawns, a swimming pool, handball court, all landscaped, manicured and spread out like a college campus. The jewel in the crown of this setting is an old Georgian-style 23 room manor house built in 1915, situated in the center of the property. The manor originated as a gentleman's mansion with working orange groves, to the thriving educational business that it is today. Originally used as the headmaster's residence, it now serves as a meeting place for the Board of Trustees, the Clairbourn Families Associates, and the Student Council.

There is a feeling of orderliness throughout —everything in its proper place. The school was strictly for Christian Science families from its inception in 1926 until 1967 when the board of directors voted to open the enrollment to people of other religions. Today, while the school considers students of different religions and ethnic backgrounds for admission, the staff, faculty, and administration remain active Christian Scientists. Please note: there is NO religion taught in school.

The curriculum is a strong academic one with an emphasis on math, science and the development of higher-level thinking skills, such as analysis, synthesis and evaluation, and original observation. There are specialists in physical education, music, art, and computer skills. The music teacher really impressed me, she was very passionate about her work with the students and answered all the parents' questions with enthusiasm and wit.

The following is taken from the Clairbourn brochure, and are included here to give prospective parents a clear understanding of the school's approach:

> Purpose: To demonstrate practically the unlimited nature of all true instruction through educational opportunities which are harmonious with the teachings of Christian Science and in accordance with accepted professional standards of educational excellence.

> Premise: The achievement of this purpose is formulated on the following collective premise:

> 1. That any student who is receptive to instruction can experience success in proportion to his/her receptivity and application.

> 2. That the best education is one that assists the student in acquiring basic study habits including active listening, critical thinking, disciplined effort, and obedience to principle.

3. That the joy of learning is enhanced and enriched through the use of variety, creativity, and self-expression in developing essential physical, mental, and social skills.

4. That the gift of understanding carries with it certain moral and spiritual obligations to mankind for its constructive use in a way that fosters noble ambition, unselfish service, and world brotherhood.

5. That a deep respect and reverence for God as an active power in human affairs provides the foundation for strength, courage, integrity, humility, and compassion, and leads to an establishment of sound Christian character and a respect for the conviction of others.

6. That the education of children is a shared responsibility between the school and the family, requiring the school to carry forward its instructional program in a way that preserves, supports, and enriches the basic family unit of which the student is a member.

7. That the protection and preservation of our democratic form of government requires an alert, informed, and active citizenry, anchored in a love of country, appreciation of heritage, and a deep respect for law.

The West Campus includes a multimillion dollar preschool with three new classrooms, an age-appropriate play yard that will feature areas to bike, climb, swing and slide, sections for digging and planting, and an outdoor theatre area for dramatic play.

HISTORY

Clairbourn school started in the music room of Mr. and Mrs. Arthur K. Bourne's home in San Marino, California in 1926. The idea of a kindergarten for children of parents interested in Christian Science grew from four students to a full elementary school, and high school. By 1931 the school had acquired 3.5 acres of the present property for that purpose.

In 1938 the school returned to the original idea of educating younger students and discontinued the high school grades. During the early 40s Clairbourn struggled along with thirty-five students, half of whom comprised the Nursery school. With increased enrollment through the late forties, money was raised to buy more property at the present site and to add buildings. In 1953 the kindergarten building was added, while in 1958 the Manor house and its properties (including orange groves and swimming pool) were acquired. In 1967 the school opened its doors to students of other faiths and established three sister schools in San Gabriel, Redwood City, and San Rafael.

During the late 1980s and through the early 90s, a library was added as well as an art studio, music room, multipurpose building, a facility to house the second, fourth, and fifth grades, and a faculty lounge.

AT A GLANCE

APPLICATION DEADLINE	February 2
OPEN HOUSES	Contact school
UNIFORMS	Yes
AFTER-SCHOOL CARE	Yes
SUMMER SCHOOL	Yes
SEE MAP	A on page 255

THE COUNTRY SCHOOL

5243 LAUREL CANYON BLVD., VALLEY VILLAGE, CA 91607
TEL: 818.769.2473 FAX: 818.752.3097
country-school.org

HEAD OF SCHOOL:	**HOLLY NOVICK**
DIRECTOR OF ADMISSIONS:	**JOY MCCARTHY**
TYPE OF SCHOOL:	**CO-ED DAY**
GRADES:	**PRESCHOOL–8**
ENROLLMENT: 200	TUITION: $17,220 - 23,296
APPLICATION FEE: $150	NEW FAMILY FEE: $1,000
ACCREDITATION: CAIS	FINANCIAL AID: YES

THE COUNTRY SCHOOL has a warm and cozy feeling starting with its pleasant campus setting, well arranged classrooms, and kind, friendly staff. Over the past couple of years The Country School site has been expanded to over two acres. It is located on busy Laurel Canyon, but once inside the compound, you leave the traffic and dust behind and step into a protected little community of offices and classrooms.

The preschool and elementary school classrooms are wrapped around a common courtyard, which houses a well-equipped playground. There is a new grass playing field, and a large paved area for basketball and other group sports located at the back of the property, which houses the after school athletics program. There is also a playground area (with sand) for the older children.

The campus expansion includes a new library and Art Studio. The kindergarten room is large, bright, and modern, with high ceilings, which gives it a lovely open-air feeling.

Here is the Country School's description of their approach for grades kindergarten through sixth grade:

> At the elementary level, the school continues to provide a strong, nurturing environment where students' academic needs are met. During elementary years, development varies from child to child. Our school makes every effort to serve each child's readiness and potential, by creating a smaller student-teacher-ratio, insuring that the learning process takes place within an environment that is attentive and supportive for the individual child.

Each class has two full time teachers, with specialists in music, physical education, art, science, and computer skills. Portfolios of the children's work are kept and reviewed during the year to show change and progress.

Note: The Kindergarten has space for up to 25 children, but priority is given to those already enrolled in preschool.

The feeling here is warm and nurturing, an atmosphere that is created by the staff and by the small size of the school with a surprisingly diverse student body. Many of the parents that I spoke with loved the school but worried that it was not academic enough for their children. They were mainly concerned with the transition from sixth grade to another, perhaps more academically challenging school, although The Country School has an excellent matriculation record to secondary schools and on to some top notch universities.

The best way to know if this school is right for your family is to see it. Be sure to take along a list of questions to ask the staff and parent volunteers who will be at the open house.

HISTORY

The Country School was founded in 1948 by Rafe and Laura Ellis to offer children a chance to reach their own individual potential within the atmosphere of balanced freedom and structure. For twenty-four years it operated as a preschool, then in 1972 was expanded to include grades K-6.

In 1979, Paul Singer became the Head of School. His strong belief in the importance of diversity, multiculturalism and inclusion redefined the student population and curriculum in both the preschool and the newly-founded elementary school. A new revolution began. With the enthusiastic support of the Board of Trustees, Paul opened the doors to those who would otherwise never have had the opportunity to experience an independent school education. He created a safe haven where cooperation between family and school became a central key to success. Paul remains an active member of the Country School's Advisory Board.

With the 2005 expansion into their Middle School program and their custom-designed "sustainable" campus, TCS continues to draw upon the fundamental principles of a progressive philosophy, which have guided the school for many years.

AT A GLANCE

APPLICATION DEADLINE	Call school
OPEN HOUSES	October
TOURS	Contact school to schedule
UNIFORMS	Yes
AFTER-SCHOOL CARE	Yes
SEE MAP	A on page 255

CRESPI CARMELITE SCHOOL FOR BOYS
5031 ALONZO AVENUE, ENCINO, CA 91316
TEL: 818.345.1672 FAX: 818.705.0209
www.crespi.org

PRINCIPAL:	**DR. JONATHAN SCHILD**
DIRECTOR OF ADMISSIONS:	**ROBERT KODAMA**
TYPE OF SCHOOL:	**CATHOLIC ALL-BOYS DAY**
GRADES:	**9–12**
ENROLLMENT: 550	TUITION: $17,910
APPLICATION FEE: $90	REGISTRATION FEE: $750
ACCREDITATION:WASC/NCEA/WCEA	FINANCIAL AID: YES

CRESPI CARMELITE SCHOOL for boys is a fairly small school in Encino, just off the 101 and Ventura Blvd. The walls here are white, with very little to distract a young man from his studies. In fact, discipline and character development is what Crespi is all about. The Dean of students who conducted my impromptu tour said, "The Campus itself is not a large footprint, but more important is what we do in the buildings, not the building itself."
Crespi is a Catholic school but is open to students of other faiths. All students, however, must take the religion courses required for graduation. Crespi cherishes three fundamental values: Lifelong learning, productive and mature behavior, along with a moral and spiritual life. Is your son a "Crespi Man?"

Here's what a Crespi Man is according to the school's brochure:

> Life-long learner uses logical, analytical creative thinking skills; uses appropriate methodologies, strategies, and current technologies to solve problems and extend his knowledge. He acquires, interprets, organizes, synthesizes, applies and evaluates knowledge; and speaks, writes and uses other forms of expression accurately, effectively, and creatively.

> As a productive and mature person, a Crespi man strives to improve community, takes risks in order to grow and claims responsibility for his actions. He understands and participates in the democratic process, and strives to enhance and maintain physical, mental, and emotional well-being.

> And lastly, as a moral and spiritual person, he models Christ by learning and practicing Gospel values; committed to living an ethical life, is involved in service to others and social justice. He also recognizes and respects the uniqueness, dignity, and personal gifts of all people.

Most students enter in the ninth or tenth grade, and admission is based on four considerations:
1. Academic and testing records from previous school
2. Recommendations from previous school
3. Entrance exam taken at Crespi
4. Personal Interview

Of these four, the personal interview with prospective students and parents is perhaps the most important. They want to be sure that Crespi Carmelite High School is the right place for you and your son. Not a lot of boys want to go to an all boys school, but it delineates activities, school time is school time, and social time is social time.

One of the most impressive and unique elements at Crespi is that they work very closely with the Gurion Institute, which is developing a program for educating young boys. This research includes how genders think and learn, which allows them to teach specifically to the way boys learn best. This teaching method also works for each boy's character development and discipline.

For example, in the art room, and in an all-male environment students might prefer to build architectural structures, carving from rocks, or sculpting in clay. Of course, students still get in a fair amount of painting and drawing, which is often what girls would choose to do more than carving out of rocks, although I know many a girl who would jump at the chance so it's not that easy to pigeon hole the sexes! Art at Crespi is about exploring imagination in a fun way and being surprised and rewarded for your creativity. Although the Dean of students added, "I don't know how many students come here for Art". If you are seeking a more art-oriented school for your son, this probably isn't the best choice for you.

Crespi has recently created more classrooms, which allows them to have smaller class sizes, and a better teacher/student ratio. The past few years has seen new construction for a commons area, a new chapel, audio/visual, counseling, and music departments. There are also new locker rooms and a relatively new gymnasium.

Academics and athletics are stressed at Crespi. They recognize the important role that science plays in the world and have invested in technology, and are constantly upgrading their equipment to give students every opportunity to become cognizant of progressive developments. There are two computer labs, and up-to-date science and biology labs.

Crespi has a strong tradition of athletic excellence. Students are encouraged to try one or more sports during their high school years. Many young men find they do better in the classroom when they play sports. They emphasize sportsmanship, teamwork, body conditioning, and skills. Crespi teams have won State Championships, CIF championships, and 80 league championships at all levels. Crespi fields teams in 12 sports: baseball, basketball, cross country, football, golf, soccer, tennis, track, volleyball, water polo, and wrestling.

There are also many extra curricular activities, and if two or more students get together they can even create a new club based on their interests for that particular year. Besides excellent academics, with the majority of students going to major universities and Ivy League Schools, the school has a very strong Alumni Association. Many students come back to teach, volunteer, and coach. Alumni can often be seen in the stands during football season and other sporting events, for there is a fraternal bond that is created in an all-boy school, a brotherhood, that Crespi men carry with them for life.

HISTORY

Established in Encino, California in 1959, Crespi Carmelite is a non-profit, Catholic, four-year, college preparatory school for young men, owned and operated by the Carmelite Order. Dedicated to excellence and responding to the challenges of education in our time, Crespi offers a holistic model of education emphasizing the spiritual, intellectual, moral, physical, and social development of their students.

AT A GLANCE

APPLICATION DEADLINE	February
OPEN HOUSES	November
SEE MAP	A on page 255

CRESTVIEW PREPATORY SCHOOL

140 FOOTHILL BLVD, LA CAÑADA, CA 91011
TEL: 818.952.0925 FAX: 818.952.8470
www.crestviewprep.org

PRINCIPAL:	**BAUDELIA TAYLOR**
DIRECTOR OF ADMISSIONS:	**MICHELE POTEET**
TYPE OF SCHOOL:	**CO-ED DAY SCHOOL**
GRADES:	**K-6**
ENROLLMENT: 230	TUITION: $17,710
APPLICATION FEE: $75	NEW FAMILY FEE: $1,000
ACCREDITATION:CAIS	FINANCIAL AID: YES

CRESTVIEW has a wholesome, old-fashioned feeling of a small school set in a by gone era. The children play in a large, grassy play yard equipped with swings and climbing structures, among them a wonderful rocket ship that I was very tempted to climb into! The school has a soccer/baseball field as well.

What appeals to many of the parents considering Crestview is:

1. It's not high-pressure.
2. The property has a large, grassy play yard.
3. It has a small-town feel to it.
4. It's less expensive than many of the other area-schools.

Crestview follows the 'whole child' philosophy of teaching. The core curriculum includes reading, creative writing, spelling, mathematics, science, handwriting, social studies, and language arts. There are specialists in physical education, music, computer, art, library, and Spanish.

The teachers are described in the brochure as holding Bachelor's degrees and appropriate teaching credentials. Fifty percent of the faculty at Crestview have, or are in the process of obtaining, advanced degrees.

Crestview suggests that new students should attend their summer school, unless family situations prevent attendance. This is probably a great idea to help the children get used to the school before the beginning of a new school year. They will arrive on the first day of school knowing other kids they've met over the summer which will make them feel more at home.

As a guideline for parents who are always wondering about how much homework their children will be getting, they suggest that homework should be about 15 minutes per grade level per night. So first graders have 15 minutes, all the way up to grade 6 who have approximately one and a half hours – yes, that's 1 1/2 hours, not the 2 1/2 to 4 hours that are given at some of the schools we visited!

If you are interested in applying, go for the tour. They are very open to answering all your questions and will take the time to explain anything you might want to know about the school. So give them a call!

HISTORY

Crestview Preparatory School was moved to La Cañada and incorporated as a non-profit corporation in 1986. It has been located on its present site since 1988. Originally, there were 100 students in the school and currently there are 230 students in kindergarten through sixth grade.

AT A GLANCE

APPLICATION DEADLINE	February 1
OPEN HOUSES	November
SCHOOL TOURS	October through January
UNIFORMS	No
BEFORE AND AFTER SCHOOL CARE	Yes
SUMMER SCHOOL	Yes
ENRICHMENT CLASSES	Yes
SEE MAP	B on page 255

CROSSROADS SCHOOL FOR ARTS & SCIENCES

ELEMENTARY CAMPUS: K - 5
1715 OLYMPIC BLVD, SANTA MONICA, CA 90404
TEL: 310.829.1196 FAX: 310.392.9611
MIDDLE/UPPER CAMPUS: 6 - 12
1714 21ST ST, SANTA MONICA, CA 90404
TEL: 310.829.7391 FAX: 310.828.5636
www.xrds.org

PRINCIPAL:	**BOB RIDDLE**
DIRECTOR OF ADMISSIONS:	**CECILIA LEE**
TYPE OF SCHOOL:	**CO-ED DAY SCHOOL**
GRADES:	**K-12**
ENROLLMENT: 1,159	TUITION: $31,872 - 38,002
APPLICATION FEE: $150	NEW FAMILY FEE: $2,500
ACCREDITATION:CAIS/WASC	FINANCIAL AID: YES

CROSSROADS LOWER SCHOOL (K-5), the admissions office, and the K through 12 athletic facility are located two blocks away from the middle and upper schools. The school buildings are in a variety of styles ranging from aesthetically distinguished to urban industrial. There are fully equipped laboratories, multi-disciplinary classrooms, a 25,000-volume library, theater, music performance space, computer centers and a photography lab. Then there is the magnificent Peter Boxenbaum Arts Education Center, with two dance studios, art studios and a screening room. They also have their own gallery, The Sam Francis Gallery, which I visit from time to time and always see interesting exhibitions.

The teachers are the heart of Crossroads Elementary. They are focused, passionate, lively, dedicated and have (if you'll excuse the pun) done their homework. Usually every school has at least one truly outstanding educator on staff, but at Crossroads they all stood out as exceptional in one way or another.

If I had to use one word to describe Crossroads School it would be 'balance.' There seems to be a respect for people and nature as well as an equal mixture of academics, the arts, and science. Crossroads was founded upon five basic commitments: academics, the arts, the greater community, student development, and the attainment of social, economic and racial diversity in its student population.

The curriculum in the lower school (K-5) is social studies based, which becomes the unifying content for the learning of reading, writing, and math skills. For example, children may apply math skills by making scale maps of a country they are studying and by developing 'businesses' like operating a store, or by calculating the amounts of food needed for a camping trip.

In language arts children are encouraged to work at their own pace sharing both works-in-progress and finished compositions, thus providing each other with questions and feedback.

Each child receives instruction in art, drama, music, and dance movement – all taught by specialists. (Crossroads is one of the few schools where drama and dance are offered during the school day and not as part of an after-school program). The general music program is based on the principles of Orff Schulwerk. There are also specialists in science, computers, physical education, and library science.

By the sixth grade, students have been taught writing, literature, math, social studies, and science in self-contained classrooms. The overall theme is immigration and multiculturalism. Note taking, vocabulary development, writing skills, discussion techniques, and literary analysis are emphasized. Students are grouped by skill level in math. There are specialists in visual arts, drama, chorus, instrumental music, life skills, and physical education. Again, this inclusion of chorus and drama in the school-day is unusual.

In the seventh and eighth grades, Latin is required along with English, history, math, science, physical education, arts and electives. A two-year Spanish course is optional for sixth and seventh-grade students. The upper school (or high school as it was formerly known) is demanding and rigorous, and designed to prepare its students for top notch colleges.

In order to graduate, students must meet the departmental graduation requirements, as well as take a minimum of four academic classes every semester of enrollment. Advanced placement courses are available to qualified students in English, U.S. history, mathematics, biology, physics, chemistry, music theory, French, Spanish, Latin, visual arts, and art history.

At the upper school level students with long-standing, focused talents, interests and skills in a particular discipline may apply to the Specialized Majors Program in one of the following areas: languages, computer science, dance, film and video, music and visual arts.

The school has a great curriculum guide, take a look at it if you have time.

HISTORY

Crossroads Elementary School was founded in the mid-fifties as a day school for the Parish of St. Augustine By-the-Sea Episcopal Church. In 1970, Paul E. Cummins became Headmaster and one year later simultaneously started Crossroads upper school with a group comprised of sixth-grade parents and educators. After separating the elementary school from the church affiliation in 1982, Dr. Cummins merged it with his Crossroads School (Grades 7-12), and in the spring of 1982 the Crossroads School for Arts and Sciences (K-12) was born.

AT A GLANCE

APPLICATION DEADLINE	K due in October, Grades 1-12 due in December
OPEN HOUSES	Call school for dates.
SUMMER SCHOOL	YES
UNIFORMS	No
BEFORE AND AFTER SCHOOL CARE	Yes
SEE MAP	D on page 255

CURTIS SCHOOL

15871 MULHOLLAND DRIVE, LOS ANGELES, CA 90049
TEL: 310.476.1251 FAX: 310.476.1542
www.curtisschool.org

PRINCIPAL:	**PETER W. SMAILES**
DIRECTOR OF ADMISSIONS:	**MIMI PETRIE**
TYPE OF SCHOOL:	**CO-ED DAY SCHOOL**
GRADES:	**DK–6**
ENROLLMENT: 491	TUITION: $26,700
APPLICATION FEE: $150	NEW FAMILY FEE: $1,500
ACCREDITATION: CAIS/WASC	

CURTIS SCHOOL is located on Mullholland Drive's 'restaurant row' of schools which includes: Berkeley Hall, Westland, Mirman and Steven Wise Temple Elementary School.

I arrived at the school one morning recently. There was a new guard booth with a security officer who really knew his stuff! He was very pleasant but thorough. Mimi Petrie, the admissions director was waiting for me. She had been a mother at the school and had been so involved that the school asked her to help with the admissions process. She agreed and now is the Head of Admissions. She gave me a very informative tour of the school. Let me tell you, If I were a parent applying to the school, I would be thrilled to find her across the desk at my interview!

In describing the physical setting, one word that comes to mind is "deluxe!" The school's 27 hilltop acres make it both beautiful and very private. The administration building houses the 14,000 volume library and provides 10,000 square feet of space. There are fields for football, soccer, and track. Other athletic facilities include: an outdoor gymnastic pavilion, a 25-yard heated swimming pool, a volleyball court, three tennis courts, a handball/racquetball court, and three basketball courts. The school is proud to tell you that the facility is valued at over $20 million. You can certainly see where your tuition goes at Curtis!

At an Open House a few years back, a full auditorium of parents listened to a description of the school and the admission process. The Headmaster was encouraging, but did not hide the fact that it was very difficult to gain acceptance to the school. He told of application files containing letters from senators and foreign dignitaries all recommending a child for kindergarten! Who do you know? But seriously, take advantage of the fact that this school accepts letters of recommendation. Oh and they will only accept the first 200 applications so please check the date you can start sending them in.

The goal of Curtis is to provide a college-preparatory academic program. The school also places a major emphasis on physical education and athletics. Central to the school's mission is its commitment to providing an excellent, well-rounded education for the whole child. Academics, the arts, and athletics are taught in an environment that encourages personal growth and excellence. Curtis has a strong tradition of developing character in young people through its' emphasis on critical thought, good citizenship, sportsmanship, and social responsibility. Curtis also prides itself on being a family school and welcomes the involvement of parents in fulfilling its' mission. It's an inclusive community that does not discriminate on the basis of race, religion, sexual orientation, or national or ethnic origin in the administration of its' admission and educational policies, scholarship and loan programs, or other school activities.

In the early grades the focus is on teaching children to read. Curtis has a Developmental Kindergarten (DK) that feeds into the kindergarten class. DK is not preschool and accepts children who are either slightly younger or not developmentally ready for reading instruction.

Mathematics instruction moves through basic skills to familiarity with fractions, decimals, positive and negative numbers, probabilities, and elementary algebra. Computers are introduced early, and the computer lab is state-of-the-art and equipped with many games too!

Science instruction is incorporated into language arts in first grade and deals with plants, animals, and environment. In fifth grade, children go to a science lab with a specialist teacher.

The music program is primarily a vocal one, but also incorporates listening, writing, reading, conducting (yes conducting!), and playing instruments. There's an orchestra that meets weekly where children have the opportunity to learn an instrument beginning in grade 3. The art program is based on a study of art appreciation and applied skills: drawing, painting, graphics, sculpture, and ceramics projects. Latin is required in grades 5 and 6.

The yearbook was filled with large, bright photos of all the teachers and children, and beautiful photographic layouts of all the year's events. Included were many pages of the children's poetry and eight pages in full color called 'the art gallery' showing beautiful reproductions of the children's art work during the past year. It was a magnificent piece of work, and it put my own high-school yearbook to shame. When I got up to leave, I handed the book to Mimi who waved me off and said, "Oh that's all right, you may keep it." How kind of her!

The school's goal is to develop in every child, a sound mind in a sound body governed by a compassionate heart. They believe that childhood is brief and precious. It is a time of limitless potential and essential development. A Curtis education honors these truths within a caring and inclusive community. They foster an active partnership with their families based on a shared commitment to their mission, their values, and the special joys of childhood.

The school is always looking to increase its' diversity, that means both in ethnicity and from a larger pool of preschools. This is very good news. If your child is going to a preschool that's not the "flavor of the year" don't despair. This could work in your favor. Fill out the application, buy a nice outfit for the interview, and keep your fingers crossed!

HISTORY

Curtis School was founded in 1925 by Carl Curtis, and in 1937, was reorganized by his nephew, Carl F. Curtis. In 1964, Willard E. Badham took over as Headmaster and ran the school for the next three decades. In 1983, the school moved to its current site on Mulholland Drive. Badham retired in 1992 and was succeeded by Clay V. Stites. Stites revitalized the academic programs and oversaw the campaign that enabled the school to build many of the modern facilities Curtis enjoys today. Stephen E. Switzer, former Headmaster of Le Jardin Academy in Hawaii, was appointed in 1997 and spearheaded the campaign that made it possible for the school to increase its endowment, build facilities, and expand its programs.

In 2009, Peter W. Smailes was named the sixth Headmaster. During his thirteen year tenure at Curtis he has had many titles including English teacher, Dean of Upper School, and Head of Middle School. Long respected as an educational leader in West Los Angeles and widely credited for many of the structural and programmatic improvements over the last decade, Peter Smailes is committed to leading the school in a manner that is both forward-looking and that honors the traditions and mission of the school.

AT A GLANCE

APPLICATION DEADLINE	February
OPEN HOUSES	October and November
UNIFORMS	Yes
SUMMER SCHOOL	Yes
BEFORE AND AFTER SCHOOL CARE	Yes
SEE MAP	D on page 255

ECHO HORIZON SCHOOL
3430 McMANUS AVENUE, CULVER CITY, CA 90232
TEL: 310.838.2442 FAX: 310.838.0479
www.echohorizon.org

PRINCIPAL:	**MARTHA SCHUUR**
DIRECTOR OF ADMISSIONS:	**LISA MARFISI**
TYPE OF SCHOOL:	**CO-ED DAY SCHOOL**
GRADES:	**PK-6**
ENROLLMENT: 214	TUITION: $19,000 - 25,125
APPLICATION FEE: $125	NEW FAMILY FEE: $1,500
ACCREDITATION:CAIS/WASC/NAIS	FINANCIAL AID: LIMITED

Martha Schuur became the Head of **ECHO HORIZON** School in 2013 bringing with her years of experience from her leadership position at Marlborough School and as Assistant Head of School at Echo Horizon. She has raised the bar academically at all grade levels, added a design thinking curriculum with a maker space and steam space and has introduced more global education opportunities. She also added sports teams and a mascot (Hawk). Echo Horizon School has been recognized as an Apple Distinguished School for 5 years in a row for the way technology is seamlessly integrated into the curriculum in innovative ways. The large yard also benefitted from Martha's dream to have shade and soft scaping for the students. There is a new astroturf yard with lots of shade. Echo Horizon School prepares students to think, question, create, collaborate, innovate and communicate their ideas. Students participate in innovative, creative time in the Centers of Inquiry and Innovation on a weekly basis.

The original school building was formerly a public elementary school in the Culver City Unified School District. It is a beautiful two story structure with wide hallways and huge sash windows. It was renovated in 2006.

Echo Horizon School is proud to also include Echo Center. Through their Echo Center they have an auditory-verbal mainstream program for deaf and hard of hearing children. These children are fully integrated into regular classrooms and learn in that environment. They receive the support they need to be successful from Echo Center teachers, who are credentialed in deaf and hard of hearing education. The ratio of deaf and hard of hearing children to hearing children is approximately 1 to 10.

The school's teaching methodologies are well researched and provide a wonderful example of progressive and traditional educational practices melded together in a program that values balance as well as high achievement.

The following is the school's Educational Approach:

> At Echo Horizon School, we value character education as highly as we do academic rigor. We believe that the education, care, and nurturing of the elementary age child is best accomplished in our Pre K-6 grade setting. Nationally recognized for our ability to leverage technology that optimizes and creates multi-dimensional learning, Echo Horizon's teaching emphasizes character education to facilitate social and emotional growth, critical thinking, autonomy, resilience, and social responsibility.

Their pedagogical approach underscores Echo Horizon's dedication to ongoing research and the utilization of evidence-based teaching practices to inform curricular decisions. In the classroom, they provide their students with opportunities and guidance to make productive choices and decisions.

In this environment, their students acquire 21st century skills to be effective collaborators, problem solvers, and innovators utilizing cutting-edge technologies. With these tools, their graduates are sought after by secondary schools not only for their academic readiness, but also for their love of learning, values and principles, technical fluency, and global awareness. Echo Horizon alumni are prepared for life-long learning and thrive in a myriad of academic and social environments in secondary school, college, and beyond.

They research all curricular initiatives before implementing them. For instance they have melded the California standards and the Common Core to establish a curriculum that merges best practices into the class work at each grade level. Their emphasis on project-based learning engages each student. The Director of Curriculum meets weekly with all grade levels to assure high quality curricular continuity throughout the school. Faculty are involved in curriculum design at all levels and meet frequently to discuss best practices. They administer standardized testing (ERBs) starting in 3rd grade. They assess reading fluency and comprehension levels starting in Kindergarten.

- Language arts instruction encompasses speaking and listening skills as well as the development of and writing competency. Reading is rooted in a whole language approach with appropriate emphasis on phonics and other decoding skills in the early years.
- Singapore Math is the core of their math curriculum based on conceptual understanding, number sense, and problem solving. The focus for thier students is not only knowing how to do math, but also understanding and being able to articulate why the algorithms work as they do.
- Science is taught at all grade levels. Grades 5 and 6 have all science classes in the science lab. Science classes are informed by the Next Gen Science Standards.
- Social Studies is taught at all grade levels following the California State Standards. All grade levels utilize primary and secondary sources in their social studies classes. Cultural diversity is a common theme throughout a student's course of study.

All children participate in an extensive arts curriculum and take visual art, dance theater, and music every week. Students also participate weekly in PE and Library.

Students use technology for productivity, research, and creative expression. They gain proficiency in keyboarding, publishing, digital storytelling, and finding, synthesizing and presenting information in a variety of formats. Students learn to be responsible digital citizens as they make local and global connections, and publish work that honors the intellectual property of others. The Echo Horizon graduates move on to secondary school with a variety of skills in their digital toolbox and the ability to determine which tool will be most effective to communicate their ideas in different situations.

Students are well prepared for top middle schools in Los Angeles having spent their 5th and 6th grade years with departmentalized teachers. Not only are their students well equipped academically, but also well equipped for transitioning from class to class seamlessly when they are in middle school.

Last year Echo Horizon graduates were accepted to and enrolled in many different secondary schools. These schools include: Harvard-Westlake, Marlborough, Windward, Archer, Crossroads, Oakwood, Wildwood, and Campbell Hall. Their graduates are sought after for being great people who are well prepared, enthusiastic learners in the middle school environment.

The Echo Horizon School community is diverse, talented, motivated, inclusive and supportive, and it represents the multi-faceted diversity of Los Angeles.

HISTORY

In 1970 the Carol L. Proctor Echo Center, formerly known as Oral Education Center, was created by parents, educators and interested community leaders. In 1983, Kent and Carol Landsberg established Kent H. Landsberg Echo Horizon School as a school that would educate deaf and hard of hearing children alongside their hearing peers.

AT A GLANCE

APPLICATION DEADLINE	December 15
UNIFORMS	No
BEFORE AND AFTER SCHOOL CARE	Yes
OPEN HOUSE TOURS	See Website
SEE MAP	D on page 255

THE EPISCOPAL SCHOOL OF LOS ANGELES

6325 SANTA MONICA BLVD, LOS ANGELES, CA 90038
TEL: 323.462.3752 FAX: 310.706.4204
www.es-la.com

PRINCIPAL:	**REV. MARYETTA ANSCHUTZ**
DIRECTOR OF ADMISSIONS:	**KELSEY PEDERSEN**
TYPE OF SCHOOL:	**CO-ED DAY SCHOOL**
GRADES:	**6-12**
ENROLLMENT: 115	TUITION: $28,500
APPLICATION FEE: $100	NEW STUDENT FEE: $1,500
ACCREDITATION: WASC/UC	FINANCIAL AID: YES

Walking into the **ESLA** for the first time, I was just a little bit confused. Is this a school? It looks like the hippest, coolest office building in town. A historical Hollywood building, the Schoolhouse at 6325 Santa Monica Blvd at one time housed one of the City's first color film studios. More recently it served as office space for several tech and creative companies. With large open spaces, tall ceilings, exposed brick walls, funky wall colors, and not one traditional classroom in sight, it now sets the stage for one of Los Angeles' most innovative and unique new independent schools.

ESLA has its roots in the STEM (Science, Technology, Engineering and Math) Institute - an after school program for students in the 5-7th grades. The Scientific Method practiced in this program, along with a strong focus on ethics and innovation, has served as the base and inspiration for the curriculum and culture at ESLA.

As per the ESLA website: "The mission of the Episcopal School of Los Angeles is to create and sustain a campus devoted to nurturing souls and minds in an intellectually rigorous and spiritually curious academic community. The purpose of the school is to enable young people to thrive in an atmosphere of diversity and to become ethical leaders in communities of faith, the nation and the world."

As I began my tour of the ESLA, admittedly my first reaction was 'can you really teach children like this?' But I walked out of the Schoolhouse convinced that this school may well produce some of our future leaders. ESLA offers a unique space, as well as a unique and progressive approach to learning, so it won't suit everyone. Being aware of this, ESLA is also quite selective in its admission process. But make no mistake that the curriculum offered at the school is no less rigorous and challenging. There are multi-level math classes, eight different languages offered, high school AP classes and much more. The expectations are high that students will thrive at ESLA and go on to the best colleges and universities.

Although my visit was during the summer months with no classes in session, I did see the newly renovated science lab, which showcased beautiful photos from the research trip that took the 9th and 10th grade classes to the rainforest of Costa Rica to research Howler Monkeys! The students were given the task to come up with research topics, create proposals as well as budgets, and pitch them to the school. They did so quite successfully, the result being an extended research trip to a professional research lab in the Costa Rican rainforest. As shown by the photographs as well as the writings of both students and teachers, it was an amazing experience for all. This is the perfect example of the school's goal to educate students who not only do 'research,' learn 'laboratory skills' or take math or science just because they need it for their college application - or because a teacher or a parent told them they had to - but rather because they have come to understand how these subjects can be applied and firmly rooted in real life work. "Learning by doing, not memorizing."

The upstairs of the building have been renovated to house more classrooms as well as the new POST lab, ESLA's space for photography, film-making, and media arts. This houses professional equipment, and connects students and teachers with professionals from Hollywood through subjects such as journalism, cinematography, and photography. Also upstairs is the music classroom. Musical instruments are provided for students to learn not only playing, but also song-writing, music production and sound engineering. The immersive nature of the music program captures the school's emphases on collaboration, risk, and creativity, all of which are echoed throughout the curriculum. At ESLA, everyone is a rockstar, an athlete, a creative, and a scholar.

The student body comes from a diverse background where about 30% live below the poverty line, 30% come from affluent homes, with the rest from somewhere in the middle. This is by design and makes for a truly unique student body that cannot be found at any other school, public or private. Technology and social media are considered a natural occurrence in the students' lives and implemented at all levels of teaching. The school provides iPads and computers to students, and make sure all students have access to internet at school as well as at home. The goal is to give students the tools to make the correct decisions and ability to use this new media responsibly and to their advantage. The value of this unique approach to education crosses curriculum, daily life, and relationships – indeed, Maryetta views an ESLA student as "one who grows to understand that he can make his own choices and pursue his goals; one who grows to understand that she holds, with these choices and actions, a great deal of responsibility to herself and to those who rely upon her."

The school day runs from 7.30 AM to 6 PM. While students make their way through the academic day, there are two events for which the entire community joins together. Three days a week, classes break midmorning for a traditional Episcopalian chapel service. And each day at noon, the entire community converges in the Commons for family style lunch, where faculty and students spend time together, sharing in food and conversation. All food and snacks throughout the day are provided by the school's own kitchen. Both chapel and shared lunch strengthen the bonds in the community. When classes finish at about 3:30 PM, after school programs such as sports and/or arts commence after which the students return to the Schoolhouse for 'think tank,' ESLA's reimaging of study hall. Teachers are present all day and available to students always, whether during class, for homework questions, advisement, or 'just' a chat or a pep talk.

While ESLA requires and expects parents to be supportive of their student and his or her school work while at home, parent involvement at and/or visits to the school during the school day are uncommon. Tutoring is done by the school's teachers during think tank and as needed. This is quite different from other independent schools in the Los Angeles area.

HISTORY

The School was founded by The Rev. Maryetta M. Anschutz. For over a decade, Maryetta has been at work changing the landscape of education and service in Los Angeles and beyond. An ordained priest educated at The Berkeley Divinity School at Yale University, The University of the South, and The Madeira School, Maryetta has dedicated herself to "creating and sustaining a school in Los Angeles that bridges the gap between financial limitations and access to rigorous education." ESLA was incorporated in 2009 and opened its doors to 28 new students (6th, 7th, 8th grade) in 2012. They will add one class per year until the first class graduates in 2017. Current enrollment in 6th - 11th grade is about 110 students, and the School is admitting 6th - 12th grade for the year 2016/2017. With the upstairs of the building renovated and readied for classrooms and new students, the plan is to grow the school to about 350 students total and expand the campus to surrounding buildings in the neighborhood. Class size is small, about 9-12 students per class. Teachers are handpicked not only based on their expertise, teaching ability, and passion for their subject, but also their ability to multi-task across several roles at the school and willingness to engage with the students as mentors.

AT A GLANCE

APPLICATION DEADLINE	Mid-January
OPEN HOUSES	Visit School's Website
SCHOOL TOURS	See Website
UNIFORMS	Yes
SEE MAP	B on page 255

FLINTRIDGE PREPATORY SCHOOL

4534 CROWN AVENUE, LA CAÑADA-FLINTRIDGE, CA 91011
TEL: 818.790.1178 FAX: 818.952.6247
www.flintridgeprep.org

PRINCIPAL:	PETER H. BACHMANN
DIRECTOR OF ADMISSIONS:	ARTHUR STETSON
TYPE OF SCHOOL:	INDEPENDENT CO-ED
	NON-PROFIT
GRADES:	7–12
ENROLLMENT: 500	TUITION: $33,600 - 34,200
APPLICATION FEE: $85	FINANCIAL AID: YES
ACCREDITATION:WASC	

FLINTRIDGE PREP is situated at the base of the San Gabriel Mountains in the community of La Cañada. It's a wonderful area, the sort of place where you don't have to lock your doors at night. The kind of place where your kids can hop on the 'free' bus and get around on their own without your having to be the chauffeur 24/7!

The school is made up of 1950s bungalows and pleasant vine-covered walkways that lead you around the campus with grassy areas and lots of shade. The newer additions resemble a combination of Frank Lloyd-Wright architecture and buildings you would find on the South Bank in London built in the late 70's.

Mission Statement (as taken from school brochure):

> Flintridge Preparatory School offers a rigorous, moral, and intimate learning environment, nurturing in its students the skills, knowledge, values, and inspiration essential to a rewarding college experience, a lifelong embrace of education, a devotion to community, and a full and responsible life.

In the center of the campus is the Jorgensen Memorial Library equipped with books, periodicals, reference materials, audio/visual equipment, new computers, and a complete technology media center. The art studios offer ceramics, painting, and drawing. Flintridge Prep's fully equipped photography studio includes professional camera and developing equipment and a darkroom.

The School's cultural/science center includes the Norris Auditorium, the Keck Biology Lab, the Braun Computer Lab and the Murfey Chemistry Lab.

The Randall Performing Arts Center includes classrooms for dance, drama and music, as well as a state-of-the-art performance venue in the Miller Black Box Theatre.

Athletic facilities include: the Olympic size Lowery Swimming Pool, the James Wood Memorial Field, a gymnasium for basketball and volleyball, the Swift Tennis Courts and a well- equipped weight room.

The list of the names of benefactors in the generous parent body both now and in the past reads a little like "who's who." The school doesn't mince words about asking for donations as you can see from their statement taken from the school brochure: "We strongly hope that parents will contribute to the school. This contribution may take several forms. Parents can support Flintridge Prep by giving to the Annual Fund, or by participating in activities associated with the Mothers' Club or the Fathers' Club."

I must make one observation about the noise from the freeway that passes directly above the swimming pool. It is quite loud. The school could have better thought out the placement of the pool in relation to the freeway overpass. On a positive note, the parking lot has been cleverly built directly underneath the freeway, which provides great shade and protection from the rain.

There's no doubt about it, this is a wonderful school, and one that is going to prepare your child for entrance into all the top colleges or universities, both here and abroad. Your money will be well spent here. Just look at the curriculum for English and Foreign Language Programs:

English:

Literature/Composition: 7th grade
English: 8th Grade
English I: 9th Grade
English II: composition/American Literature, 10th Grade
English III: Advanced Composition/British Literature (Regular & Honors), 11th Grade English IV: 11th-12th Grade
American Identity
The Beat Generation
The City in Literature
Contemporary Fiction
Contemporary Latin American Literature
Imitations of Genius
Language, Style and Sounds in Modern American Literature Language, Style and Sounds in Modern American Poetry
Literature in Translation (H)
Literature of Dissent
Shakespeare (Regular & Honors)
Short Story
Writing Fiction in a Modern World

Foreign Language:

Latin I, II, III/IV, V (AP Lyric Poetry)
French I, II, III, IV, IV/V (AP Literature & Language †) Spanish I, II, III, IV, IV/V (AP Literature & Language †), VI (Latin-American Women Writers)

The academic curriculum at Flintridge Prep includes a full complement of regular, honors, and Advanced Placement classes which prepare students for attendance at the most selective colleges in the nation. Prep's graduation requirements exceed the subject requirements for the University of California. A yearly appraisal of each student's composite performance determines if that student will be recommended for placement in honors and Advanced Placement classes.

In grades 10 to 12, there are honors and regular sections in all subject areas. Honors Courses (H) cover extended content and require more work than do standard courses. Advanced Placement Courses (AP) are available in French, Spanish, Latin, calculus, and computer science. All students enrolled in AP classes take the AP exam, the majority of students enrolled in honors classes also sit for AP exams.

HISTORY

Founded in 1933, Flintridge Prep is a nonprofit, independent, co-ed college preparatory day school. Flintridge Prep is one of only four schools in the U.S. to receive a leadership grant from the Edward E. Ford Foundation. The grant supports the school's commitment to an innovative Idea Lab in which faculty-driven ideas are nurtured. Four initiatives are supported by the grant: the Nicaragua Collaborative, which engages students in several organizations in Nicaragua; a Community Impact Project program that enables students to create ongoing community service projects; Engaging Los Angeles, which seeks to broaden students' understanding and interaction within the Los Angeles area; and a Mentoring Initiative, which matches students, parents, and alumni based on their interests, career goals, and college choices.

AT A GLANCE

APPLICATION DEADLINE	January 30
OPEN HOUSE	December
ISEE	Yes
UNIFORMS	No
SUMMER SCHOOL	Yes
SEE MAP	B on page 255

FLINTRIDGE SACRED HEART ACADEMY

440 ST. KATHERINE DRIVE, LA CAÑADA-FLINTRIDGE, CA 91011
TEL: 626.685.8500 FAX: 626.685.8555
www.fsha.org

PRESIDENT:	**SISTER CAROLYN MCCORMACK**
PRINCIPAL:	**SISTER CELESTE MARIE BOTELLO**
DIRECTOR OF ADMISSIONS:	**LUANA CASTELLANO**
TYPE OF SCHOOL:	**ALL GIRLS CATHOLIC DAY & BOARDING SCHOOL**
GRADES:	**9–12**
ENROLLMENT: 500	TUITION: $23,600
APPLICATION FEE: $85	FINANCIAL AID: YES
ACCREDITATION:WASC	

FLINTRIDGE SACRED HEART ACADEMY occupies 41 acres on a hilltop in the city of La Cañada- Flintridge. The views are spectacular overlooking the San Gabriel Valley and the Pasadena Rose Bowl from the crest of the San Rafael hills. Follow the directions carefully as there are many turns and a long steep climb up the hill. Arriving at the main building and walking up the steps and into the lobby one couldn't help but wonder if it is not in fact a fabulous hotel – well it once was! (See History).

Today the main building provides housing for boarding students and staff, a convent area for the Dominican Sisters, a dining room and administrative offices. My friend Sue and I were given an impromptu tour by one of the staff who was more than happy to show us around, even inside one of the girls' dorms. Having once been a hotel, the rooms hardly looked like the ones I slept in as a child, each one with a bathroom en suite! Two or three boarders share a dorm, and there's plenty of room. The dining room is a beautiful hall with high ceilings and wonderful furniture. The menu looked delicious – plenty of choice and variety. On our way out, we were shown a model of the school and its grounds, and it was only then one really got a feeling for just how big the campus was. Our guide talked about how much she loved working for the school. It was obvious she adored it.

Between the main building and the swimming pool lies Senior Lawn, home of the FSHA's graduation ceremony for most of the school's history. It was there we were introduced to two girls who were on their way to their next class. They stopped and chatted with us and gave us an overview of 'a day in the life' . . . it sounded great. They were articulate and extremely amusing, and told us that they were treated with the utmost respect and loved everything about the school. They couldn't think of one negative thing to say about anything. They were especially proud of their math teacher, and boasted about the recent award she had been given and wanted to take us into class with them so we could see what they were talking about. Unfortunately we had to decline. As we walked over to the admissions office to pick up a brochure, we noticed a landmark of the school, the bridge connecting the old campus to the new. Oh and did I mention the fabulous tennis courts!

A high school classroom building and an auditorium for the performing arts were built in the 1950s. The Visual and Performing Arts Department produces two theatrical productions each year. The fall production usually takes places in November, and the spring production (often a musical) is generally in March. Music students give recitals throughout the year and FSHA's dance students produce a dance concert in late spring. Both perform at Flintridge assemblies, liturgies, and various other functions throughout the year. Art students also have the opportunity to display their work. Through courses and co-curricular activities students are allowed to express abilities different from those found in traditional academic courses. Particular emphasis is placed on the experimental, the interpretive, and the creative in order to enrich students' lives through self-expression, self-awareness or through response to the expression of others.

The science and athletic complex is quite outstanding – over 26,000 square feet. In addition to the gymnasium and multi-purpose athletic field, the complex includes a sizeable aerobics room and a weight room. There's also a training room with massage tables and whirlpools for the students to use. Flintridge athletes compete in CIF (California Interscholastic Federation) as members of the Mission League. Their teams often reach league and state finals and have achieved numerous championships over the years. Their basketball team is known all over Los Angeles as one of the best. The state-of-the-art science wing, including biology, chemistry, and physics class- room/laboratories, as well as a computer research lab, is located on the second level. This site also provided a space for the Byrnes Amphitheater. The new area, named for an alumnus from the class of 1935, has provided a new location for student gatherings and annual events.

The Academy has been honored by the United States Department of Education as a Blue Ribbon School of Excellence for its success in meeting National Education Goals through the conditions of effective schooling. These include leadership, teaching environment, curriculum and instruction, student environment, parent and community support, and organizational vitality.

The curriculum includes 70 University of California-approved college-preparatory courses. Following the Academy's mission, their curriculum is intended to prepare students for the next level of education. The program is designed to provide students with effective oral and written communication skills, to teach students to think conceptually, to encourage students to share their artistic skills, to be effective problems solvers, and to help students explore moral, political, social, and economic issues.

The school offers 15 honors and advanced placement courses for more capable students. In addition, it administers a comprehensive English as a Second Language (ESL) program in order to mainstream the international students into the college preparatory curriculum. Here are some of the courses offered:

Advanced Computer Applications; honors English II, AP English IV; Spanish I-IV; Latin I-IV; French I-IV; AP Spanish IV; AP French IV; algebra I; geometry; Honors calculus; advanced algebra I; honors geometry; AP calculus-AB; algebra II; pre-calculus; honors algebra II/trig.; honors pre-calculus; physical education.

The student-teacher ratio is 10:1. Almost 100 percent of the students go on to attend four- year colleges and universities all over the country and beyond.

The students have the opportunity to pursue interests, and test and expand their leadership skills in a variety of clubs and organizations such as:

Alpha Sigma Mu (science club); Ambassadors; Amnesty International; Art Club, California Scholarship Federation, C'est la Vie (French club), Christian Action Movement (CAM), ComedySportz, Junior Statesmen of American, La Vanguardia (Spanish club), Multi-cultural Club, National Honor Society, Students Against Driving Drunk (SADD), Student Alumnae Relations Council (SARC), Saltatrix Dance Company, Theatre Club, Thespian Troupe, Varsity Club and the Young Writers Society.

In addition to curricular demands, students must complete 15 hours of Christian service each year. The Academy's Christian service program seeks to expose students to the responsibility of service as Christians, while helping them discover their own individual gifts and talents.

Approximately 25 percent of the students receive financial aid. Endowment funds and foundation grants support annual need-based tuition aid. Merit-based scholarships are awarded to qualifying incoming freshmen.

From the school brochure:

> "From its opening days, the Academy's college preparatory curriculum has attracted to its resident program international boarding students seeking an education in the United States. Today, approximately two-thirds of the Academy's 90 resident students are international. Now with nearly 400 students, the Academy continues to enroll vibrant, gifted young women who mirror the diversity of cultures, ethnicities, religious affiliations, and socio-economic backgrounds found in southern California. Over the years, this mosaic of students and their families has built a truly global community essential to the 'Flintridge experience.'"

HISTORY

Southern California architect Myron Hunt designed the main buildings of the school as a luxury resort hotel in the 1920s. The resort opened in 1927 as the Flintridge Hotel. It was soon sold to the Biltmore Hotel chain and renamed the Flintridge Biltmore. Unfortunately, the hilltop retreat was deemed too expensive, especially after the onset of the Great Depression in 1929 and was unable to attract more than eight to ten paying guests at one time.

When the resort failed, Archbishop Cantwell contacted the Dominican Sisters of Mission San Jose, who were seeking to open a girls' boarding school in the Los Angeles area. In 1931 they purchased the abandoned resort, including the nine original buildings, hotel furnishings, and surrounding land at an auction for the unbelievably low price of $150,000.00. According to Sister Frances, FSHA's first principal, Mother Dolorosa, Sister Thomasinia and Sister Odelia travelled up the hill to take possession of their new school. They carried with them "only a statue of the Blessed Virgin and a single five-dollar bill." Just two weeks later the school opened for the first day of classes on September 2, 1931 with 200 students enrolled in grades one through twelve.

In the 1930s and 1940s, all students were boarders. It wasn't until the high school building was constructed in 1951 that the Academy began to accept day students. The new high school campus was complete following the construction of the auditorium in 1956. At about the same time, the school began to phase out the elementary grades, and in 1963 the elementary school was closed and the old elementary school building was later sold as a private residence.

Originally governed exclusively by the Dominican Sisters, the school today is a California, non-profit corporation governed by a Board of Directors. It includes both lay and religious leaders who seek advice in the areas of finance, development, and community relations from volunteer committees of alumni, parents, and friends. The Academy's ongoing desire for outstanding faculty and educational facilities is supported by a development program, which seeks voluntary contributions to support the annual and capital needs of the school.

AT A GLANCE

APPLICATION DEADLINE	January 4
OPEN HOUSE	December
SCHOOL TOURS	October - December
UNIFORMS	Yes
SUMMER SCHOOL	Yes
SEE MAP	B on page 255

FOUNTAIN DAY SCHOOL

1128 N. ORANGE GROVE AVENUE, WEST HOLLYWOOD, CA 90046
TEL: 323.654.8958 FAX: 323.654.5214
www.fountaindayschool.com

DIRECTOR:	**MARY NOUSAKAJIAN**
PRINCIPAL:	**JANE DWINELL**
DIRECTOR OF ADMISSIONS:	**ANDREW RAKOS**
TYPE OF SCHOOL:	**CO-ED DAY SCHOOL**
GRADES:	**PRESCHOOL-K**

ENROLLMENT: 118   TUITION: $21,000
APPLICATION FEE: $125   NEW FAMILY FEE: $1,250
REGISTRATION FEE: $150   FINANCIAL AID: YES

As you enter **FOUNTAIN DAY SCHOOL**, you will be surprised how sweet and unassuming the exterior is, with, of course, a fountain! You will be surprised when you enter to find a successful school that has been there since 1957. " Mr. Andrew" was my utterly charming tour guide, the school's Head of Admissions. Here at Fountain Day School teachers and administrators are addressed as Miss or Mister, and their first name to continue the family type feel and relationship. This gem of a school was inspiring. That is how I knew I had stumbled upon something truly special, and by the time I completed the tour, I was excited and energized, and wanted to attend the school myself!

The campus itself is impressive. They are constantly improving and evolving as a campus and community. Wait for it, there is a year round indoor/outdoor pool where children get 2 swim lessons per week (4 swim lessons per week in the summer), a science yard, a completely revamped playground, and a brand new parking lot. This is not a traditional drop-off, the school doesn't really encourage just dropping your child at school, but creating a short transition into the school day with them when you are 'leaving' them at school. " We guide them into the things that make the family stronger and united, " says Mr. Andrew. Fountain Day school really services the working parent, and understands the need for flexibility and support. "Most of the time its really helping parents deal with their feelings" says Mr. Andrew.

They follow a curriculum that is fun and engaging that incorporates all your child's senses! Learning can be fun when you provide an environment that builds confidence and excitement. They also have the latest media technology, including Smart Boards. They have themes every month with creative projects that incorporates concepts and traditions. Additionally they have wonderful school wide monthly "parties" that have included Lunar New Year Celebrations, Bollywood Dancing performances, a Mardi Gras Parade and even a learning experience where parents and students rode camels. Lunches are provided by WHOLE FOODS and offer a hot and wholesome opportunity for your children to try new tastes and treats. They understand how busy parents can be and so they also provide 2 snacks per day. Though the school is non-denominational, they pray at lunchtime. Its an opportunity to share gratitude.

Though the majority of the students start at 2 years old, they typically have spaces available for 3 and 4 year olds as well. Kindergarten is something special here that truly prepares children. Although primarily known as a preschool Fountain Day Kindergarten is known as a top transitional class for those children that have a late birthday or just need that extra year of maturing.

Children eagerly greeted me and proudly showed me what they were working on. There is a definite confidence and full-self expression in this huge extended "family." As I completed my tour, I and the parents on the tour we're given

HISTORY

Fountain Day School was founded in 1957 by Ms. Evangeline Brooks. It began as a pre-school for working families and single mothers who found themselves in need of childcare. Ms. Brooks was a big-hearted woman who cared for children as if they were her own. The original building included her personal apartments upstairs. Often in those days, Ms. Brooks would end up babysitting children late into the night.

58 years later the school had a student population of 140 students. Fountain Day School is now operated by her daughters Ms. Mary and Ms. Jane.

Today the hours of operation are 8:00 am-5:00 pm (with service till 6:00 pm for an extra fee). Parents can use any portion of the day or month. So you can stay part time but your tuition is the same as full time. At the time of this review their tuition for the most part is all-inclusive. They have a parent association that raises money for financial aid for parents who cannot readily afford the tuition. Since they are open 12 months a year this amazing school offers amazing service with great value.

AT A GLANCE

APPLICATION DEADLINE	Preadmission in December
SCHOOL TOURS	Tuesdays
UNIFORMS	Yes
BEFORE AND AFTER SCHOOL CARE	Available 7:30am-6pm and inclusive in tuition
SEE MAP	C on page 255

FRIENDS WESTERN SCHOOL

524 E. ORANGE GROVE BLVD, PASADENA, CA 91104
TEL: 626.817.2481 FAX: 626.793.2727
www.friendswesternschool.org

HEAD OF SCHOOL:	PETER DAY
TYPE OF SCHOOL:	CO-ED DAY SCHOOL
GRADES:	K-6
ENROLLMENT: 56	TUITION: $10,920
APPLICATION FEE: $100	FINANCIAL AID: YES
NEW FAMILY FEE: $500	

FRIENDS WESTERN SCHOOL is a very special Quaker school. As the school tells me, "When we add new students, it is important for us to maintain diversity in many aspects. Economic diversity is very important to our school. Our scholarship students are among our best and brightest, and we hope to be able to accept children based on who they are, how they learn, and their magnificent gifts, instead of whether or not their parents can afford the tuition."

The school is located on the grounds of the Orange Grove Friends Meeting house in Pasadena. Trees surround the two-story building that serves as the school and a wonderful playground full of climbing equipment and different areas to play in. Upstairs in the schoolroom I was delighted to see how well organized it was. There are books galore, brightly painted walls, and a very well-designed area for the students to study in, there's even a built-in low-cushioned area, where kids may relax.

Who are Quakers?

George Fox founded the Religious Society of Friends 400 years ago in England. The most fundamental belief of Quakerism is that there is a part of God within everyone. There is an Inner Light within us that will guide us if we listen to it. Although Friends have no formal creed, out of experience they have developed 'testimonies:'

"The Peace testimony (Harmony) goes far beyond the simple idea that war is wrong. It is a commitment to try to solve conflicts without violence or threats. The testimony of Simplicity is a commitment not to live beyond their needs. This doesn't mean that they live spartan and monastic lives. Friends go to movies, have DVD's, and enjoy a good meal like the rest of us but feel that living a life of excess and conspicuous consumption gets in the way of the true joys of life. Simplicity also applies to speech and behavior. It means saying what they mean, being honest and fair, and acting in moderation. Equality is the oldest of Friends' testimonies and is the idea that all people are equal in God's eyes. It has led to a conscious effort to eliminate all words and behavior that arise from distinctions such as class, race, sex, or social status. Equality also means that for nearly 400 years women and men have shared in the leadership in Quakerism and from the beginning, Friends educated girls as well as boys."

Friends have a long and respected tradition of educating children to approach problems with knowledge and creativity, and to treat their fellow humans with respect and compassion, while maintaining high academic standards.

There is a daily silent worship held in the beautiful Victorian Meeting House that allows the children to begin the school day with a few moments of centering and reflection. Multi-age grouping allows the children to advance at their own pace in each academic subject. Physical education focuses on developing physical intelligence rather than solely learning rules for games. Students may participate in dance, gymnastics, martial arts, or other rigorous activities. Music is taught three times a week using percussion instruments.

During a typical day there will be a central theme: growth, point of view, character, and turning points. For example, if the theme were growth, the children might plan and build a flower box, work in the garden, measure and graph how high their flowers have grown, pretend to be a plant, sing a growing song or read a book together about gardens. They might write about their observations on growth, add things like charting their heights and foot sizes and observe the changes. Students might talk about how characters in a story grow, or perhaps create a computer model projecting the growth of a community.

In seventh grade, the students will serve in the community, as their social studies class. They will be set up in intern-like situations with time to work in the community and to discuss their services back in the classroom with their classmates. This will allow them to compare their theories of society to their actual experience.

Friends Western School is a small school and they can give your child personal attention and teach in the way your child learns best. They design their instruction to balance skills and challenges so that each student experiences success. Each person in their learning community is treated with respect and compassion. As the school explains, "We will do our best to discover and develop your child's unique intelligence. We believe that all children have unique talents. What gift does your child have?"

If you are currently home schooling your child, Friends Western School is interested in including those children in selected instruction and activities. This allows these children some socialization and group learning, which are often difficult to incorporate at a home school. While Quakerism is in the liberal Christian tradition, there are Friends who also draw from other faiths and practices. Families of all faiths are welcome among Friends.

Most of the children are gifted in one way or another, and a few have identified learning disabilities. I am a Quaker and went to a Quaker boarding school in England. It was one of the first co-ed boarding schools there and I loved every minute. I have been to many of the meetings held here in Pasadena with my own children. I would suggest prospective students and their families attend a Meeting for Worship at the Orange Grove Meeting in Pasadena which also oversees the development and spiritual life of Friends Western School, or at Pasadena Options Nights.

HISTORY

The school was founded in 2002 by Robin Durant who had been an educator for 14 years, teaching in the Alhambra and Pasadena school districts.. In addition, Ms. Durant had her multiple subjects teaching credential through Pacific Oaks College, and a specialist credential from CSULA. She has worked in both public and non-public settings, and has been a Quaker all her life.

AT A GLANCE

APPLICATION DEADLINE	Rolling Admission
OPEN HOUSES	See website
UNIFORMS	NO
AFTER SCHOOL CARE	Yes
SEE MAP	B on page 255

GLENDALE MONTESSORI

413 W. DORAN, GLENDALE, CA 91203
TEL: 818.240.9415 FAX: 818.240.8089
www.glendalemontessorischool.net

HEAD OF SCHOOL:	**ARNOLDA C. UTRECHT**
PRINCIPAL:	**ANITA TUCHRELLE**
TYPE OF SCHOOL:	**CO-ED DAY SCHOOL**
GRADES:	**PRESCHOOL-6**
ENROLLMENT: 120	TUITION: $1,000 - 1,200/mo.
APPLICATION FEE: $200	NEW FAMILY FEE: NONE
ACCREDITATION:AMS/NCME	FINANCIAL AID: NO

GLENDALE MONTESSORI is such a wonderful little gem that I am tempted to keep its whereabouts a secret! At first glance, the school appears to have an urban setting, with a paved front yard and three classroom buildings grouped around a common courtyard. However, if you look behind the caretaker's bungalow in the adjoining lot, you'll discover that the entire space has been converted into a shaded playground with several climbing structures and loads of (dust-free) sand to romp in. The children at GMS are blessed, and here's why. They have outstanding teachers, many of whom have been with the school for many years.

The classroom environments are cooperative, peaceful, clean, and well stocked with materials that are state-of-the-art. At GMS one thing is very clear: All of the school's resources go back to the students with the goal of providing the best education possible. The children are the focus.

The big news since my last edition is that the school now goes up to 6th grade. It used to stop at 2nd grade, which caused much anxiety amongst parents who then had to find a 3rd grade spot for their children. Obviously all those parents trying to convince Mrs. Utrecht to expand the school worked! I am thrilled to hear this as it truly is a wonderful school and the more years a child can stay there the better!

Speaking of Mrs. Utrecht, she runs the school with an understated grace, in a reserved but always approachable manner. I respect her enormously and hope that in the future she may even expand it to 8th and beyond, but I won't hold me breath. Going up to 6th is wonderful enough.

Mercifully absent is the non-stop plea for funds over and above tuition that is standard issue at most of the other private schools in Los Angeles. GMS does not do fundraising. Yes you heard right, DOES NOT DO FUNDRAISING! It also doesn't heckle parents to put in x amount of volunteer hours per year, although there are many opportunities to give of your time for the school's special events. One of the events is at Halloween where the whole school dons costumes for a parade around the block (chaperoned by teachers and parents), an event enjoyed by all!

The Montessori curriculum provides a carefully planned, sequential course of study in the areas of Practical Life, Sensorial, Mathematics, Reading, Language, Literacy, Science, Geography, and what I love and believe in teaching children, Grace and Courtesy. The classroom is designed to meet the needs of the individual student, whether primary (ages 3 to 6) or elementary (ages 6 to 12). The prepared classroom environment is beautiful, orderly, furnished with appropriate-sized furniture, and equipped with attractive Montessori materials. Many of the materials are designed to be self-correcting to encourage practice and mastery. So if you're talking about the "sensory" component and example of this would be when a child gets to the point where he/she is writing numbers, that final step represents many preliminary ones such as writing the number in sand or tracing a sandpaper number with his or her finger.

Their program has two extended work periods in which children are free to choose, move, and manipulate materials with guidance from their experienced teachers. Carefully monitored guidance of academics is given to the individual student. Large group discussions and small group collaboration are also key components of the Montessori classroom. The reason they are able to really teach to each child is because there are two fully accredited teachers in each classroom, which translates to approximately 12:1 teacher to student ratio.

Special programs in Music and Spanish complement their core curriculum. Elementary students meet daily for P.E. but it's optional. They also take part in curriculum-related field trips and other experiential education such as island exploration and camping experiences. The Montessori's cosmic curriculum, where the child is encouraged to see her/his place within a universal perspective, is very much part of their credo.

Their multi-aged classrooms provide the students with wide boundaries for social interaction. Students are in constant interaction, teaching and learning from each other. The classroom itself mimics a small community in which the student becomes an integral member. This same environment provides wide boundaries for academic achievement as well. The beauty of the Montessori program is that it allows children to work at their own pace and developmental level. There is no need to rush a child who is not ready to grasp certain concepts, or to hold back a gifted child who is ready to fly past his or her age appropriate work.

Learning Expectations for their Students:

- o To develop a solid academic foundation and a desire for lifelong learning.
- o To practice independent decision-making and to develop problem solving skills.
- o To become an integral member of a respectful school community.
- o To view the world as a vast, mysterious and inspiring place, replete with opportunities for intellectual and emotional growth.

The attending families represent a wonderful mixture of every culture present in Los Angeles. Once each spring the school holds a luncheon inviting the students to bring a favorite or traditional family dish. The banquet table goes on for miles and is filled with the most extraordinary and delicious food. It is not only an opportunity for the children to set all the tables and play host to their families, but a great chance for parents to visit, break bread, and get a sense of the school community.

HISTORY

Glendale Montessori was opened in 1971 by Arnolda C. Utrecht, and expanded in 1989 to include the bungalow (now the caretakers' cottage) and adjoining property. It includes a half-day primary, full-day primary, and elementary school through sixth grade.

AT A GLANCE

APPLICATION DEADLINE	March
TOURS	September-June, call school to schedule
UNIFORMS	No
AFTER SCHOOL CARE	No
SEE MAP	A on page 255

THE GOODEN SCHOOL

1921 N. BALDWIN AVE., SIERRA MADRES, CA 91204
TEL: 626.355.2410 FAX: 626.355.4212
www.goodenschool.org

HEAD OF SCHOOL:	**PATRICIA PATANO**
DIRECTOR OF ADMISSIONS:	**MARIANNE RYAN**
TYPE OF SCHOOL:	**CO-ED DAY SCHOOL**
GRADES:	**K-8**
ENROLLMENT: 170	TUITION: $14,950 - 15,950
APPLICATION FEE: $75	YEARLY REGISTRATION FEE: $850
ACCREDITATION: CAIS/NAES/WASC	FINANCIAL AID: LIMITED

The GOODEN SCHOOL has such a quaint, small-town feeling to it that you might believe you were on a movie set! This is a K-8, Independent Episcopal school where students attend chapel services held in a beautiful, old stone church across the street. Strong academics and Service-Learning are additional hallmarks of a Gooden education. The curriculum provides core subjects: reading, writing, math, science and social studies. All students play musical instruments and in middle school are either in the band or the orchestra. Spanish is taught in grades K-8 and Latin is taught in grades 4-8. Technology is integrated throughout the curriculum in all grades. The average class size is 20 students. Teachers are credentialed and half hold masters degrees.

Here is the Gooden Mission Statement:

> The Gooden School offers a firm educational foundation, using both traditional and progressive approaches. Our caring community allows students opportunities to grow in body, mind and spirit, to gain confidence, and to discover their unique gifts. We value diversity and promote character development and responsibility within a framework of Episcopal values. We foster a life-long commitment to learning, to compassion and to service by emphasizing respect for self, respect for others, and respect for the world.

There is an on-site library with 3,000 plus books, a computer lab, mimio boards and iPads in each classroom and a 1:1 iPad program in middle school. Classes in art and physical education compliment the curriculum. Additionally, each class stages a theatrical performance each year.

Parent participation is encouraged in the yearly events, (the annual Holiday Party, Shrove Tuesday Pancake Supper and the Barn Sale) as well as the annual giving campaign, which raises funds for enrichment programs at the school.

As far as life after junior high, Gooden states that, "Most graduates are accepted at their first choice college preparatory high school." This is an area always worth serious consideration at any school that ends at sixth or eighth grade. Choose a potential high school and ask, "How many of your students applied here last year, and how many of those applicants were accepted?"

It may seem like a long way off, but you don't want to be stuck later on if the elementary school you choose for your child does not sufficiently prepare him/her for the middle/high school.

HISTORY

The Gooden School was started by The Reverend and Mrs. Spencer P. Edwards Jr. It bears the name of the Right Reverend Robert B. Gooden, a longtime Episcopal Bishop. Bishop Gooden served as Headmaster of Harvard School for many years, and in that role was considered the patron of Episcopal Schools in Southern California. He maintained a life-long interest and involvement in education and remained active in affairs of this diocese throughout his life. The Bishop dedicated The Gooden School in 1975 in his 101st year.

AT A GLANCE

APPLICATION DEADLINE	February
OPEN HOUSES	November
SEE MAP	A on page 255

HARVARD-WESTLAKE

MIDDLE SCHOOL:
700 N. FARING ROAD, LOS ANGELES CA 9007
TEL: 310.274.7281 FAX: 310.288.3331
UPPER SCHOOL:
3700 COLDWATER CANYON, STUDIO CITY, CA 91604
TEL: 818.980.6692 FAX: 818.487.6624
www.hw.com

HEAD OF SCHOOL:	JEANNE HUYBRECHTS
DIRECTOR OF ADMISSIONS:	ELIZABETH GREGORY
TYPE OF SCHOOL:	CO-ED COLLEGE PREP DAY SCHOOL
GRADES:	7-12
ENROLLMENT: 1,595	TUITION: $35,900
APPLICATION FEE: $200	NEW STUDENT FEE: $2,000
ACCREDITATION: WASC	FINANCIAL AID: YES

In case you are new in town, **HARVARD-WESTLAKE** is considered to be one of the top private schools in Los Angeles. What used to be the Hollywood Country Club back in 1937 is now home for Harvard Westlake's upper school, which occupies 22 acres in North Hollywood's Coldwater Canyon and it's gorgeous. The middle school is comfortably nestled close by in Bel Air.

Competition to get into this school is tough since there are many more applicants than there are spaces. The program at this school is clearly designed for students who are highly motivated and independent learners. Your child needs to have extremely good study habits in order to survive here. The Harvard-Westlake experience is not for everyone. I have known some very able students drop out and leave because the pressure was simply too much. But then there are the others who stay and blossom into future world leaders!

The Admissions process is rigorous but well thought out. If your child excels, for example in soccer, then the school might arrange that he or she be interviewed by the soccer coach. Don't feel left out, you will have your own interview too!

The school will hold a number of 'Parent Coffees' for applicant parents. This is where you are handed the curriculum guide, which is almost as thick as this book and will become your favorite bedtime reading! These informal gatherings are where you hear the Director of Admissions, and the Headmaster speak, and it's here that you can ask questions. There is a sibling and legacy policy, but admission is not automatic. There are 209 faculty members and the facilities are amazing. There are eight academic halls, two lecture halls, two libraries, three gymnasiums, football/soccer fields, one track and one auditorium. Besides having two orchestra rooms, there are instrumental rehearsal studios, two electronic music studios and additional fully equipped MIDI stations, and music practice rooms. Two art centers boast ceramic studios, two photography labs. Computer labs are available throughout both campuses. To top it off there's a seven lane Olympic-size swimming pool!

Harvard-Westlake has its fair share of celebrity families but it also strives to include a student/parent body, which is diverse, socio-economically, culturally and geographically. Harvard- Westlake parents are told that the tuition doesn't cover all of the costs. Parents give what they can, and if you look at the school's annual report, you will see a long list of donors. Some give a few hundred a year while others tens of thousands. Of course there are the usual list of fundraisers where you can donate your time to if you aren't able to contribute financially.

Middle school students are required to take three years of English, foreign language, history/social science, science, math, computer science, P.E., as well as human development, performing arts, visual arts and communications courses. Emphasis is placed on the Classics. Seventh graders take an introduction to language course and can choose from Latin, Russian, French or Spanish.

Sports is big at Harvard-Westlake, and competition is fierce. In addition to interscholastic sports in the traditional teams, there are other sports offered such as: Jiu Jitsu, fencing, equestrian team, aerobics and dance production. Ninth graders are encouraged to choose a sport very carefully since trying-out for a team does not guarantee a place and they should have another P.E. class picked out as a backup.

All middle school students must participate in community service (12 hours a year), and there's a magazine called "Reach" which the students publish themselves.

The upper school students are required to complete three years of English, two years of history/social studies, two years of math (though three is recommended), and two years of laboratory sciences. One foreign language is studied up to level III, or two years of modern language and two years of Latin may be substituted. Students take two semesters of visual and/or performing arts in addition to five trimesters of physical education. For good measure, students do three years of community service, a semester of social service and health and human development.

If your child shows an aptitude for the sciences, then you're in the right place. The Munger Science Building is choc-a-block full of the most sophisticated equipment, which includes a scanning electron microscope, an infrared, ultra violet and visible light spectrometer, as well as a gas chromatograph and a NMR spectron. Students can study Oceanographic Biology, enroll in a SCUBA certification (NAUI) program, while learning the physics, chemistry and geology of the oceans. Meanwhile back in the math department, once students have completed their basic math courses, there are advanced level classes offered in calculus, linear algebra and math competition.

The Performing Arts Department is an integral part of the program with courses given in theatre and drama. Your child might be happier 'behind the scenes' – no problem, there's a course entitled "Technical Theater." With a full-time set designer, part-time box office manager and professional level lighting, your child's school theater production can be quite the night out!

The music department offers a vast number of classes. The music room is home to rows of cellos and just about every other string instrument you can think of as well as five kinds of drums, horns and a piano. Students really enjoy this department and meet there daily to play and record all styles of music.

Be warned that homework at this school is given to the tune of two to three hours per night for Grades 7 and 8 and count on three to four hours for grades 9 through 12. If your child is up for the challenge and you don't mind them being up into the wee hours of the night sometimes it's a wonderful school.

HISTORY

In 1989, Harvard, a boys' school founded in 1900 as a Military Academy, and Westlake, a girls' school founded in 1904 as a college preparatory school merged and Harvard- Westlake was born. The school's present headmaster, Thomas C. Hudnut has been with the school since 1987. Under his leadership the Munger Science Center was completed and is considered to be one of the most sophisticated science centers at any level.

AT A GLANCE

APPLICATION DEADLINE	January 15
OPEN HOUSES & TOURS	Call school for dates
ISEE	Yes
UNIFORMS	No
SUMMER SCHOOL	Yes
BUSING	Yes
SEE MAP	D on page 255

HIGH POINT ACADEMY

1720 KINNELOA CANYON ROAD, PASADENA, CA 91107
TEL: 626.798.8989 FAX: 626.798.8751
www.highpointacademy.org

HEAD OF SCHOOL:	**GARY STERN**
DIRECTOR OF ADMISSIONS:	**KRISTIN HAINES**
TYPE OF SCHOOL:	**CO-ED DAY SCHOOL**
GRADES:	**K-8**
ENROLLMENT: 350	TUITION: $13,600 - 13,900
APPLICATION FEE: $90	NEW STUDENT FEE: $200
ACCREDITATION: CAIS/WASC	FINANCIAL AID: NO

HIGH POINT ACADEMY is located in northeast Pasadena where it borders Altadena at the base of the foothills. The main building has an outside balcony walkway for access to the upper classes. There is a spaciousness to the surrounding land, a feeling of being in the high desert. Huge eucalyptus and pine trees shade the two outside play yards and basketball courts, and down below is a well-groomed soccer field.

The school's facilities include twenty classrooms, two play areas, P.E. locker rooms, a football/soccer field, a computer room, and a library. In the last few years, the classrooms and the school office have been enlarged and/or remodeled. A state-of- the-art science lab and an art/music room have also been added as well as a new arena-type seating area that allows parents and students to watch games being played the athletic field.

Kindergarten observation takes place by appointment, and parents shuttle between the two classes to watch quietly while the teacher goes through the normal schedule. This is a good time to see the "Carden Method" of teaching in action. The teachers in kindergarten through third grade are trained in the method first developed by Mae Carden in 1934. Simply stated, the Carden Method is a phonic based method of teaching reading. A simple example:

a + = a and another vowel says "a" as in gate

a = a alone says "a" as in mat

These are called vowel controls and help the children learn to decode the words for reading. During the school visit the teacher will talk about Carden phonics and answer parents' questions. Children in third grade are transitioned into more traditional phonics and dictionary markings.

Here is the school's philosophy:

> High Point Academy strives to awaken in each child the joy of learning and to educate by emphasizing the acquisition of basic skills to master all subjects. The rigorous academic curriculum stresses command of both the written and oral language and mathematical concepts as tools for analytical thinking. The school provides a safe and nurturing environment which enables the child to flourish academically, emotionally, morally, socially, and physically. Through careful fiscal responsibility and resource management, High

Point Academy seeks to make this quality education economically accessible to as many families as possible. With faculty and family support, the school's program develops in our students the ability and desire to pursue and organize knowledge throughout a lifetime.

The Kindergarten curriculum includes: manuscript printing, beginning reading (phonetic approach), vocabulary, high frequency sight words, learning to tell time, addition, subtraction and counting, identifying coins, foundations for spelling phonetically, daily physical education (every day), music, computers, library, art and French twice per week. I was very impressed with the website. It is easy to navigate and has so much information for the children to use as a research tool.

High Point is a structured, traditional academic school. There are specialists in art, music, computer, library, French and Spanish. Each year there are drama productions in kindergarten through third grade. The school often uses the church facility across the street for events such as plays and assemblies.

High Point's primary and elementary program is designed to give students a well-balanced academic schedule for core subjects while also preparing them for the challenges of junior high and high school. The junior high program has a strong academic emphasis that offers students a comfortable transition to high school.

In the special curricular offerings students receive a variety of enrichment programs each week. All students in kindergarten through eighth grade have a daily physical education class. They also have (on a rotating basis) art, music, computers, and library time. Students in kindergarten through fifth grade have French twice a week, while sixth grade students can choose either Spanish or French. For a nominal fee, band is offered once a week after school to interested students, as well as science and chess classes.

Students in grades 7 and 8 can participate in an after-school sports program. They also take either French or Spanish daily. High Point belongs to the prep league which offers students an opportunity to compete in a variety of major and minor sports.

Dollar for dollar, this school offers good value. This is due to sound fiscal management and a board policy that tuition covers all operating costs.

HISTORY

High Point Academy is an independent day school for boys and girls grades K-8 founded in 1965. It is located in northeast Pasadena. Students come from Pasadena, Arcadia, Sierra Madre, Monrovia, Altadena, and other neighboring communities in the San Gabriel Valley. The school has a non-discriminatory admissions policy.

AT A GLANCE

APPLICATION DEADLINE	January
UNIFORMS	No
AFTER SCHOOL CARE	Yes until 6:00pm
SUMMER SCHOOL	Yes
SEE MAP	B on page 255

THE HOLLYWOOD SCHOOL HOUSE

1233 NORTH McCADDEN PLACE, HOLLYWOOD, CA 90038
TEL: 323.465.1320 FAX: 323.465.1720
www.hollywoodschoolhouse.org

HEAD OF SCHOOL:	**STEPHEN BLOODWORTH**
DIRECTOR OF ADMISSIONS:	**LISA BEIRAS**
TYPE OF SCHOOL:	**CO-ED DAY SCHOOL**
GRADES:	**PRESCHOOL-8**
ENROLLMENT: 270	TUITION: $15,101 - 18,366
APPLICATION FEE: $150	NEW FAMILY FEE: $1,000
ACCREDITATION: WASC	FINANCIAL AID: YES

The **HOLLYWOOD SCHOOL HOUSE**, formerly The Hollywood Little Red School House, is situated on Highland Avenue near Fountain. From the outside, it looks exactly like its old name, a very quaint, very small, and very red school house, but when you enter the campus you realize why they changed the name. It has grown considerably over the years. The campus extends back an entire city block and is over half a city block in width. It also has its own 35-foot pool! When you arrive at the front desk, you must sign in before they buzz you into the main school through a locked door. Once in the school, you realize how deceiving the front of the building is...it goes on and on.

There are four separate buildings: Building I houses the preschoolers and the administration offices. Building II is the home of junior kindergarten and the kindergartners; Building III accommodates the elementary and middle school grades. Building IV contains a very well stocked library, a dance studio, an up to date computer lab, and classrooms for third-and fourth- graders.

I have been told by a number of people whose children attend the school that, if there is trouble out on the streets, they send their security people out to deal with it! I felt incredibly safe every time I went to pick up my neighbor's children. They have a state-of-the-art security system installed, and there is a heavy presence of staff out on the playground at all times. In fact, I saw a young boy sitting alone one day, and it wasn't long before one of the staff was right there beside him asking if everything was okay. It was reassuring to see that sort of concern. The child jumped right back up and began playing with his friends.

There is a delightful preschool playground filled with playhouses and climbing equipment, surrounded by flowers and plants. The courtyard playground has plenty of shade while the back playground is a large area in which the kids play basketball. Every time I have visited the school, I have been delighted to see the level of interaction between child and teacher. The kids really do seem to be very happy here – lots of smiling faces.

Most recently, a new building was added with classroom space, a multi-purpose room, a computer laboratory (with full internet access and multimedia capabilities), and a fully equipped kitchen facility. They have also added a new art studio, two new playground areas, an up-to-date technology program in each class and a new library program. As part of their Science curriculum the students maintain a community garden.

The teachers at Hollywood Schoolhouse bring a variety of experience and educational specialties to the program. They meet all state requirements and have further training in Early Childhood Education. In addition, the staff's continuing education is assured through in-service training, college courses, workshops, and professional conferences. From the school brochure:

> The mission of the Hollywood Schoolhouse is to attend to the intellectual, psychological, social, and physical needs of the students so that they will become responsible, literate, thinking, contributing citizens who are technologically prepared for the twenty-first century. The school environment provides the warmth and care that nurtures a child's self-esteem and positive self-image. The school has developed a program that ensures an opportunity for individualized academics, while fostering creative learning through a fine arts curriculum. The school recognizes that each individual possesses special characteristics and talents. Our commitment to individualized growth is reflected in our small class size. Success at the Hollywood Schoolhouse is measured by the ability to confront new situations with confidence, assess information creatively and analytically, and act on that information intelligently.

They believe that:

- All students can succeed academically when given the opportunity to learn in a balanced program which includes directed/undirected, individual, and cooperative activities.
- Students should be taught environmental awareness, including a basic knowledge of and respect for all life.
- Students should be life-long learners who are encouraged to strive for personal excellence.
- School is an integral part of the community, and everyone (parents, teachers, children, and administrators) must work together to build a strong, caring, and stimulating community environment.
- Change is positive and new ideas and experiences provide opportunities for growth and creative thought.
- Diversity is a strength and by enhancing each student's self-esteem, all students will achieve their highest potential.
- Instruction should be culturally responsive, free of bias, and compatible with the values of students' own cultures.
- All students possess multiple intelligence and should be taught strategies to enhance their strengths and compensate for their weaknesses.
- All students must develop skills that will prepare them to meet the future and allow them to function in a technologically changing society.
- Students learn best from hands-on, child-centered, curricular experiences that encourage them to explore their world creatively and analytically.
- Students learn best from passionate and enthusiastic teachers.
- All students should be guided into becoming self-determined citizens who do what they believe is right and are able to make responsible choices.

The elementary and middle school offers the following academic subjects:

Language Arts: reading, vocabulary building, comprehension and rate building, creative writing, oral language, grammar, spelling, dictionary skills, listening skills development and literature.

Mathematics: concepts, computation, problem solving, graphs and tables, practical application.

Science: experimentation, concepts and data collection, reporting and practical application of natural, earth and life sciences, physics and chemistry.

Social Studies: historical concepts and patterns, current events, understanding maps and using maps, critical thinking skills, reporting and practical application, multi-cultural studies.

Library: The students visit the library at least once a week. The library also has after-school reading and writing programs, and mentorship programs.

Computers: The commitment to state-of-the-art technology includes networked computers with color printers in every classroom. The world wide web and interactive-telelearning is accessible. They also have a mobile computer lab featuring "alphasmarts."

Fine Arts: art, dance, music, drama.

Spanish and Physical Education: Part of the regular weekly curriculum, swimming is a part of P.E. during warm weather months. Classes are taught by specialists.

Once a parent has visited the school and filled out an application, his/her child may be invited to spend time at the school. The visit gives your child the opportunity to interact with the teachers and students, and experience the school day first-hand. Using standardized assessment tools, an individual evaluation of the student's current academic skill level, plus social, verbal, and physical skills, are all carefully noted and assessed.

While the child is experiencing "a day in the life", the parents will meet with a member of the Admissions Committee. It is very important for both parents to attend this interview. The director maintains that the match between a school's program and the needs of the student and the family are paramount. The interview process gives you the opportunity for personal dialogue and helps in assessing the appropriateness of the program for your child. All qualified applicants are considered equally based on their commitment to a multi-cultural, socioeconomic student population, and a balance of boys and girls in their classes. But please know that the completion of all of the above steps does not guarantee admission.

This school is smaller than some, but with its caring and dedicated staff, It is to be recommended, especially to working parents who want not only a good education for their children, but also need after school care.

HISTORY

The Hollywood Schoolhouse, (formerly the Hollywood Little Red School House, and originally the Small Fry Nursery School), was opened in 1945 by Ruth Pease on Highland Avenue in the heart of Hollywood. The school was a response to the county's request for help in meeting the child care needs of the post-war community. For more than 23 years, it served the area by providing preschool activities for 20 children. However, by the 1960s the need for child care was growing. To meet the need the school expanded, and in 1968 the current preschool building was constructed with enrollment more than doubling to 50 children.

As years passed, the school prospered. Still, the ever-burgeoning demand for quality child care and an enhanced educational program beyond the early formative years, enlarged. To serve that demand, the Elementary Division was born in 1984. The campus expansion included the first elementary building with classrooms, a computer lab, and library. Two years later, a 35-foot swimming pool was built, and in 1987, the new kindergarten building, as well as an art and science workshop, were unveiled. In 2002, the school became 'non-profit' with a board of directors.

AT A GLANCE

APPLICATION DEADLINE	January
UNIFORMS	No
AFTER SCHOOL CARE	Yes until 6:00pm
SUMMER SCHOOL	Yes
SEE MAP	B on page 255

IMMACULATE HEART SCHOOL

5515 FRANKLIN AVENUE, LOS ANGELES, CA 90028

TEL: 323.461.3651 FAX: 323.462.0610

www.immaculateheart.org

PRESIDENT:	**MAUREEN DIEKMAN**
PRINCIPAL:	**VIRGINIA HURST, IHM**
ADMISSIONS DIRECTOR	**JENNIE LEE**
TYPE OF SCHOOL:	**CATHOLIC, ALL GIRLS DAY SCHOOL**
GRADES:	**6-12**
ENROLLMENT: 750	TUITION: $14,600
APPLICATION FEE: $75	REGISTRATION FEE: $450
ACCREDITATION: CAIS/WCEA/WASC	FINANCIAL AID: AVAILABLE

IMMACULATE HEART MIDDLE SCHOOL is a Catholic private school for girls, grades 6 through 8, located on the corner of Franklin and Western in the Los Feliz area. It's a great location surrounded by some of the largest homes in Los Angeles. Being a stone's throw away from Griffith Park, one has this feeling of not even being in the city once you enter the campus.

The middle school shares the rolling seven-acre hillside with Immaculate Heart High School, grades nine through twelve, and there's plenty of room for both. Please note that if you want your daughter to continue her education through the high school she must still apply to it as if it were a new school, entrance test and all.

It's a beautifully laid out campus, with gardens for students to use during the day or at lunchtime. There are pathways that wind their way through the property past the science building and student/faculty center, around the large playing field and four-lane competition- size swimming pool. There's volleyball and basketball courts and an impressive auditorium that serves as a gymnasium and performing arts center. My daughter pointed out the very charming, intimate chapel. Above it sits the dining room/cafeteria, where the children can enjoy lunch sitting outside on the patio perched high up on the side of the hill, with wonderful views over the city.

As we were walking through the grounds admiring our surroundings, we were greeted by a couple of girls who recognized my daughter from AYSO soccer. They could not have been more polite and bubbled with pride about their school.

The philosophy of Immaculate Heart is firmly rooted in Christian principles based on a primary belief in God. They also view technology as an essential educational tool and have a very in-depth computer program that integrates computers into the students everyday lives.

The library and audio-visual center serve both the middle and high school students and faculty. It's a wonderful place bursting with state-of-the-art equipment. The school's deep belief that the Library Information Center is essential to the learning process is plainly apparent when you enter this well organized, large and airy building. Here the students are encouraged to use both computers and the virtual library to help them in their studies.

Immaculate Heart Middle School's curriculum is designed to provide a sound academic foundation and allow the student to move with confidence into a strong college-preparatory high school program. Honors classes are offered in English, literature and mathematics. Students may qualify for membership in the California Junior Scholarship Federation as well as for a listing on the principal's Honor Roll.

Curriculum Components: Computer science, mathematics, religious science, Spanish, English, science, literature, social studies, art and physical education. Electives include: chorus, computer lab, dance, drama, leadership, newspaper, speech, and the Yearbook.

There are also many field trips planned throughout the year to places such as: The Will Geer Theatricum Botanicum, LACMA, the Museum of Tolerance, and The Norton Simon Museum. Recent two-day trips have been to San Francisco, Sacramento and Catalina Island. Sixth graders experience a three-day outdoor educational trip. In the annual Celebration of Cultures, students recognize and embrace their cultural diversity through music, dance, stories, and a vast array of international foods.

There is a Father/Daughter picnic and Mother/Daughter luncheon and only one fundraising event per year, which is a 10K walk. It is a great way for the kids to raise money for their school, and for children and their parents to get some serious exercise!

The average class size is only 22 students, and with 41 full-time faculty members there is a student/instructor ratio of 1:16, which means lots of extra attention. There is a school psychologist on staff to help students resolve personal problems. In the middle school, the homeroom teacher, along with the school director, oversees the academic progress of each student.

If it's the Middle School you're interested in, then there's an open house in early December. But if you miss it, don't worry, you can fill out the application and student essay form and return it to the Admissions Office by early January. For seventh grade, the application due date is early February.

Immaculate Heart's HIGH SCHOOL curriculum offers students a wide choice of classes in addition to those required for college admission. A typical freshman program of studies might include: religious studies I, English I or honors English I, algebra I or honors algebra I, or geometry or honors geometry; French I or Spanish I, and world civilizations I.

Honors classes are also offered (after the freshman year) in Spanish, French, chemistry, algebra, geometry, biology, physics, world civilization, design layout and advanced art. Students are encouraged to participate in advanced placement classes, which qualify them for college credit and include: English, calculus, U.S. history, U.S. government, comparative government, Spanish and studio art.

The Visual and Performing Arts program offers studio arts, chorus, speech, and drama. The school is proud of their drama troupe, "The Genesain Players," who present major productions yearly. The school competes in CIF volleyball, cross-country, basketball, tennis, swimming, softball, soccer, and track.

As with the middle school, there is a school psychologist available on staff to help students resolve personal problems, and an academic counselor who supervises the progress of each student.

When it comes time for your daughter to find a college or university, there is a college counselor who helps in the research and application processes, plans college admission informational programs for parents and students, and coordinates the visits of college representatives to the school. I was impressed to hear that 98 percent of Immaculate Heart's high school graduates enter many prestigious colleges and universities immediately after graduation.

If you are looking at ninth grade, your child is invited to attend an academic playday. Each year in November, the faculty and students present a 'playday' for eighth grade girls to acquaint them with the campus and members of the school community. The half-day event features student-led campus tours and informal workshops followed by a barbecue. It's a great way for your child to see the school and experience a day in the life of a high school student at Immaculate Heart. Oh and did I mention it's a fraction of the price of some of the other private schools!

HISTORY

The school was founded in 1906 by the Sisters of the Immaculate Heart of Mary, a Catholic religious order of women who trace their origin to Olot, Spain. In 1996, Ruth Anne Murray, IHM, stepped down from the position of principal to become President of Immaculate Heart High School, and Virginia Hurst, IHM, became the new principal. A new sixth grade class was added to the middle school and Immaculate Heart celebrated its 100-year anniversary in 2006. To see more, visit their website. The children have worked very hard on a most impressive look at Immaculate Heart's long history. It's also a great way to take a 'virtual tour' around the campus.

AT A GLANCE

APPLICATION DEADLINE	January 8
OPEN HOUSES	December
ENTRANCE EXAM	Yes
UNIFORMS	Yes
SUMMER SCHOOL	Yes
SEE MAP	D on page 255

JOHN THOMAS DYE

11414 CHALON ROAD, LOS ANGELES, CA 90049
TEL: 310.476.2811 FAX: 310.476.9176
www.jtdschool.com

PRINCIPAL:	**ANDREA ARCHER**
DIRECTOR OF ADMISSIONS:	**JUDY HIRSCH**
TYPE OF SCHOOL:	**CO-ED DAY SCHOOL**
GRADES:	**K-6**
ENROLLMENT: 320	TUITION: $27,390
APPLICATION FEE: $125	NEW FAMILY FEE: $2,000
ACCREDITATION:CAIS/WASC/NAIS	FINANCIAL AID: YES

JOHN THOMAS DYE occupies eleven beautiful acres in Bel Air and feels very exclusive from the moment you drive up to the campus until the time the tour is over. Included in the application packet is an exquisitely detailed little map –don't lose it –because the school is quite difficult to find!

At first I thought I had taken a wrong turn and stumbled upon an Arabian Horse farm enclosed by an impeccably kept white split-rail fences. But, of course, I still had that little map clenched in my hand so eventually I made my way to the parking lot.

The whole facility is gorgeous and generously laid out on the property with spectacular views. It is so removed from the chaos and smog of the city that it feels more like a vacation resort, but don't be fooled, there's a lot of learning going on there! A multi-purpose facility located on the lower field houses an art studio, a large gymnasium, and a 13,000+ volume library. The younger children enjoy two large play areas. Physical education and after-school sports programs take place on the athletic field.

The school began in the home of the Dye family in 1929, so the buildings were designed with a warm, homey feeling about them. The John Thomas Dye Hall contains administrative offices, an assembly hall, a computer lab and two music rooms. Two identical wings extend east and west from the main building housing classrooms. The two story MAC center is a new addition housing the Fifth and Sixth grade classrooms and has a wonderful roof-top vegetable garden. Three Kindergarten classrooms are housed in a separate adjoining facility. They accept 70 boys and 70 girls into the Kindergarten applicant pool, on a first-come, first-served basis. There are 45 available openings at the Kindergarten level. Siblings of present students get first priority. The school also admits students at First through Sixth grades depending on the available openings.

Dye is a traditional academic school using an integrated curriculum. Students learn specific subjects and also how these subjects relate to each other. Emphasis is placed on the development of problem-solving abilities, effective written and oral communication skills, good study skills, and work habits.

Each class is taught by two full time teachers. Courses taught in each self contained classroom include language arts, mathematics, and social studies. Grades five and six are taught by separate departments of English, math, science, and social studies. All students receive instruction from specialists in art, computer science, library, music, physical education and science. Students are given homework assignments, which become more challenging at each grade level. Written reports are issued three times a year and parent-teacher conferences are held twice a year. Educational Records Bureau Tests are administered each spring.

The First grade class that I observed was working in independent groups spread out among all the different 'centers' in the room (i.e. the reading area, the science area, etc.). The teachers were assisting students as they came up to them with questions, but they were fully aware of what was going on. The children were aware of my presence, but always stayed focused on the tasks at hand. The classroom was impeccably organized with every scholastic aid one could imagine. There were computers and iPods available for each student, a miniature library, a large fish tank, and lots of state-of-the-art audio/visual equipment. I got the feeling that this group of children got many things accomplished in a day, and that the teachers kept them interested in what they were learning.

One couple I spoke with told me that they were so terribly excited to send their child to Dye. They had toured at least 11 other schools and nothing compared to what they saw on campus. They told me that Judy Hirsch, the Director of Admissions, had welcomed them so warmly that they knew what it would feel like if they were chosen to become part of the Dye family. Parents often ask me "what will it be like meeting Judy," I always tell them she's passionate about what she does in making sure the child is the right fit for JTD and that she's funny and kind and always puts you at ease, so don't worry about what to say, she knows what to ask! It's so true. She is such a big part of what makes Dye the school it is today. She sets the tone, along with her trusted assistant Kim Bublitz who greets everyone with a huge smile and is always happy to answer any questions you might have forgotten during your tour/interview.

Traditional Dye events include Grandparents Day, a Winter Carols Program, Open House, the Sixth grade Awards Program, the Sixth Grade Musical and the Spring Fair. If you have a chance, tour the school in the Spring and go to the Spring Fair (always held the first Sunday in May) because these events will give you a clear picture of what the school is all about.

This school prepares their students really well for their next step; a full one hundred percent of the last year's graduating class went on to leading independent secondary schools. The list is very impressive and most years the majority go on to Harvard-Westlake with Brentwood close behind and after that Marlborough, Windward, Crossroads, St. Matthews, Archer, Campbell Hall and other top notch schools. In case you haven't already guessed, to enroll in JTD is difficult but possible!

HISTORY

Cathryn Robberts Dye and her husband, John Thomas Dye II, founded the school in 1929. It was originally called Brentwood Town and Country School and was started in their home for their only son, John Thomas Dye III, and his friends. By 1949 the school had outgrown its original home. It moved to its present site and was renamed The Bel Air Town and Country School. In 1959 the name was changed to the John Thomas Dye School in honor of John Thomas Dye III who was killed in action in WWII.

Today the vision of the founders is being carried into the 21st century as the school starts it eighty-sixth year of operation under the guidance of the New Head of School, Andrea Archer, who took over from the much beloved prior Head Raymond Michaud Jr. who ran the school from 1980 to 2014. Ms. Archer joined JTD in July 2014 having come from the prestigious Derby Academy in Hingham, MA. Prior to that she was Head of School at Dutchess Day School in New York and started her teaching and administrative career at Crossroads for the Arts and Sciences here in Santa Monica. The school is very excited to see what she has in store for them!

AT A GLANCE

APPLICATION DEADLINE	Applications available in August
SCHOOL TOURS	April through January
UNIFORMS	Yes
BEFORE AND AFTER SCHOOL CARE	Yes
SUMMER SCHOOL PROGRAM	Yes
SEE MAP	D on page 255

LAURENCE SCHOOL

13639 VICTORY BLVD, VALLEY GLEN, CA 91401
TEL: 818.782.4001 FAX: 818.782.4004
www.laurenceschool.com

HEAD OF SCHOOL:	**LAURIE WOLKE**
PRINCIPAL:	**GARY STERN**
TYPE OF SCHOOL:	**CO-ED DAY SCHOOL**
GRADES:	**K-6**
ENROLLMENT: 118	TUITION: $26,325
APPLICATION FEE: $125	NEW FAMILY FEE: $1,250
REGISTRATION FEE: $150	FINANCIAL AID: YES

LAURENCE SCHOOL is a beautifully landscaped, five-acre campus located in Valley Glen in the heart of the San Fernando Valley. Affectionately referred to as a "Secret Garden" that magically comes to life upon entering the campus where you witness the smiling faces of students who feel secure and confident, and faculty and administrators who are deeply devoted to students' growth and development.

The campus is brimming with student-inspired artwork, an Edible Garden, and a regulation size Athletic Field. The facilities include a newly-renovated science center that provides an ideal venue for exploration, experimentation, and STEAM (Science Technology Engineering Art Math) projects, a new spacious dance studio and drama room, a beautiful and well equipped music studio, a state-of-the-art library with reading and storytelling room, and expansive classrooms with an interactive Air Server technology utilized by all students – the ultimate modern overhead projector! Technology is incorporated into the curriculum with a 2:1 iPad program in kindergarten-4th grade and a 1:1 iPad program in 5th and 6th grades. Coding/programming is taught as early as the 1st grade and continues all the way to 6th grade. There's digital photography, graphic design classes, and there's also a dedicated Technology Center with Macs and 3-D printers. A modern 10,000 square-foot gym and indoor/outdoor theatre provide exceptional athletic facilities and a venue for musical theatre productions, school-wide assemblies, and special events. There's a full kitchen, which can accommodate school-wide special events. I also liked the secure, fast, convenient, and safe drop-off/pick-up area, and Laurence encourages carpools to ease traffic and has four different bus routes to offer families a convenient and safe alternative to get to and from school.

Kindergarten students have Art, Literacy Centers, and Music/Drama/Dance every day, and enjoy an impressive playground with rubber flooring and raised ski slope type shapes. The playground includes misters for hot days. I haven't seen that before at a school! Students are also put into small, ability-based groups at their age level in reading and math to provide a customized program. Perhaps ten will do art, and the remaining ten are placed into even smaller groups to work on academics. Later, the groups switch.

Laurence's educational philosophy is a good mixture of being warm and nurturing with a whole-child developmental approach, but also states that it has a 'strong academic curriculum.' The program provides an excellent balance of tradition and innovation. The academic curriculum is tailored to meet the needs of highly gifted children, as well as those progressing at grade level. The goal is to have children develop into creative thinkers who seek out innovative solutions to complex problems. They proudly report that their graduates routinely receive multiple acceptances into all of the highly competitive and selective secondary schools such as Harvard-Westlake, Marlborough, Brentwood,

Archer, Oakwood, Buckley, Campbell Hall, and more. All graduating sixth graders speak at graduation, and each year the sixth grade class leaves a parting gift to the school. This year, it was a beautiful fountain and a Zen Garden.

I was most impressed by the sense of unity and oneness at the school, the deep feeling of community and family. The children all have "buddies" (for example, a sixth grader with a kindergarten student) and they get together once a week. Many extend the friendship outside of school with "play dates". Every family new to the school gets a "host" family, to help teach them the ropes of Laurence and help them become acclimated. The families communicate year round. It's simply a very family oriented community with a great deal of parent involvement. In fact, many people who work at Laurence have children there, or have had children there. It is as if the kids leave, but the parents don't!

Here is the School's Mission Statement as taken from the school brochure:

> Laurence's purpose is to develop the unique abilities and potential of its students by offering a personalized, developmentally appropriate,and enriched educational program. Our focus and concern is for "The Total Child." A multidisciplinary approach encourages intellectual, creative, ethical social, and emotional growth and awareness. Laurence is dedicated to academic excellence, pride in oneself, mutual respect, compassion, and interculturalism. Rich traditions and innovative curriculum endow our students with the life skills needed to meet the challenges and opportunities of citizenship and leadership in the global community.

There is an average of 18 students per class, with a student-teacher ratio of 8:1. There are specialists in science, music, drama, dance, physical education, art, computer, library, and Spanish. All specialists are experienced in their fields, and all teachers are credentialed. A school-wide Red, White, Blue and Green assembly is held every Friday morning, with lots of American flags waving while students receive recognition for outstanding achievements, noteworthy participation, birthday celebrations and special events. All Laurence families are invited to attend.

After school programs include art, chess, musical theatre, school orchestra, and technology, in addition to interscholastic sports teams in basketball, soccer, flag football, baseball, and volleyball. There is an extensive theatre program at Laurence, and all students are comfortable speaking to adults and in front of a group. The school maintains a Global Education program in which students learn about sister countries across the globe and engage in collaborative projects with their buddies in China, Japan, England, Mexico, Kenya, and Israel, to name a few. Other special programs include Kids' Court, which involves students in a simulated courtroom trial and further hones their public speaking and debate skills, and a celebration of the Elizabethan-era and Shakespearean literature. Student Council representatives hold town meetings, publish a student newspaper, and organize weekly collection drives for a local food pantry.

The school is a recipient of an award from the National Character Education Partnership and has received commendations for its community service programs, class meetings, and cross-age buddy programs. Their Character Education program is designed to teach the concept of values: honesty, respect, self-control, good judgment, caring, and responsibility. These values are continually reinforced in the classroom and at assemblies where children are recognized and awarded for their good deeds by Representing the "L" (Laurence).

According to Head of School, Lauren Wolke,

> As you enter our "Secret Garden", you will be able to feel the magic that is Laurence School. In addition to our beautiful state-of-the-art facility, you will witness our exceptional faculty, administration, and staff, who are deeply devoted to our students' growth and development. You will see the smiling faces of students who feel safe, secure, and confident to take advantage of the numerous opportunities we provide. You will be embraced by a diverse community that draws families from the San Fernando Valley, as well as the Greater Los Angeles area including Beverly Hills, Brentwood, Hancock Park, Hollywood, and Los Feliz, thanks to our bus service. Laurence is a one-of-a-kind elementary school experience. Our

highly personalized, close-knit community – where everyone knows each child and is dedicated to his or her overall development – will always be Laurence's distinguishing trademark.

The Laurence School brochure is full of happy, smiling faces, a true representation of our city's rich cultural blend, as well as the acres of beautiful gardens and learning spaces that adorn the campus. My general impression is that Laurence provides an excellent, traditional academic education (with a multitude of enrichment opportunities) for its students, and all interested should go for a visit.

HISTORY

Founders, Marvin and Lynn Jacobson, are very proud of their school, and lovingly refer to it as "our secret garden where children grow." Founded in 1953, as a one room schoolhouse with 10 students, Marvin Jacobson is still at the school on a daily basis. After all these years, his "Total Child" philosophy and belief that everything around children affects their learning, is evident in his caring interactions with children and parent. The attention to detail and the user-friendly nature of everything on the stunning five-acre campus, is a testament to the vision of the School's founders.

AT A GLANCE

APPLICATION DEADLINE	January 15th
OPEN HOUSE	October - January
AFTER SCHOOL CARE	Yes
SUMMER CAMP	Available month of July
UNIFORMS	Yes
SEE MAP	A on page 255

LILA - LYCEE INTERNATIONAL DE LOS ANGELES

1105 W RIVERSIDE DRIVE, BURBANK, CA 91506
TEL: 626.695.5159 FAX: 818.859.7355
www.lilaschool.com

HEAD OF SCHOOL:	MICHAEL MANISKA
DIRECTOR OF ADMISSIONS:	JULIETTE LANGE
TYPE OF SCHOOL:	BILINGUAL (FRENCH/ENGLISH)
GRADES:	PRESCHOL-12
ENROLLMENT: 1000	TUITION: $16,400 - 19,500
APPLICATION FEE: $125	NEW FAMILY FEE: $3,000
ACCREDITATION: WASC	FINANCIAL AID: YES

LYCEE INTERNATIONAL DE LOS ANGELES (LILA) opened its fifth campus at the beginning of the 2013 school year in Burbank. It houses the secondary school (6th-12th) and is to handle the large influx of 5th grade graduates from the Los Feliz, Pasadena, and West Valley elementary school campuses. Moving the secondary school off the Los Feliz campus has also allowed LILA to expand its elementary classes. There is currently a two-year waiting list for the PreK classes at Los Feliz.

There are currently over 1000 students enrolled at LILA's five campuses.

Part of LILA's academic program includes annual Artist-in-residence guest instructors - professional working artists who create ongoing projects with students. Another component of the carefully designed program are regular "Writing To Share" events where students display and share their writing (in French and English) with the school community.

There is an interactive SMART Board in every LILA classroom which instructors and students are able to utilize for lessons. ipads are also available for every student's school use.

LILA's 2014 graduating seniors had a 100% pass rate in the French Baccalaureate (all with "mention"/distinction) and a 98% pass rate in the International Baccalaureate full Diploma program 100% pass rate in the full bilingual Diploma and in IB certificates.

87% of LILA's 93 teachers and 15 classroom aides hold at least a master's degree and/or teaching credential, including a Ph.D and/or university-level teaching credential. Due to the nature of the pedagogical program, the majority of the teaching staff are selected from France. All teaching staff undergo a rigorous selection process.

LILA has earned an esteemed reputation with the placement of graduates in top universities all over the world including Princeton, Columbia, Stanford, Cornell, Dartmouth, UC Berkeley, Chicago, Carnegie-Mellon Universities (U.S.); McGill, Concordia and British Columbia Universities (Canada); Oxford and Edinburgh Universities (UK); and Sciences Po and Sorbonne Paris (France).

The Cycle Program

This system was inaugurated in France in 1991 and allows elementary students to develop at their own pace. These first years are a time of intellectual curiosity, but young students do not learn at the same rate in all subject areas. The cycle system allows children to acquire knowledge according to their ability. By the time students finish their elementary curriculum, they have been prepared for a demanding secondary curriculum and given solid study habits and learning skills which will enable them to excel through college and beyond. At the Pre-Kindergarten level, children are placed in a typical French classroom situation whether they speak French fluently or not. In Kindergarten, English is added as part of the reading curriculum. From this grade on, the percentage of English in the curriculum will increase from 20% to 40% in 5th grade. This dual language approach has specific objectives: by the end of Cycle 1 (Kindergarten), students begin to read in English. By the end of Cycle 2 (2nd grade), students read in both English and French. By the end of Cycle 3 (6th grade), students are capable of reading and writing in both languages.

LILA aims to offer more than the mere knowledge of at least two languages. The ultimate goal is to form fully bi-literate students capable of functioning in two linguistic worlds. To achieve this goal, LILA specifically avoids dividing students based upon their dominant language. At the very foundation of the educational program is a policy of integration: young Americans must be integrated into French classes and French children must study English along with their American classmates.

The French "Brevet" is a rite of passage for all LILA 9th graders, but the French "Bac" and the IB (International Baccalaureate) DIPLOMAS often allow LILA graduates to enter universities with up to two years' worth of class credits.

LILA offers the International Baccalaureate DIPLOMA program to their high school juniors and seniors. This is the full diploma program, not merely IB certificate classes which some area-schools offer. In addition, many LILA students opt to pursue the full bilingual IB Diploma.

HISTORY

LILA was established in 1978 by visionary educators who felt that the Los Angeles community needed a school, which would prepare children for life in an increasingly international environment. They chose the proven French educational system as the foundation for LILA's curriculum. Since its inception LILA has continually evolved and has grown out of the very first campus – a small house in Van Nuys with seven students – to five formal campuses in the greater Los Angeles area, with over 1,000 students.

AT A GLANCE

APPLICATION DEADLINE	November 30
OPEN HOUSE	November
UNIFORMS	Yes, West Valley Campus, Strict dresscode all other campuses
BEFORE AND AFTER SCHOOL CARE	Yes
SEE MAP	A on page 255

LOYOLA HIGH SCHOOL

1901 VENICE BLVD, LOS ANELES, CA 90006

TEL: 213.381.5121 FAX: 213.368.3819

www.loyolahs.edu

PRINCIPAL:	**FRANK KOZAKOWSKI**
DIRECTOR OF ADMISSIONS:	**HEATH UTLEY**
TYPE OF SCHOOL:	**ALL BOYS CATHOLIC DAY SCHOOL**
GRADES:	**9-12**
ENROLLMENT: 53	TUITION: $18,700
APPLICATION FEE: $75	FINANCIAL AID: YES
ANNUAL REGISTRATION FEE: $350	

The **LOYLA HIGH SCHOOL** campus is magnificent-looking, with handsome three-story brick buildings that remind one of the University houses in Cambridge, England. A sweeping circular driveway deposits you outside one of the finest Catholic all-boy schools in the city. Students at Loyola enjoy the spacious school buildings with wide corridors and large, bright classrooms overlooking the huge playing fields and gardens.

The campus is close to downtown and centrally-located, which is convenient for Loyola students who come from Malibu, Santa Monica, North Hollywood, Beverly Hills, Hancock Park, San Gabriel Valley, Whittier, Long Beach, Palos Verdes and Pasadena, and with Uber there's really no excuse not to get your kids there!

In any one year, this school may receive applicants from as many as 225 Catholic, public and private elementary schools. The competition is tough, last year they had 800 applicants for 300 slots. They generally give preference to Catholic boys, although they do take in about 14 percent non-Catholics each year.

Mission Statement (as taken from the school brochure):

> Loyola High School of Los Angeles is a Catholic College preparatory school for young men who represent the racial, ethnic, and socio-economic diversity of greater Los Angeles. Drawing upon the Jesuit tradition, Loyola is committed to the development of the whole person through a challenging educational experience of academic, co-curricular, and religious opportunities. By teaching as Jesus taught, Loyola is dedicated to inspiring its students to develop as conscientious leaders and agents of change who are intellectually distinguished, morally courageous, and compassionate in service to others.

The average student/teacher ratio is 15:1, so your child won't be lost in huge lecture-size classes and will have plenty of individual attention. This is a traditional school, which offers many advanced placement courses (see below). If your child enrolls in these classes, and then passes the exams set by the College Entrance Examination Board, he will receive college units, which can earn him credit in University.

In his freshman year your child will choose from the following subjects: English I, algebra, accelerated algebra, foreign language with a choice of Spanish, French, German, and Latin, Honors Spanish, theology, global studies, global science, biology, physical education, touch typing/word processing.

His sophomore year will include: English II (British Literature), AP English language and composition position, foreign language, Honors Spanish, geometry, theology, community service project, western civilization, biology, health, Earth science, AP environmental science, honors French.

In his junior year: English III, AP English language and composition, foreign language III, honors Spanish IV, algebra II, honors algebra II, honors pre-calculus, theology, community service project, U.S. history, AP U.S. history, chemistry, honors chemistry, AP chemistry, Earth science, fine arts (photography, painting, design, ceramics, music, drawing, chorus, acting work- shops), AP environmental science, AP Latin III, honors French III.

Finally, in his senior year, your child must take at least ten courses in required and elective subjects. The required subjects are: English, mathematics, fine arts, foreign language IV, science, social studies electives, and theology. He must also complete a senior internship in community service.

Loyola is well known for its sports programs. It fields 11 varsity teams: football, cross country, and water polo in fall, basketball and soccer in winter, baseball, volleyball, swimming and diving, track and field, golf, and tennis in the spring. As a Loyola athlete, your son will have the chance to compete with and against some of the best athletes in southern California, often reaching the CIF finals and then winning those, too. However, if your son does not make it onto one of the interscholastic CIF teams, the school offers a wide range of intramural sports.

Your child is not expected to 'sail through' this very rigorous 4 years, and that's why they allocate each student a personal counselor and an academic advisor to help when needed. They take a personal interest in your child at Loyola, and that's an important reason why their students are so successful, extremely polite and well-mannered. Visiting the school is a delightful experience, and I thoroughly recommend it.

Another reason to consider this school is that 99 percent of their graduates go on to college immediately (97 percent of those to four-year universities). The most popular choices are the UC campuses, UC Berkeley, and UCLA, although many have gone on to a Jesuit college or university, to USC, and others to one of the Ivy League schools.

HISTORY

The school was founded 137 years ago and follows the Jesuit tradition of education, which spans over 450 years. There are 85 faculty members at Loyola, and of these, 10 are Jesuits.

AT A GLANCE

APPLICATION DEADLINE	January 6
OPEN HOUSE	Call school for dates
UNIFORMS	No, but there is a dress code
SEE MAP	C on page 255

LE LYCÉE FRANÇAIS DE LOS ANGELES

OVERLAND CAMPUS-MAIN CAMPUS

3261 OVERLAND AVENUE, LOS ANGELES, CA 90034

TEL: 310.836.3464 FAX: 310.558.8069

RAYMOND & ESTHER KABBAZ HIGH SCHOOL

10309 NATIONAL BLVD, LOS ANGELES, CA 90034

TEL: 310.836.3464, ext. 331

www.lyceela.org

SCHOOL PRESIDENT:	MRS. KABBAZ, ESQ.
HEAD OF SCHOOL (HIGH):	MR. PETAUTON
HEAD OF SCHOOL (MIDDLE):	DR. ANGELINI
HEAD OF SCHOOL (ELEMENTARY):	MRS. COLE
DIRECTOR OF ADMISSIONS:	MME. SOPHIE DARMON
TYPE OF SCHOOL:	COLLEGE PREP DAY SCHOOL
GRADES:	PRESCHOOL-12
ENROLLMENT: 900	TUITION: $19,400 - 24,800
APPLICATION FEE: $100	NEW STUDENT FEE: $1,000
REGISTRATION FEE: $500	FINANCIAL AID: YES

In a quiet, residential area of West LA, a small sign and friendly gate guards indicate that you have indeed made the right turn as you wind your way up the hill to the Main Campus of **Le Lycée Français** in Los Angeles. Situated on a tucked away historic lot, the Administrative Offices overlook the Elementary School Campus on one side, and parts of a beautiful garden on the other. "When you reach 6th grade, you are allowed to have lunch in the garden, and the students like to spend time there on their breaks," says School President Mrs. Kabbaz. "They always used to cross through the planters, so we built a walk-way for them and we created a covered area where they could sit. I love to see them in the garden."

As you enter in to the original buildings, now housing the Elementary School and the Administrative Offices, what strikes you is how lovingly and meticulously maintained they are. This theme runs through the entire Main Campus. It seems every item has its place, and it is clear that the people here, students, teachers, and staff alike, take pride in keeping their school impeccably clean and organized - from garden paths to lunchrooms to classrooms. The general atmosphere and reception from everyone I meet is professional and efficient on one hand, and genuinely warm and friendly on the other.

Founded by the current President's parents in 1964, this is the first Lycée in the West, and the third Lycée in the U.S. At the time of its founding Code of Education forbade teaching in a foreign language, and immersion programs were non-existent. Thanks to the persistent lobbying by the founders, Esther and Raymond Kabbaz, California law was changed, opening the possibility for many other language immersion schools to exist in the Golden State.

Enter through its gates, enter history. Le Lycée runs on its founders' vision , which is very much alive and respected. Le Lycée offers a blend of tradition --old school European manners, with children standing up when an adult enters the classroom, with a relaxed and congenial atmosphere. The feeling is not "stodgy." (Mme la presidente used that word). The gardens, grounds and buildings are beautifully maintained.

There is no theft in the high school lockers, no disciplinary issues. Any behavior problems are dealt with directly and immediately. The school does not hesitate to expel students if there are on-going problems and school feels that student is not a good fit for Lycée and its community.

The student-teacher ratio is 12 to 15 students per teacher. 55% of students are American, 20% French, 25% International (roughly!!). 66% of students are "lifers," which means they go from Preschool through 12th grade graduation at Le Lycée. This school is not only for French students – the majority of students are American, and most graduates continue on to American universities.

Le Lycée offers two different tracks starting in 3rd grade : The French School Program (FSP), where students learn all subjects in French, and the International School Program (ISP) where students learn in English while studying French and another modern language. Both tracks lead to a US high school diploma, and are college preparatory, with almost all students continuing to selective US Universities.

From Preschool through 2nd Grade ALL students are in a bilingual immersion program. After that parents, students, and teachers decide on one of tracks described above. Most students in the French track are American , and many of their parents don't speak French.

At end of the French School Program, students can test for the Classic French Baccalaureate degree, or the new FAB Franco American Baccalaureate (a brand new degree). Lycée students score very high on both.
A US Student who passes the FAB can go to any university in the EU, French and other European Universities are free. The US System holds FAB and Classic French Bac in high regard. You place out of many university classes with the FAB and AP-classes.

The International School Program (ISP) offers up to fourteen different Advanced Placement courses starting in 10th grade and culminates in the College Board's brand new prestigious "Capstone" diploma or certificate, along with a California high school diploma. The AP offerings include AP Calculus A/B and B/C, AP Biology, AP English Literature, AP English Language, AP Human Geography, AP Latin, AP Macroeconomics, AP Microeconomics, AP Spanish, AP Studio Art, AP US History, and AP US Government.

Students lead in organizing extra-curricular classes and activities. Student-invented programs and clubs are very much encouraged, such as Global Outreach, where funds are collected to install water filters in African and Haitian homes, for the LA Foodbank, etc. Students turned Classroom without Borders, into a graded and approved for credit class. The Environmental Club was turned into the Environmental Science Class. The Drama Club is complemented by a course in Dramatic Literature, and another extra-curricular course in World Cinema.

Lunch is cooked on premises every day by cooks on staff. Each campus has its own kitchen and chef. Students learn to sit down at the table and enjoy learning and using European table manners. They serve each other water and pass the bread basket. Table settings use real silverware, and waste is discouraged. Students are taught how to handle table settings and eating using the fork in the left hand.

Madame President speaks of her staff with same tone as she uses for her family, the founders of the school. The Staff has been with the school for a very long time, for example one of the custodians retired this year after 35+ years.

The Arts: Art is taught formally up to 9th grade. Elementary and Middle School have art and music as part of their curriculum. The Performing Arts are now taught in the Kabbaz family's former home (across from Main Administration building) Madame Kabbaz's mother loved ballet.

Middle School students hold performances in a bucolic outdoor amphi-theatre on school grounds. They perform Moliere in French and Shakespeare in English. They even perform skits in Latin and Ancient Greek ! These are peer performances only, as it takes pressure off the students. The Drama Clubs at all levels, elementary, middle and high-school, put on 5 to 6 plays and musicals per year in the Theatre Raymond Kabbaz at the Century City Campus, to which parents and family members are invited.

CAMPUSES:

What is unique about Le Lycée is that, unlike other multi-campus schools, each location is age-appropriate and children can look forward to matriculating smoothly from one campus to the next along with their classmates.

Starting with **CAMPUS 55**, which includes PRESCHOOL and K1, just three minutes from the Main Campus, students can enjoy a charming learning garden, green spaces, comfortably furnished classrooms, a cozy eating area, a large, comfortable reading library and a spacious indoor area for dance and movement. Mme. Haustete is the director of Campus 55's complete French/English immersion program.

K2 and First Grade at the beautiful **CENTURY CITY CAMPUS**, is located on Pico Blvd across from the Rancho Park Golf Course. Mr. Zala, is director of this large campus with colorful and spacious classrooms, a garden, a dedicated gymnasium, an airy art room and a bilingual library. It is also home to Le Lycée's legendary Theatre Raymond Kabbaz, LA's number one theatrical venue for French and European talent, including student performances.

THE PACIFIC PALISADES Campus, convenient to Malibu, Pacific Palisades, Santa Monica and the West Valley, is headed by Mme Leloup – located in a serene, residential neighborhood, it offers Preschool through Second Grade and a tightly-knit school community with lovely, green outdoor spaces. At 2nd or 3rd grade, students move to the Overland Main Campus in West L.A.

Starting in 2nd or 3rd grade all students attend the **MAIN CAMPUS** "up the hill" through 5th grade at the lush, expansive Elementary School Campus, headed by Mme Cole. This is one of the original campuses since the early sixties.

THE MIDDLE SCHOOL CAMPUS is "down the hill" from the main campus and houses Grades 6 through 8. The Middle School offers a superior academic curriculum with a wide range of electives, including Latin, Ancient Greek, Mandarin, Spanish and German along with mandatory French for all students. Strong focus on math, sciences, and humanities prepares students for the robust academic program offered in the High School. Outside the classroom, the Middle School offers many activities such as modern and jazz dance, the Student Council, middle school newspaper The Cub, chess, community service opportunities, choir, and dances. Sports include karate, soccer, basketball, volleyball.

THE RAYMOND AND ESTHER KABBAZ HIGH SCHOOL, located on National Blvd, just two blocks from the main campus, is a brilliant work of architecture completed in 2009. A state-of-the-art educational and sports facility, under the leadership of Mr. Petauton, it was commissioned precisely from the ground up over a period of nine years, custom-designed to create spaces that engender a sense of collegiality and independent learning... It is clean-lined, warm and imaginative, with massive floor-to-ceiling windows in almost every classroom and laboratory. It is the home of a world class gymnasium, and a dining hall that overlooks the gym through a wall of glass as well as partially covered outdoor dining terraces. Up to fourteen Advanced Placement classes are offered, along with preparatory classes for the Capstone Diploma in the International School, the French Baccalaureate, and the French-American Baccalaureate. Students often accelerate their college careers by receiving credit for their AP work. There is a multitude of clubs, sports, and other extra-curricular activities.

HISTORY

Two career educators, Mr. and Mrs. Raymond Kabbaz, founded Le Lycée Français de Los Angeles as a dual language, international school in 1964. Due to a law that prohibited teaching in California in a language other than English, the opening of this French school was delayed for a year as Mr. and Mrs. Kabbaz hired consultants and attorneys to lobby for a change in the education code in Sacramento. This historical change in the law not only paved the way for the opening of Le Lycée Français de Los Angeles, but also for many other multilingual, international schools, dual language programs and language immersion.

The school officially opened in 1965 with no outside financial help. The first campus was located on Doheny Drive in Beverly Hills. In 1967, the school moved to their present location at 3261 Overland Ave in 1967. The school quickly became well known for its quality of education, its devotion to the needs of students as individuals, and its "open arms" policy for pupils from all walks of life. The uniform with its classical and timeless style was established during the first year and has remained the same since.

In those many and exciting years, the school expanded to six campuses including two preschool and kindergarten campuses, a lower elementary campus, an elementary campus, and a middle school. In September of 2009, the much-anticipated new 96,000 sq. ft. Raymond and Esther Kabbaz High School opened, providing the school with a gymnasium as well as spacious classrooms, various state-of-the-art learning areas, and a well-equipped cafeteria. In 2000, the modern performing arts theater, Théâtre Raymond Kabbaz, opened at the Century City Campus with professional quality facilities.

Sadly, Le Lycée's community lost the Founders of the school during the last decade. However, their values and passion have been passed on in the fundamental structure of the school. Many of the people they trusted and worked with over the years are still active in the school. The most notable is Clara-Lisa Kabbaz who has been associated with the school from the beginning (as a kindergarten student) and now serves as President of the school and Chairman of the Board, continuing her parents' work of providing a unique and outstanding international educational experience.

In the future, much will change, but the values and standards of Le Lycée Français de Los Angeles will remain the same. It will always be the top French School in Los Angeles with an exemplary American college prep program.

AT A GLANCE

APPLICATION DEADLINE	Call School for Deadline Dates
OPEN HOUSES	RSVP on website
UNIFORMS	Yes
SUMMER SCHOOL	Yes
AFTER SCHOOL PROGRAM	Call School for Information
SEE MAP	D on page 255

MARLBOROUGH SCHOOL

250 S. ROSSMORE AVENUE, LOS ANGELES, CA 90004

TEL: 323.935.1147 FAX: 323.933.0542

www.marlboroughschool.org

HEAD OF SCHOOL:	DR. PRISCILLA SANDS
DIRECTOR OF ADMISSIONS:	JEANETTE WOO CHITJIAN
TYPE OF SCHOOL:	COLLEGE PREP DAY SCHOOL FOR GIRLS
GRADES:	7-12
ENROLLMENT: 530	TUITION: $36,365
APPLICATION FEE: $150	NEW STUDENT FEE: $2,000
ACCREDITATION: CAIS/WASC	FINANCIAL AID: YES

MARLBOROUGH SCHOOL is an independent day school offering young women an outstanding education. The four-acre campus located in the middle of Hancock Park includes a gymnasium and training room, seven science labs, a computer center, facilities for photography, painting and sculpture, a 75-foot six-lane pool, and several outdoor courts. The school built a new parking lot across the street, which was designed with a great deal of style and taste. There is a 22,000-volume library offering over 90 periodicals and newspapers, and it is connected to UCLA's card catalog (ORION). The Performing Arts Annex includes two dance studios, a music room, a 100-seat performance theater and a 500-seat auditorium. A girls' school education is not for everyone. One father, whose daughter was accepted at Marlborough, was tearing his hair out because she refused to go. He tried to convince her that it was the opportunity of a lifetime, while she insisted that a co-ed experience was the only one for her.

The benefits of a single sex education for our daughters are well documented. Marlborough grads say that it helped them to develop leadership skills, self-confidence and enabled them to focus on their goals. Research sponsored by the Women's College Coalition has found that graduates of single sex women's schools are six times more likely to sit on the boards of fortune 500 companies than women attending co-ed schools. The Coalition also found that 41 percent of the women who ran for U.S. Senate were graduates of women's colleges. This is an amazing figure, since it only represents two to three percent of the women in this country.

Upper School Grades 10-12:

Minimum graduation requirements, as defined by the academic program in grades 10-12, include three years of English, foreign language through level III, three years of mathematics, three years of science (Biology required), Modern History and US History, and four semesters of fine and performing arts in grades 9-12. In addition, students must complete six semesters of physical education in grades 9-12. Most students exceed these basic requirements.

Advanced Placement Courses (AP)

These are classes that prepare students for the Advanced Placement examinations administered by the College Board. Marlborough offers the following AP courses: Art History, Studio Art, Calculus AB & BC, English, European History, US History, World History, French Language, Spanish Language, Latin, Chemistry, Biology, Physics (1 and C), Computer Science, Environmental Science, Statistics.

Student Government

Student government is an important means of cultivating leadership qualities in young women. Each class elects a Class Council that includes a president, vice president, secretary, treasurer, athletic representative, fine arts representative, and community service representative. Class Council members work as a team to facilitate weekly class meetings and organize class activities, including class traditions such as Colors, Banner, and Mascot presentations.

Each graduating class designs a Banner using elements and ideas that tell a visual story of what the group is all about and what they have experienced in their years at Marlborough. It is so impressive to walk through the hallways where banners dating back to the turn of the century are on display. Now that's tradition!

Marlborough offers classes in photography (complete with dark room), video production, and ceramics (there are several kilns). Displays of the remarkable artwork in its own art gallery are located in an atrium/lounge area at the center of one of the campus buildings.

Philosophy

Marlborough School provides a learning environment where young women develop self-confidence, creativity, a sense of responsibility and moral decisiveness. The school's program encourages students to discover their potential, to think critically, and to develop intellectual curiosity. Students learn to set priorities, develop decision making skills, and value the process of the educational experience. Marlborough believes that for women, academic excellence, leadership skills and confidence flourish best in a school exclusively devoted to their education. The Marlborough community enables each student to develop her fullest potential so that she may contribute in a global society.

HISTORY

Marlborough School was founded in 1889 as Mrs. Mary S. Caswell's School for Girls by Mary S. Caswell. A former resident of Maine, Mrs. Caswell brought her 20 years of East Coast educational experience to Los Angeles. In 1916, Mrs. Caswell moved her school to the (then) far western edges of the city at Third and Rossmore. The new buildings were surrounded by barley fields, with the nearest paved intersection at Third and Arden.

Upon Mrs. Overton's retirement in 1948. She and her husband, Kenneth (the school's business manager), established the Marlborough School Foundation and sold the school to the Foundation trustees in 1960, at which time the school became a nonprofit organization.

AT A GLANCE

APPLICATION DEADLINE	January
OPEN HOUSES	October and November. Please RSVP.
UNIFORMS	Yes
ISEE	Required
CO-ED SUMMER CAMP	Very Varied
SEE MAP	C on page 255

MARYMOUNT HIGH SCHOOL

10643 SUNSET BLVD., LOS ANGELES, CA 90077
TEL: 310.472.1205 FAX: 310.440.4316
www.mhs-la.org

HEAD OF SCHOOL:	**JACQUELINE LANDRY**
DIRECTOR OF ADMISSIONS:	**PATTI LEMLEIN**
TYPE OF SCHOOL:	**CATHOLIC, INDEPENDENT**
	ALL GIRL DAY SCHOOL
GRADES:	**9-12**
ENROLLMENT: 391	TUITION: $31,400 - 32,000
APPLICATION FEE: $100	BOOKS: $300 - 700
ACCREDITATION: CAIS/NAIS/NCEA/WASC	FINANCIAL AID: YES

MARYMOUNT is located on Sunset Boulevard across the street from UCLA. My daughter and I drove down there one afternoon from Hancock Park. The traffic was light and it only took us about 20 minutes door-to-door. I began to see why parents might choose to send their children to school on the other side of town, but then I wasn't driving in rush hour and sitting bumper to bumper with several hundred other frustrated mother/chauffeurs!

We turned up the steep driveway and parked right outside the school. It's an impressive looking building – manicured lawns abound. Built on five-and-a-half acres, the original buildings were declared cultural historical monuments in 1982. In addition, the campus is home to the Marian Hall Library and Learning Center and the Pavilion, a sports complex that includes a state of the art gymnasium and weight room. Athletic facilities also include a soccer field, tennis courts, and an Olympic-size swimming pool.

Hand-carved wood, frescos, stained glass and expansive lawn are some of the things that create the stately elegance of this Spanish Colonial Revival architecture. They even have a three-hole golf course, which borders onto a private club on the Westside, so it gives the impression of being somewhere out in the middle of the country. It's an idyllic setting on Sunset Boulevard.

The classrooms are big, bright, and airy with lots of space. I could imagine running through the corridors of this school feeling like quite the special daughter, especially when I looked at the wonderful walls of photographs depicting beautifully clad girls in their graduation robes.

My friend's daughter was accepted into Brentwood and Marymount. We all thought for sure that she would choose Brentwood because it was mixed and had a tad more cache to it . . . but she opted for Marymount. I asked her why, and she told me that she wanted to concentrate on doing well in school and that she would be too distracted by the boys at Brentwood. I'm sure it was music to her mother's ears!

Admissions are selective. Drawing from communities as far away as the South Bay to the San Fernando Valley, and from central Los Angeles to the Westside, the student body reflects a broad spectrum of ethnic, economic and religious backgrounds. The average class size is 15, with a student/teacher ratio of 8:1. There are 60 faculty members, all of whom hold a B.A. or B.S. degree. Typically 99 percent of Marymount's graduates go on to universities and colleges that include: Amherst, Barnard, Brown, Columbia, Duke, Georgetown, Harvard, MIT, NYU, Princeton,

Tufts, UC Berkeley, UCLA, Notre Dame, USC, Vassar and Yale.

Marymount offers a rigorous and challenging academic program. The students must complete a minimum of six courses per semester. Requirements include four years of English and theology, at least three years of foreign language, mathematics, science, social studies, three semesters of visual and performing arts, three semesters of physical education, and one semester of computer science.

There are Honors courses at every grade level and in every subject and 16 Advanced Placement (AP) classes. There are independent study projects. A very healthy 64 percent of the student body is enrolled in honors or AP classes. Each year, the college board names several Marymount students as AP Scholars in recognition of their exceptional achievement on the college-level AP examinations. In addition, each fall several Marymount seniors are selected as scholarship winners, a National Merit Finalists, semifinalists or commended students. This places them in the top five percent of the over one-million students who take the qualifying exam - very impressive.

Important in the review of a school are the elective courses offered. At Marymount they offer a wide range of self-expression in diverse areas such as oceanography, engineering and robotics, music, drama, art, photography, physical education, journalism and yearbook. At each grade level, the Guidance Department coordinates with the Human Development Program, enabling each student to develop her personal resources and helping her to make the right decisions in life issues.

Students are encouraged to maintain balance in their lives by participating in co-curricular activities and, as you can see, they are have a wide choice of clubs, student organizations and athletic teams in which to take part. Speaking of athletics, Marymount fields 22 sports teams, including baseball, crew, cross-country, equestrian, fencing, golf, soccer, softball, swimming, tennis, track and field, volleyball and water polo.

If your child is interested in the performing arts, she may participate in the fall play, the spring musical, the Marymount Singers choral group, the handbell choir, the orchestra, the pop bank, the jazz/rock ensemble, and the annual student produced talent benefit. In the publications department, the school offers an award-winning student newspaper, The Anchor, and the literary magazine, Sunset, winner of a gold medal from the Columbia School of Journalism.
Other clubs include: French Club, Spanish Club, Art Club, Science Pre-Med Club, Creative Writing Club, Mock Trial, Marymount Ambassadors, Model United Nations, History Club, Action!, The Film Club, The Book Club, Rainbow Coalition, Current Affairs Club, National Honor Society, Spirit Club and Amnesty International. Shall I go on?

Marymount offers a number of internships open to sophomores and above. This program, the Internship and Mentoring Program, has rapidly grown from two girls to fifty. This opportunity is providing our students a chance to work with extraordinary leaders who are not only role models, but who have made important contributions ranging from neuroscience, STEM fields, art conservation to animation, public policy, and public health. I really love this program as it can really help focus a young woman on what career she may want to pursue.

For several years running Marymount High School has hosted an All-Girls Leadership Conference open to rising 6-8th grade students, and incoming Marymount 9th grade students. Their goal is simple: to give young girls the tools necessary to better themselves as well as the world. Middle school is a crucial time for young girls to build strong friendships, find inspiring mentors and recognize themselves as leaders in their local and global communities. This conference is completely run and organized by current Marymount students. The conference title "A Better Self for a Better World," conveys exactly how Marymount students want to inspire middle school girls.

You as parents are expected to support the Marymount Annual Fund Drive. Last year 91 percent of the parents participated. Money goes to faculty salary and benefits, daily bus transportation, and contributes to the academic and co-curricular program that is so extensive at Marymount. Plans are underfoot to improve student restroom and eating/study areas.

Recently, funds from the Board of Trustees have helped to redesign and refurbish the parking facilities and to create a beautiful new Pavilion Courtyard. New computers have been acquired so that every classroom has them. New security lighting was also installed to help maintain the safety of the campus.

If you are looking for an all girl education for your child please visit the school and see for yourself what a truly spectacular school this is.

HISTORY

Founded in 1923 and rooted in the tradition of the Religious of the Sacred Heart of Mary, Marymount High School is a Catholic, independent, college prepatory school for girls.

AT A GLANCE

APPLICATION DEADLINE	January 5
OPEN HOUSES	November
UNIFORMS	Yes
ISEE TESTING	Yes
SUMMER SCHOOL	Yes
SEE MAP	D on page 255

MAYFIELD JUNIOR SCHOOL OF THE HOLY CHILD

405 S. EUCLID AVENUE, PASADENA, CA 91101
TEL: 626.796.2774 FAX: 626.796.5753
www.mayfielddjs.org

DIRECTOR:	**MARY NOUSAKAJIAN**
PRINCIPAL	**JANE DWINELL**
DIRECTOR OF ADMISSIONS:	**ANDREW RAKOS**
TYPE OF SCHOOL:	**CO-ED DAY SCHOOL**
GRADES:	**PRESCHOOL-K**
ENROLLMENT: 118	TUITION: $19,504
APPLICATION FEE: $125	NEW FAMILY FEE: $1,000 - 2,000
REGISTRATION FEE: $150	FINANCIAL AID: YES

MAYFIELD has a large, attractive campus with an athletic field, hard court play areas and a primary playground. The elementary and middle schools have science and foreign language labs as well as art studios, performing arts center and a beautiful well-stocked library. Students have an indoor gym and there is a school chapel.

The campus has an old-fashioned air about it with a collection of buildings from the 30s, 60s, 70s, and 90s as well as modern structures. The classrooms are large and bright with lots of windows. The feel of the campus has changed slightly with the South Campus Expansion. In 2008, the Primary Center opened to house K to second grade classes. It also includes a hands-on science center and elementary art lab. The new Performing Arts Center replaced the old auditorium, and the old convent buildings were transformed into Connelly Hall with new offices. There is an underground parking facility under the new complex. The Multipurpose Building houses the gym, art studio, chapel and P.E. offices all on one level. The lower level houses the Kids Club After School Program and music rehearsal rooms. The library is located in the Pike Resource center and is beautifully laid out with lots of large, round tables. It has a lower level, with pillows on the floor for a more relaxing read. Above this reading area is a large, round window allowing lots of natural light to come.

Mayfield is a Catholic school committed to the philosophy of Cornelia Connelly, (founder of the Society of the Holy Child), who believed in the spirit and talents of the individual. The school provides a traditional academic and religious education challenging each child to reach his or her potential.

There is also an emphasis on athletics. The competitive sports programs for seventh and eighth grade boys and girls include: volleyball, basketball, soccer, track, softball, golf, and swimming. A tennis program takes place once a week from September through May.

The school is run by a board of directors and the Society of the Holy Child Jesus. There are additional committees for finance, educational planning, building and grounds, and the executive committee. There are specialists in art, technology physical education, music, drama, French and Spanish. The average class size is 17 with a student/teacher ratio of 12:1.

Mayfield Junior School implements the philosophy of the Holy Child Schools. School personnel are committed not only to the religious and educational development of each child, but also to maintaining a sense of community and family spirit.

Here is the definition of a Holy Child school, from the brochure:

> The educational philosophy of Mother Cornelia Connelly seeks to educate the whole child. Thus, a Holy Child school educates the body, mind, and spirit in a context which is values-based and responsive to individual needs. Instruction takes place in a learning climate based on trust and reverence for the uniqueness of the individual.

I was particularly interested to hear about the Reach Out Program that includes individual classes, parents, and the outside community. With a constant emphasis on learning to be there for others.

HISTORY

Mayfield Junior School was founded in 1931, and named after the Holy Child School in Mayfield, England. It was founded by the Sisters of the Holy Child Jesus and dedicated to the educational philosophy of Mother Cornelia Connelly, a tradition and a history which began in England in the year 1856.

AT A GLANCE

APPLICATION DEADLINE	K: December; 1-8: January
OPEN HOUSE DATES	October to January
UNIFORMS	Yes
AFTER SCHOOL CARE	Yes
SEE MAP	B on page 255

MILKEN COMMUNITY SCHOOLS
15800 ZELDIN'S WAY, LOS ANGELES, CA 90049
TEL: 310.440.3553 FAX: 424.270.2365
www.milkenschool.org

HEAD OF SCHOOL	**GARY WEISSERMAN**
DIRECTOR OF ADMISSIONS:	**PAOLA GANCMAN (MIDDLE)**
	JESSICA FEIVOU (UPPER)
TYPE OF SCHOOL:	**JEWISH CO-ED COLLEGE PREP**
GRADES:	**7-12**
ENROLLMENT: 750	TUITION: $37,500
APPLICATION FEE: $150	NEW FAMILY FEE: $1,500
ACCREDITATION: CAIS, WASC	FINANCIAL AID: YES

Milken School is located just off of Mulholland Drive, close to where it intersects with Sepulveda Blvd just off of the I-405 Freeway. Well-protected and gated, the campus is divided into two parts, the Middle School and the Upper School. It stretches across a 10-acre beautifully landscaped and neatly kept hillside property.

The school's website states: 'Milken Community Schools is a place of rigorous academic preparation and intellectual inquiry: a place of profound and trans formative experiences, with learning, spiritual practice, and ethical practice at the foundation of those experiences. Students at Milken learn that their education is responsibility for family, community, country, and the world.'

What was immediately apparent to me was that I was entering into a very close-knit community. The guards at the gate, the staff at the Admissions Office, the teachers and students at summer camp, the parent volunteer at the Milken Mart-everyone was extraordinarily warm, welcoming, helpful, and happy and excited to share in their experience at the School. While Milken rightly boasts its 'rigorous academics', the school consciously creates a strong focus on community, family, faith and culture, and it shows. My guide, Mr. Gancman, pointed out that Milken Schools is home to a broad spectrum of observance levels of the Jewish faith. The community welcomes and encourages intellectual, ethical, and spiritual questioning. The Jewish Study Program runs through the entire curriculum at the Schools, and Milken offers in-depth programs such as the Beit Midrash Fellowship, the Global Beit Midrash, and the Tiferet Israel Fellowship-all unique to Milken and created with the goal of fostering innovative, independent thinkers, and future leaders in the Jewish Community.

The Upper School consists of four buildings. The campus is on a hill side, so there are stairs and lots of walking between class rooms in different buildings which create a nice 'college feel'. There is ample outdoor space, such as an amphitheater where students can have lunch and/or spend their free periods. The buildings are neat and orderly with beautiful landscaping throughout. The Upper School houses the large gymnasium and Theater, which are utilized by both Upper and Middle School students. The 'student hub' is naturally the Milken Mart where students can buy freshly-cooked meals, snacks, school supplies and so on.

In contrast to the more mature Upper School campus, the newly constructed Middle School building was designed with the younger student in mind. Located a short walk up the hill from the Upper School via a nice and secure walk-way, the circular drive-way where parents can drop-off and pick-up opens up into one large building where the Administrative Offices overlook the entrances to the classrooms. Floor to ceiling windows and tall ceilings create classrooms that are light and bright, and outside there are running creeks, shady trees, and offices with glass walls that all give the campus a warm and secure feeling. The Middle School has its 'mini-Mart', a nice outdoor amphitheater with a small basketball court and climbing wall, a beautiful dance studio/performing space, a brand new science classroom, and the Beith Midrash utilized by both schools as a community room for gatherings and town hall meetings.

As the school was kind enough to open its doors to me during the summer months, there were few students on campus and no classes to observe, but the teachers I met and the projects and student work that they shared really impressed me and showed me that these students are performing at a very high level. They are clearly encouraged to not only excel pen-to-paper in the classroom, but to go above and beyond and be hands-on, independent, follow their own leads and initiatives, explore, and think outside the box.

For example, the professor in the Robotics, one of Milken's signature programs, showed me on of their latest projects: a Frisbee throwing robot that made it to the 2013 Robotics World Championships! This is a machine that the students themselves dreamed up and created from scratch. The Robotics Team also works in exchange with MIT in Israel.

The Upper School Architecture Program, The Architecture and Design Institute, teaches students residential and commercial design, how to build models to scale, operate CAD, practice environmental awareness, as well as hands-on design experience through field trips and guest lectures. According to the Admissions Director, the students who wish to pursue Architecture and/or Design in College are at least one year ahead of their college peers.

The Mitchell Academy of Science and Technology, MAST, is one of Milken's flagship programs. Students learn how to conduct independent research, they find professional mentors in their research field, and work in professional laboratory environments. The 12th graders submit their original research to the Intel Talent Search-the country's most prestigious science contest for high school students.

There is also an extensive and equally impressive Arts Program with Creative Writing, Performing Arts, Visual Arts, and Media Arts. The publication 'blueprint' from the Creative Writing students blew me away with it's breadth and depth, and the Media Arts program expose and trains students in TV-studio production, News Broadcasting, and Photography. The broadcast studio is state-of-the-art, and the students write, direct, and produce a live 'Milken Newscast' for their peers. The Performing Arts program has a large stage with high-tech sound booth, and sets up productions such as 'Grease', 'Macbeth', as well as offer performances by the Israeli Dance Company and Kol Echad. There are Jazz and Chamber ensembles, Music Theory, and technical classes offered for those who are more inclined to work behind the scenes.

Milken Schools and their students aim high, and sometimes this can create a competitive and cold environment. This does not seem to be the case at Milken-quite the opposite. If you are considering a Jewish, college-prep a tory education for your child, I would highly recommend a visit to the Milken Campus.

HISTORY

In 1981 Milken Middle school was founded, located in a handful of dormitory rooms on the American Jewish University campus (formerly the University of Judaism). Based on the success of the middle school, the upper school was founded in 1991.

AT A GLANCE

APPLICATION DEADLINE	January
OPEN HOUSE DATES	Fall
UNIFORMS	No
SEE MAP	D on page 255

MIRMAN SCHOOL

16180 MULHOLLAND DRIVE, LOS ANGELES, CA 90049

TEL: 310.476.2868 FAX: 310.471.1532

www.mirman.org

HEAD MASTER:	**DAN VORENBERG**
DIRECTOR OF ADMISSIONS:	**JEN LEGITT**
TYPE OF SCHOOL:	**CO-ED DAY FOR GIFTED CHILDREN**
GRADES:	**UNGRADED, AGES 5-14**
ENROLLMENT: 118	TUITION: $27,460 - 30,270
APPLICATION FEE: $125	NEW FAMILY FEE: $1,250
REGISTRATION FEE: $150	FINANCIAL AID: YES

Mirman School is located on Mulholland Drive, a beautiful setting with views of the San Fernando Valley to the north and West Los Angeles to the south. The school's mission statement sets forth an educational philosophy to serve highly gifted students:

Mirman School is passionately committed to the education of highly gifted children:

> We are dedicated to: academic excellence; the social, emotional, and physical development of the student; academic programs that offer depth, complexity, and differentiation tailored to each student's needs and abilities; and developing creatively productive and ethical world citizens.

The school gives students the opportunity to reach their intellectual potential through individualization and differentiation while fostering their social and emotional development. Students must score in the 99th percentile on an IQ test before officially beginning the admission process. The first step for entrance is the WISC or WPPSI, IQ tests, administered by a local psychologist. The school maintains a list of testers located throughout the Los Angeles area, but any licensed psychologist may administer the test and submit a report.

Dan Vorenberg, the Head of School, has been at Mirman School since 2013. With his vision and 31 years of independent education experience, Vorenberg has positively impacted the school culture and the education of gifted students. Originally from Boston, Vorenberg began his career as an elementary school teacher at Milton Academy in Massachusetts. He served as Head of School at Atrium School, a pre-K through sixth grade school, and subsequently served as Head of elementary and middle schools in Indianapolis and Albany, New York. Before coming to Mirman School, Vorenberg became Head of the Lower School, then Assistant Head of School at Columbus Academy, a college preparatory school in Columbus, Ohio. In addition, Vorenberg has been a faculty member for the New Teacher Institute for the Association of Independent Schools in New England, a member of the Principal's Center at Harvard University, as well as the Assistant Director of the Massachusetts Advanced Studies Program.

The campus includes a Lower and Upper School with science labs, an innovation lab, art and music rooms, amphitheater, library, and a large auditorium. Volleyball and basketball courts, along with a new regulation sized middle school football and soccer field support Mirman's mission of educating the whole child.

This is the first year they are introducing grade levels. Prior to this, students were divided by age groupings similar to a K-8 school. Students generally work at least one to two years above grade level, and in some of their curriculum, considerably more. At Mirman there is a commitment to provide students with curricula they are ready to learn when they are ready to learn it. Lap tops are integrated into the learning environment for all students.

In the Lower School (ages 5-9), the classroom teacher works with students for language arts, reading, math, and social studies. Each classroom has an assistant teacher to aid in individualizing the curriculum and working in small groups. There are additional opportunities in science, math, computer, art, music, drama, and physical education.

The Upper School (ages 10-14) follows a departmentalized program with core classes, electives, and service learning. The curriculum includes math, language arts, social studies, world languages, art, music, theater arts, innovation and design thinking, and human development. All students select from an elective pool of choir, computer programming, art, science, and speech.

The Annex, Mirman's after school program, provides further exploration in art, music, chess, drama, Mandarin, rocketry, science, and physical education. Four bus routes provide transportation to and from school with a late bus for athletics.

HISTORY

Beverly and Norman Mirman founded Mirman School in 1962 out of their love for children and a deep concern for education. Dr. Mirman served as President of the National Association for Gifted Children and was one of the founders of the California Association for the Gifted. The Mirmans' legacy continues to influence and inspire educators, parents, and generations of children today.

AT A GLANCE

APPLICATION DEADLINE	December 11
INFORMATIONAL EVENINGS	October and November. Please RSVP.
TESTING	IQ of 145 or higher is required for admission.
IQ TEST DEADLINE	Novemeber
UNIFORMS	Yes
SEE MAP	D on page 255

NEW ROADS SCHOOL

Elementary School
2000 STONER AVENUE, LOS ANGELES, CA 90025
TEL: 310.828.5582 FAX: 310.828.2582

Middle School
3131 OLYMPIC BLVD., SANTA MONICA, CA 90404
TEL: 310.828.5582 FAX: 310.828.2582

Upper School
3131 OLYMPIC BLVD., SANTA MONICA, CA 90404
TEL: 310.828.5582 FAX: 310.828.2582

www.newroads.org

HEAD OF SCHOOL:	LUTHERN WILLIAMS
ASSISTANT HEAD OF SCHOOL:	RYAN HAWLEY
DIRECTOR OF ADMISSIONS:	NANCY FASULES
TYPE OF SCHOOL:	CO-ED DAY SCHOOL
GRADES:	PRESCHOOL-K
ENROLLMENT: 651	TUITION: $21,800 - 43,900
APPLICATION FEE: $125	NEW FAMILY FEE: $2,000
REGISTRATION FEE: $150	FINANCIAL AID: YES

NEW ROADS SCHOOL in Santa Monica is an independent educational community currently set on two campuses. There is an educational village on the site where the Middle and High School is located. Being able to grow up in a village-like community is something we are losing as our cities keep growing and children spend hours in travel time instead of play time.

K through 5

The campus has comfortable classrooms, a well-stocked library, computer and science areas, and an art studio surrounding two play yards and gardens. They offer an innovative and creative developmental approach to education which includes language arts, math, science, social studies and Spanish. Other programs are music, visual art, drama, dance and P.E., as well as human development, environmental studies, service learning and information technology. This is a wonderful home for discovery and exploration. Check it out!

Middle School

The Middle School and High School campus is near Overland Avenue on Olympic Boulevard. It is a welcoming place. School Philosophy as taken from school brochure:

> Born of a felt responsibility to prepare young people for the challenges and opportunities they face, New Roads School seeks to promote personal, social, political and moral understanding, and to instill in

young people a respect for the humanity and ecology of the earth and the sensitivity to appreciate life's deep joys and mysteries.

The School rests upon several fundamental commitments: to the development of a student population of social, economic, ethnic and racial diversity; to the development of each student's full human potential; to academic excellence and excellence in the arts; to behaving responsibly and honorably as an institution and serving the larger ecological and social community.

As taken from the school brochure:

It is our goal to provide a strong college preparatory program from which each student will develop a personal dedication to learning, a respect for independent thinking and an expanding curiosity about the world and its people. We believe that education must not be a race for the accumulation of facts, but a joint venture among students, parents, and teacher to develop habits of mind; habits of character; an ever expanding awareness of the human situation; and the tools needed for effective personal, social, political and moral participation. We consider certain skills to be essential for all graduates: to read well and write clearly, to express oneself effectively; to reason and question thoughtfully, soundly and critically, and to study successfully and with determination. To be truly supportive of young people, teachers and parents must themselves continue to learn so that they may perceive the young accurately and treat them wisely.

We understand that there are many kinds of intelligence. As such our programs assist young people in developing and appreciating cognition, intuition, imagination, artistic creativity, physical expression and performance, sensitivity to others, self-understanding, and personal well-being. To neglect any of these areas is to limit students in the development of their full potential.

I felt it important to reproduce the school's philosophy in its entirety since it speaks to what we parents are striving to do for our children. The middle school has six spacious classrooms, an art room, a large gym, meeting rooms and outdoor playing fields, The children take part in many after-school activities on the site, which is located near the beach, community arts resources, and the local library. Apart from the traditional core subjects the school expects their students expect their student to be committed to learning, and so consider such affective skills as accountability and responsibility into their assessments of a student's performance. The school is very diverse in its ethnic and social background helping students to discover different people and communities.

For instance, in the middle school the students will study Spanish in a unique program that supplements classroom based Spanish instruction with more intensive immersion-type experiences, including visits to Spanish-speaking communities. They also work with the children on real world investigations, problem solving and exploration, in keeping with what will be major challenges in the future. Each week the teachers and students work in a collectively designed, holistic course of study called The Workshop for Social, Economic and Ecological Action. In high school, the students actually design and implement their own community service plans.

High School

When I attended the open house I was impressed by the campus. We visited the various class rooms and their teachers, all of whom made a very good impression, for they were enthusiastic and informative.

Grades 6-12 Curriculum:

Math— Fundamentals, algebra, geometry, algebra II, pre-calculus and calculus.

Science— An integrated program of skills: computer studies, college preparation, individualized study, biology, chemistry, physics and advanced area studies.

The Humanities— English genre studies (poetry, fiction, non-fiction, drama), vocabulary, grammar, diagramming, creative writing and essay writing, and ethical themes.

Social Science— chronology, thematic investigations, multi-cultural history and literature, application of composition skills to history essays.

Workshop— Integrated curriculum, real world explorations and applications, social justice, inclusivity, ecological regeneration, community service.

Foreign Language— Spanish, with In-class instruction, sister school in Mexico, cultural history, conversation and translation, Spanish I through AP Spanish Literature.

The Arts:

- Music — instrumental (flute, recorder, guitar, piano, strings, percussion, jazz), chamber music, music theory, choral, the piano academy.
- Visual Art — painting, sculpture, book arts, film history & film production.
- Drama and Writing — technique, improvisation, scene study, productions, creative writing, journalism.
- Dance — jazz, ballet, hip hop, tap, modern.

Physical Education and Athletics— Yoga, team sports, golf, tennis, basketball, volleyball, fencing, track and cross country, baseball, softball.

Human Development— Diversity training, human development (mysteries/connections) combining a focused music studies curriculum with a college preparatory academic curriculum.

The Spectrum Program

The Spectrum Program is a unique program designed to create educational options and interventions, within a regular school environment, for students that meet the diagnostic criteria specified in the revised DSM-5 for Autism Spectrum Disorder; formally categorized as Asperger's Syndrome or High Functioning Autism. The program targets academically capable students diagnosed with ASD and takes a fresh approach to addressing their needs by both: a) including them in neurotypical academic classes and campus activities, and b) providing concentrated, daily focus on improving our students' social and real-world functioning skills within the specialized Spectrum Life Skills Program. The Spectrum Program offers the following accommodations: extended time on tests, extended time on large projects, and preferential seating at the front of the room. Our main goal is to provide support to our students in developing executive functioning skills, organization, time management, calendaring, and self advocacy.

The Spectrum Drama Program is an all-encompassing theatrical experience for middle school students, upper school students and alumni diagnosed on the autism spectrum. Together with their neurotypical peers, students learn acting, improvisation, voice, speech, movement and dance. This ensemble-based program promotes cooperative and creative collaboration, Students are encouraged to step out of their comfort zones, develop their own voices, and take artistic risks in a safe and supportive environment.

Another very interesting aspect of the school is that New Roads has devised an Independent Studies Program (ISP) to enable students to find their own way of learning most effectively. Many parents would love their children to learn this way. I know I would.

New Roads students can participate in many after-school activities. There are art classes, music and drama production, homework tutorials, peer tutoring, student organized clubs and competitive athletic teams. Each campus makes an effort to accommodate students' interests at its facility. Students are welcome to participate in activities at either of the New Roads' campuses.

While admission is competitive, and there are many more applicants than openings, the student who is able to exhibit a genuine desire to be part of the school will help his or her chance of acceptance. Applicants must supply transcripts of previous academic work and two letters of recommendation from current teachers. The Independent School Entrance Examination (ISEE) is used for all applicants. New Roads' school code is 054243. Please request that ERB (Educational Records Bureau) send the test results to that number. Students will be notified of acceptance beginning in late March, and thereafter as openings occur.

HISTORY

New Roads School was established in 1995 by The New Visions Foundation* as a model for education in an ethnically, racially, culturally, and socio-economically diverse community. To prepare young people for the challenges and opportunities they face, the school aims to promote personal, social, political, and moral understanding, and to instill in students respect for the humanity and ecology of the world in which they live. A non-profit, non-denominational institution, New Roads School is guided by a 25-member Board of Trustees.

*Paul Cummins is the Executive Director of New Visions Foundations. He used to be headmaster, and is now President of Crossroads School.

AT A GLANCE

APPLICATION DEADLINE	January
OPEN HOUSES	October through December
UNIFORMS	No
SUMMER SCHOOL	Yes
SEE MAP	D on page 255

NOTRE DAME ACADEMY

2851 OVERLAND AVE., LOS ANGELES, CA 90064

TEL: 310.839.5289 FAX: 310.839.7957

www.ndala.com

PRESIDENT:	**NANCY COONIS**
DIRECTOR OF ADMISSIONS:	**KRISTIN CALLAGHAN**
TYPE OF SCHOOL:	**ALL GIRLS DAY SCHOOL**
GRADES:	**9-12**
ENROLLMENT: 480	TUITION: $13,200
APPLICATION FEE: $75	FINANCIAL AID: YES
YEARLY REGISTRATION FEE: $600	

I visited **NOTRE DAME ACADEMY** one Sunday in the fall for one of their Open Houses. The school is nestled in a residential area of West Los Angeles, close to the Santa Monica Freeway. The Academy is a microcosm of the ethnically-diverse community it serves. Most of the students commute from as far north as Malibu and as far south as Palos Verdes. With varied ethnic, social and economic backgrounds this seems to make up what appears to be a progressive and talented student body. Ninety-three percent of the students identify themselves as Catholic.

Mission statement (as taken from school brochure):

> Notre Dame Academy educates young women to make a difference. In a caring and nurturing atmosphere, the Academy's value-centered program stresses the importance of personal spirituality, concern for the common good, and service to one another and to the community. Each student is encouraged to set realistic goals, to take confident steps to achieve them and to realize her leadership and service potential. The student sees herself as a worthwhile, esteemed and competent woman, able to make a positive contribution to her Church and the world.

The open house was a very well-organized affair. The girls looked beautiful, all dressed in their Sunday best, and very helpful. We arrived in the auditorium, which was filled with booths the girls had set up showing off all the various clubs and organizations to which they belong. It was an impressive show of talent. We were then taken around the school in small groups and shown the students "at work" in their various classrooms.

We visited the computer labs, the art studio, and the Regal Theater, where students were singing, and watched experiments being performed. We then looked in on the Counseling Center and heard about all the resources available to the students to assist in the college selection process. The campus ministry program is the largest organization on campus and is extremely active. The campus ministry students plan school liturgies and retreats.

Members of the HOPE (Helping Other People Everywhere) service organization coordinate extensive Christian service programs and work to raise money for various local and international charities. Developing leadership skills and building a spirit of cooperation, unity and school pride are the goals of all the student organizations, including: National Honor Society, Student Council, Music Club, Queen's Council (a student service organization), Yearbook, L'Esprit, NDA International, Speech/Debate, WIMS (Women Interested in Math and Science), Journalism and the Environment Club.

Notre Dame Academy has a full and balanced program of student activities. It offers Advanced Placement and Honors Courses in Art, English, Foreign Languages, Mathematics, Science and Social Studies. In order to graduate from Notre Dame the students must have completed a minimum of 240 semester credits, including the following specific requirements: religion (four years); English (four years); social studies (three years); foreign language (two years); laboratory science (two years); mathematics (three years); physical ed/health (one year); art, dance, drama, music (one year); computer literacy (one semester), dramatic Interpretation (one semester).

Students are provided with classroom instruction, workshops and one-on-one counseling sessions to help them throughout the college selection and admissions processes. Ninety nine percent of graduates attend either a two or four-year college. Students have been offered admission to all the top colleges and universities around the country. The sports program excels on every level and stresses the importance of good sportsmanship and team play on the road to victory. Their competitive teams have won numerous championships in volleyball, cross country, basketball, soccer, track and field, softball and swimming.

At the end of our tour we were treated to the most delicious refreshments in the rather grand looking cafeteria on the lower level. It was a nice way for us to meet and talk to some of the students and the staff, who were delightful, intelligent and happy to answer all of our questions.

The school really believes in educating the whole person. With that in mind, it has academic advisors and personal counselors who are qualified professionals dedicated to recognizing and nurturing the uniqueness and potential of each student, assisting her to develop a strong sense of self as she grows from a young teenage girl into a mature young woman. As they said "The best gift your daughter can receive is open communication and support from all of us working together as a team for her." Please take a closer look at this school.

HISTORY

Notre Dame Academy is a Catholic private college-preparatory high school for young women fully accredited by the Western Association of Schools and Colleges and by the National Catholic Education Association. Founded in 1949, NDA is owned and operated by the Sisters of Notre Dame.

AT A GLANCE

APPLICATION DEADLINE	January 8
OPEN HOUSE	December
UNIFORMS	Yes
SEE MAP	D on page 255

NOTRE DAME HIGH SCHOOL

13645 RIVERSIDE DRIVE, SHERMAN OAKS, CA 91423
TEL: 818.933.3600 FAX: 818.501.0507
www.ndhs.org

PRESIDENT:	**BRETT LOWART**
DIRECTOR OF ADMISSIONS:	**ALEC MOSS**
TYPE OF SCHOOL:	**CO-ED CATHOLIC**
GRADES:	**9-12**
ENROLLMENT: 1,250	TUITION: $14,050
APPLICATION FEE: $110	NEW FAMILY FEE: $550
ACCREDITATION: WASC/WCEA	FINANCIAL AID: YES

NOTRE DAME HIGH SCHOOL is on the corner of Riverside Drive and Woodman Avenue in Sherman Oaks. If you live in Hollywood it's a quick trip north on the 101, and the exit is conveniently no more than 30 seconds from the school's main entrance. The school grounds are wonderful to walk through. It's beautifully kept with flower gardens, trees and places to sit and relax. Built in the late 40's, the architecture is "early California mission" and it's a sight for sore eyes. It made me want to go back to school!

While touring the campus, I spoke with the Director of Counseling who said, "If you're looking for a well-rounded education for your child, this is the school. Seventy percent will go to a four-year college, 20 percent to a two-year college and the rest will take a year off traveling". Coming from England where "the gap year" is very popular amongst students and their parents, I liked hearing that some of them wanted to explore the world a bit before going to University and that their parents were in favor of them doing it.

Mission Statement as taken from the school's brochure:

> Incorporating the Holy Cross educational tradition in our school community, Notre Dame strives to provide each student with a rich academic background, a strong sense of self, a willingness to take risks for the sake of growth, commitment to family and community and an appreciation for the spiritual dignity of all persons.

Sixty-seven percent of the student body are Catholic and the school does give preference to Catholic students attending a Catholic school, next to Catholic students previously not attending a Catholic school, and lastly to non-Catholics. If you are Catholic and your child's grades have not fallen below a "C" in any subject, then he/she may be accepted. There are 75 faculty members, with 36 holding master's degrees and two with Ph.D.s for a total of 96 staff members. Notre Dame offers a college preparatory curriculum with honors and advanced placement courses in art, English, foreign languages, mathematics, science, and social studies. An extensive elective program offers students courses in computer programming, acting, band, art, art history, journalism, speech, debate, advanced topics in biology, sports medicine, psychology of prejudice, law and society, sociology, and film and American history.

Graduation Requirements:

- 4 years English
- 4 years religious studies
- 3 years mathematics
- 3 years social studies
- 2 1/2 years science
- 2 years foreign language
- 1 year fine arts
- 1 year physical education
- 1 semester computers

In addition to the academic requirements, students are required to complete 90 hours of community service by the time of graduation. Freshmen are required to complete 10 hours of service within their family. Sophomores must complete 20 worship hours of service. Juniors will to complete 30 hours of service at Notre Dame, and Seniors are required to complete 30 hours of service anywhere in the local community.

The campus ministry program provides a religious experience for students, faculty, and staff by providing spiritual, prayerful experiences on retreats, prayer services, liturgies and personal counseling.

There is plenty of room to play every sport, the playing fields are vast and this is a school that really loves its' sports! Three levels of athletic teams, Freshman, Junior Varsity and Varsity levels, compete in 15 different girls and boys athletic events. During the school year, both the boys and girls will play in the Mission League. Their league opponents are Alemany, Chaminade, Crespi, Flintridge Sacred Heart, Harvard-Westlake, Louisville, Loyola, and St. Francis Notre Dame students are involved in a variety of extra-curricular opportunities. There are many different clubs on campus, ranging from the Japanese Animation Club to the Liturgical Music Club.

The Theater Department produces three very good plays every school year, and the Student Publication groups publish the school Newspaper, Yearbook, and Sports Guides. Forensics and journalism students travel around the country competing in tournaments and participating in conferences. Their award-winning Irish Knight Band competes in many parades, performs in concerts and supports their football and basketball teams. In addition to all of this, the school has an extremely active Associated Student Body group which organizes dances and other social events throughout the year.

The School has worked hard to provide the students with the most up-to-date technology to prepare them for the world. The Fritz B. Burns Center for the Arts and Technology has allowed the school to move closer to reaching its goal. In addition to two computer labs, all the classrooms have a computer for the teacher's use and all students have iPads. The library offers over 20 computers for student use.

This school is becoming a popular choice among parents looking for a reasonably priced college prep high school as tuition is about a third less than other non Catholic private high schools. I highly recommend taking a closer look at this school.

HISTORY

Notre Dame High School is a private Catholic secondary school. Founded by the Congregation of Holy Cross in 1947, Notre Dame has been co-educational since 1983. The school has the maximum six-year accreditation by the Western Association of Schools and Colleges, and is recognized as a National Blue Ribbon School of Excellence.

AT A GLANCE

APPLICATION DEADLINE	January 16
OPEH HOUSE	November
UNIFORMS	Yes
SUMMER PROGRAM	Yes
SEE MAP	A on page 255

THE OAKS SCHOOL

6817 FRANKLIN AVENUE, LOS ANGELES, CA 90028

TEL: 323.850.3755 FAX: 323.850.3758

www.oaksschool.org

HEAD OF SCHOOL:	**TED HAMORY**
DIRECTOR OF ADMISSIONS:	**NATALIE MAST**
TYPE OF SCHOOL:	**CO-ED DAY SCHOOL**
GRADES:	**K-6**
ENROLLMENT: 163	TUITION: $22,563
APPLICATION FEE: $150	NEW FAMILY FEE: $2,000
ACCREDITATION: CAIS/WASC/NAIS/ISAMA	FINANCIAL AID: YES

The Oaks School is located in the landmark Hollywood United Methodist Church in the heart of Hollywood. While The Oaks is a secular school and not affiliated with the church, the gothic architecture and stain-glassed windows create an impressive backdrop for learning. A large gym, library with over 14,000 volumes, and beautifully curated Music, Art, Drama and Maker studios provide a space to create, explore and build.

The kindergarten is separate from the rest of the school, providing an easy transition for the children coming from various preschools. The bright, spacious classroom has areas for storytelling, cooking, experimenting and sharing as well as a large, private outside area that acts as an indoor-outdoor classroom. Kindergarten has three teachers who model collaboration and work with children in small groups. The home-like environment of the Kindergarten lays the foundation for really confident kids and I've met quite a few!

1st and 2nd grades are a combined class called Multi-Age, where five teachers work together. Students will have these same teachers for two years in a row which allows for time to show strengths and problem solve. In the upper elementary grades, more collaboration is continuously modeled and more independence and responsibility is incorporated into the curriculum. Oaks students leave after 6th grade as self-possessed, confident and kind students.

The Oaks models a constructivist approach to teaching and hands-on and project-based learning are found in every classroom. Teachers collaborate and integrate their lessons with art and music teachers, and students' interests fuel the curriculum.

There is an open, friendly, inclusive atmosphere about The Oaks that is refreshing. There are a myriad of opportunities for parental involvement and diversity is celebrated in all classrooms through conversations and experiences.

HISTORY

In September 1986, eleven children from various preschools attended the first class of what was to become The Oaks School, on the premises of St. Thomas Church. The school was founded by the Head, Deborah Wyle, and concerned parents seeking to bring quality progressive education to the area. In April of 1987 The Oaks incorporated as a non-profit educational institution and moved to the Hollywood United Methodist Church. A 19-member Board of Trustees that includes parents, educators, and members of the community governs The Oaks. Families of all races, religions, cultures, and socioeconomic status are welcome.

AT A GLANCE

APPLICATION DEADLINE	Janurary 9
OPEN HOUSE AND TOURS	October through December
UNIFORMS	No
BEFORE AND AFTER SCHOOL CARE	Yes
SEE MAP	C on page 255

THE OAKWOOD SCHOOL

K-6 Elementary Campus:
11230 MOORPARK ST., NORTH HOLLYWOOD, CA 91602
TEL: 818.752.4444 FAX: 818.752.4466
7-12 Secondary Campus:
11600 MAGNOLIA BLVD., NORTH HOLLYWOOD, CA 91601
TEL: 818.752.4400 FAX: 818.766.1285
www.oakwoodschool.org

HEAD OF SCHOOL:	JAMES A. ASTMAN, PH.D.
DIRECTOR OF ADMISSIONS:	
K-6	NANCY GOLDBERG
7-12	JENNA FROST
TYPE OF SCHOOL:	CO-ED DAY SCHOOL
GRADES:	K-12
ENROLLMENT: 765	TUITION: $30,880 - 36,200
APPLICATION FEE: $125	FINANCIAL AID: YES
NEW FAMILY FEE: $2,500	
ACCREDITATION: CAIS/NAIS/WASC	

OAKWOOD ELEMENTARY is located in North Hollywood on Moorpark Street alongside the 170 Freeway. The campus property backs onto tree-lined Woodbridge Park, which lends a feeling of open space and greenery to the grounds. There is a play space at the elementary campus, along with a performance space and community room. There is a new science and technology center at the elementary campus. Oakwood is also expanding the classroom technology center. The school has expanded the arts program in both academic and performance opportunities, including the addition of four jazz bands. There are currently two buildings under construction: The Story-Center and Music Center.

The facility is not sophisticated and the buildings have a rustic feeling about them much like a summer camp. The tour begins with a question and answer session supervised by Head of School James Astman, with questions directed to eight bright sixth-grade students holding microphones.

One parent asked the question, "Which part of the program do you like the most and which the least?" Math was a popular "like-most" answer, as was art.

Dislikes included wanting bigger classrooms, cleaner bathrooms and a unanimous thumbs down to doing so many 'laps' in physical education! The students all said that there was a lot of work and homework that was sometimes overwhelming. This was in direct contrast to the impression that I had had from the school brochure, which described Oakwood as developmental. I'm sure that it starts out that way in Kindergarten, but by sixth grade, it has an academic, college preparatory curriculum with several hours of homework per night.

During the tour through the classrooms, the first graders told us about an experiment they were doing to teach each other what discrimination felt like. The class was divided into 'greens' and 'blues' and each child wore a color tag. For the whole day, the 'greens' would be treated special, have the best seats, use the 'green' designated bathroom, get called on first, have a longer recess, etc. Meantime, the 'blue' group would be frowned upon, have to sit on the floor, use the 'blue' bathroom, let all the 'greens' go first to lunch, recess, and so on. The 'green' children were also discouraged from talking to the 'blue' children. By the time our parent tour rolled through the classroom where the experiment was taking place I could tell by the long faces on some of the 'blue' children that they had learned quite a bit about how it felt to be discriminated against. However, I was surprised to hear that the experiment was ending that day without giving the 'green' children a chance to experience the 'blue' side of the experiment.

The kindergarten uses a whole-language approach to integrate reading, writing, and listening skills, and children learn at their own level and pace. The math program uses manipulative learning tools such as cuisinaire rods, pattern blocks, base ten blocks, chip trading, and collections. In social studies, (K-6) topics include: the evolution of life, the pioneers, native peoples of North America and Mexico, ancient Egyptian civilization, medieval Europe, early American History, classical Greek cultures, and current world events.

All teachers have bachelors degrees, and many have completed masters and doctorate degrees. There are specialist teachers for physical education computer, music, and library. There is now a full time director for Diversity and Outreach, and a full-time Director of Service Learning.

In addition to Oakwood's academic, art, and athletics programs, upper-elementary students may select mini-courses taught by teachers, parents, alumni, or outside community leaders. Past courses include: textile design, jazz dance, law, jewelry, teaching, futurism, theatrical make-up, drama and African-American history.

THE OAKWOOD SECONDARY CAMPUS is located on Magnolia right off the 170 freeway. There are approximately 460 students in grades 7 to 12. The average class size is fifteen students. The secondary school includes a specialized math and science building of ten classrooms, five labs, a lecture hall, and a meeting atrium. Humanities, languages, and the arts are offered in an additional 15 classrooms, plus an auditorium. The theatre is charming. In addition, they recently added a 1,400 sq. ft STEAM I-Lab with ten 3D printers, laser cutters, and power tools.

When I visited students were building sets, and one was left with the impression that it is a very creative space. Across the street is the Music, Dance and Athletic center. This is an impressive building that houses the professional-looking music and dance rooms, and a 500-seat regulation gym with a separate weight training facility. There are plans to build a bridge to connect the gym to the other facilities. At the present time the children have to cross Magnolia. However, there are two full-time crossing guards.

The sports program has improved drastically -- most teams make it to their division playoffs. They have over 52 teams, 7-12. In addition, they have a new athletic director and have added several sports. When you ask the high school students what they like most about the school they unanimously said, "our teachers." They told us that they could call them at home if they had homework problems, and that the teachers were more concerned with their understanding their work, not just doing well on tests. Mr. Astman said, "Teaching can be enthralling, unsettling, hysterically funny, or profoundly serious (or all four), but it is never impersonal."

A parent on the tour said he wished that he had gone to a high school like Oakwood because it felt as if he would have had the freedom to express himself. All students and staff in the secondary school meet twice weekly in town meetings on the basketball court. Here the students can talk about what is on their minds, read poems, or make announcements. Many schools talk about community, but here you are left believing that this is the heart of Oakwood.

If you are interested in Oakwood's Secondary school (7-12), call and ask for their curriculum handbook which gives a detailed, comprehensive description of the academic program.

Immersion (Grades 7-12):

Oakwood's Immersion Program provides an intense two-week period in the academic year for students to be fully immersed in rich and challenging learning experiences – in ways not possible during the regular academic schedule. Immersion courses are experiential: learning is hands-on, exploratory, and in the field, well beyond the boundaries of the regular classrooms. Sample Immersion Courses include: Computer Animation, Fashion Design, Marine Biology and Oceanography, Musical Theatre, Screening writing, Ocean Sailing and Navigation, The Physics of Roller coasters, and International Travel (varies per year but has included: Belize, China, Costa Rica, France, Italy, Japan, Oxford, Sierra Leone).

S.T.E.A.M. (Grades 7-12) intertwines the multiple disciplines of Science, Technology, Engineering, Art, and Math into one curriculum. Through experimentation and problem solving, students encounter real world applications of design. This unique department allows students to engage fully in every stage of the process – from conception and design to its physical production. If students can dream the idea, S.T.E.A.M. possesses all the technology and tools to bring their visions to fruition. The newly constructed I-Lab features 3D printers, laser cutters, one-to-one Macs, and numerous power tools (drill press/miter saw/band saw).

In most years 100 percent of all Oakwood graduates enroll immediately in four-year colleges and universities across the country. Oakwood provides an athletic program which includes: cross country, volleyball, equestrian, basketball, soccer, softball, track and field, tennis, and flag football. Boys' sports include the aforementioned with the addition of baseball.

Here's a word on the school philosophy taken from the brochure:

> Although our program is college preparatory, we are equally concerned with the quality of children's experiences in the present.
>
> We intend an Oakwood education:
>
> 1. To develop students' intellectual, artistic, physical, and social competence, and seek to develop intellectual curiosity, imagination, and independent thought.
> 2. To spark passion.
> 3. To foster morality and develop self-knowledge.
> 4. To help students learn about their strengths and weaknesses within a supportive environment.
> 5. To foster a learning community in which students experience respect for the integrity of their efforts, whether those efforts result in success or failure."

The word on the school from several Oakwood parents that I spoke with is that it's a great school with a challenging curriculum and wonderful teachers. My take away from Oakwood is that the students all seem mature and confident.

HISTORY

The Oakwood School is a co-educational K-12 college preparatory school. It was founded in 1950 by a group of parents who wanted to provide their children with an educational experience balanced among the arts, sciences, and humanities. It was to be challenging to creative and intellectual capacities. They wanted a learning community, which fostered independence of thought, intellectual integrity, and personal and social morality. The Secondary School was founded in 1964.

AT A GLANCE

APPLICATION DEADLINE	January
OPEN HOUSES	September through January
UNIFORMS	No
AFTER SCHOOL CARE	Yes
SUMMER SCHOOL	Yes
SEE MAP	A on page 255

PACIFIC HILLS SCHOOL

8628 HOLLOWAY DRIVE, WEST HOLLYWOOD, CA 90069

TEL: 310.276.3068 FAX: 310.657.3831

www.phschool.org

DEAN OF STUDENTS:	**IVAN BARAHONA**
DIRECTOR OF ADMISSIONS:	**MICHAEL WAGNER**
TYPE OF SCHOOL:	**CO-ED COLLEGE PREP**
GRADES:	**6-12**
ENROLLMENT: 220	TUITION: $28,550
APPLICATION FEE: $100	NEW FAMILY FEE: $1,000
ACCREDITATION: WASC	FINANCIAL AID: YES

PACIFIC HILLS SCHOOL is located on Holloway Drive just below Sunset Boulevard and a stone's throw from Book Soup. It's a small urban campus without playing fields, swimming pool or cafeteria. A catering truck does come onto the campus every day offering the students hot or cold choices for lunch.

The school believes that a thorough education must provide for the physical, social and recreational needs of the students so, as there are no school playing fields, they bus the students to local parks and often rent out the gym at other schools. Daily P.E. is required from grades 6-11 but is optional for seniors. In the middle school, students participate in team and lifetime sports such as flag football, volleyball, soccer, floor hockey, softball, track and golf. The brochure says, "While these classes emphasize participation, skill development and fitness, they are also just plain fun!" If your child is serious about sports, there is a championship athletic program that guarantees that the more competitive students are looked after. The school has won recent C.I.F. championships in both basketball and softball.

There is a strong parent involvement at the school. In fact, in the letter to the parents it clearly states that volunteer activity and support for their annual fund-raiser are important considerations during the admissions process. It also goes on to say that "admission to the school is contingent upon an evaluation of the student's ability to succeed in the academic program, and upon an indication that acceptance would benefit both the student and the school."

Its parent body is an ethnically and socially diverse group who all seem to share a commitment to their children's school. Almost 50 percent of the student body receives some form of aid and boasts 65 percent diversity. Parents can often be seen participating in classroom activities, going on overnight field trips and attending the various sports events.

The entire school curriculum fits on one page and offers the core classes in all the major subjects with the opportunity to move from standard to honors courses or (and I quote) "from honor to standard courses," based on the students' achievement in each subject. Pacific Hills leans toward being a traditional school, however, there are more progressive educational practices being incorporated into the curriculum. A variety of clubs also pop up depending on interest, including forensics, chess, robotics, etc.

The school is able to provide students with much individualized attention since the student/ teacher ratio is approximately 10:1. As students enter the upper school there is more course work, and students are expected to work independently. Teachers are available for extra help, and the school will suggest a tutor if a child falls behind, which probably happens once in a while with children who are left to their own devices and are not that motivated. It's good to know the school is looking out for them.

Upper school students are required to complete four years of English, social science and P.E., and three years each of math, science and a foreign language. In addition, students must complete classes in human development, the fine arts, speech and various electives. Electives offered in the middle and upper schools include: art, advanced art, ceramics, photography, advanced photography, computers, theater arts, music, journalism, newspaper, yearbook, law and filmmaking. A required Outdoor Education Program sends every class, every year, off campus for a week to locations such as Big Bear, Santa Barbara, Catalina, Malibu and San Diego for kayaking, rope-courses, hiking etc. The eighth grade takes an additional trip to the State Capitol and other destinations in northern California.

From the Mission Statement

> Pacific Hills School is dedicated to providing its students with a challenging college preparatory program in a warm and supportive environment. The school is committed to establishing a racially diverse, multi-cultural community, and to develop each student's full human potential through a comprehensive educational program.

If you are looking for a school that offers a family atmosphere and helps your child to foster self-awareness and self-esteem, as well as to read well, write clearly and coherently, to study effectively, to reason soundly, and to question thoughtfully, then you might wish to consider applying to this school. Many parents from the neighborhood are looking at Pacific Hills as an alternative to some of the Westside schools.

HISTORY

Pacific Hills School was founded in 1983 as the Bel Air Preparatory School. In 1993, Richard Makoff turned the school into a nonprofit organization and the school's name was changed. The school's Board is composed of a president and nine other officers. Five of these officers form the school's executive committee. The headmaster, the assistant headmaster, a faculty representative and an administrative assistant sit on the Board and are instrumental in working with other Board members to incorporate the school's policies and programs.

APPLICATION DEADLINE	February
OPEN HOUSES	November, January and February
ISEE OR EQUIVALENT	Yes
UNIFORMS	No
SUMMER SCHOOL	Yes
SEE MAP	C on page 255

PAGE PRIVATE SCHOOLS

Hancock Park Site:
565 N. LARCHMONT BLVD., LOS ANGELES, CA 90004
TEL: 323.463.5119 FAX: 323.465.9964
Beverly Hills Site:
419 S. ROBERTSON BLVD., BEVERLY HILLS, CA 90210
TEL: 323.272.3429 FAX: 310.273.0497
www.pageschool.com

PRESIDENT:	**CHANES VAUGHAN**
TYPE OF SCHOOL:	**CO-ED DAY SCHOOL**
GRADES:	**PRESCHOOL-8**
ENROLLMENT: 225	TUITION:
BOOKS FEE: $587	PRESCHOOL: $17,200
REGISTRATION FEE: $900	K-8: $18,520
	FINANCIAL AID: YES

PAGE SCHOOL is conveniently located on Larchmont Boulevard in Hancock Park, just above Larchmont Village. It is a very pleasant looking school with a gated courtyard in the front. Inside there are air-conditioned, spacious classrooms and administrative offices. There is a library, computer and science labs, as well as art and music rooms.

The kindergarten classrooms have been enlarged giving the children a lot more space for learning and playing. In fact, the overall look of the campus has greatly improved. Classrooms have been painted, new computers installed. On my recent visit, the teachers were informative, friendly, and willing to answer all my questions. Page School provides a nurturing environment for the individual child so that educational and social growth skills may be developed. The school prides itself on providing incentives for scholarship, character, and personality through individual attention.

Page is a traditional and structured school. According to the school, "There is an emphasis on the three R's." Students are required to follow a core curriculum of subjects in math, phonics and reading, spelling, English composition, penmanship, science and social studies, geography, history, computers, library science, foreign language, physical education, art, music, drama, and dance.

Here is the school Philosophy:

> To a small degree, a child may be compelled to learn. But unless he learns because he truly wants to, he will quit at first opportunity. Page strives to give students a desire to learn and thirst for knowledge, so they seek education on their own. We try to lead students into right choices, not because they will be punished if they do not make those choices, but because they want to excel. The only discipline is self-discipline.

> Each subject is taught separately. Study is departmentalized at Page to those specialties. Our system has proved superior. Again and again, students tell us they like a change of pace and a change of surroundings during the school day.

Textbooks and other classroom materials are the finest. All meet our high expectations in the classroom. At Page we also teach etiquette – the mannerly way of life. Page takes the time required to mold young ladies and gentlemen."

There are specialists in Spanish, art, music, dance, drama, computer and physical education. A strong partnership with the Music Center has been established for this academic year. Afternoon programs offer etiquette classes (possibly a vestige from its days as a girls' boarding school), music, dance, arts, and crafts.

Beginning as early as pre-kindergarten, the children not only learn to operate computers but to use them in the practical aspects of schooling. Every student is required to complete classes in technology and computers. All elementary and middle school students have supervised study halls available from 3:30 to 4:30 p.m. and 8 to 8:45 a.m. daily. Attendance is on a voluntary basis unless a teacher places the student in mandatory study hall.

Behind the school, there are several sport courts which provide children with a variety of activities including tennis, racquet ball, volleyball, basketball, and badminton. The physical education teachers work hard to instill the importance of good sportsmanship, teamwork, and character. I was surprised at how much land the school has. From the front you would never believe there was room for a swimming pool, but, there is, and it is used year-round by the students. Part of the curriculum for every student is the mastery of swimming and the understanding of water safety.

The children attend daily assemblies. There's also Back-to-School Night, a Halloween Carnival, Spring Program and Barbecue, Field Trips and Graduation ceremonies.

If you are looking for a traditional, academic school that concentrates on basic education and old-fashioned fundamentals, you might want to visit this campus and take a look for yourself.

HISTORY

The Los Angeles campus of the Page school was founded in 1908 by the Vaughan family and has been continuously operated by succeeding generations. Originally a girls' boarding school, Page became a military academy and day school in the 1950s. Today there are additional campuses in Beverly Hills, Garden Grove, and Costa Mesa. There are also three Florida campuses.

AT A GLANCE

APPLICATION DEADLINE	Open enrollment, as space is available
UNIFORMS	Yes
BEFORE AND AFTER SCHOOL CARE	Yes
SUMMER SCHOOL	Yes
SEE MAP	C on page 255

PASADENA WALDORF SCHOOL
209 E. MARIPOSA ST., ALTADENA, CA 91001
TEL: 626.794.9564 FAX: 626.794.4704
www.pasadenawaldorf.org

HEAD OF SCHOOL:	DOUGLAS GARRETT
DIRECTOR OF ADMISSIONS:	DIANE KELLY
TYPE OF SCHOOL:	CO-ED DAY SCHOOL
GRADES:	PRESCHOOL-8
ENROLLMENT: 300	TUITION: $11,895 - 23,070
APPLICATION FEE: $100	NEW FAMILY FEE: $500
ACCREDITATION: AWSNA	FINANCIAL AID: YES

PASADENA WALDORF SCHOOL is located in Altadena on a five-acre property complete with sprawling green lawns and huge old pine, oak and eucalyptus trees. The most impressive structure is a historic California craftsman house built at the turn of the century where most of the classes are held. The other buildings are of a more temporary nature – permanent trailer structures that can be set up quickly and cheaply to provide instant space. These are commonly seen on many campuses as an affordable way to keep up with a rapidly growing enrollment.

A parent interested in a Waldorf education for his/her child is given every opportunity to learn about the school philosophy and to observe the students in action. The orientation is very thorough. The teaching staff is passionate and enthusiastic about the Waldorf approach, and eager to educate visiting parents. The school follows the curriculum and educational philosophy of Rudolf Steiner, integrating academics and the arts in a developmentally appropriate manner. The school store has many books available for purchase that describe the Waldorf philosophy and method.

The school offers a preK program to keep up with the demand in the neighboring communities. Children are accepted from age four and are kept in the nursery-kindergarten class until they are ready for first grade at six plus. The adults in charge are known by name and not yet thought of or referred to as teachers. There is also a resource teacher on staff.

The atmosphere is warm and un-pressured. Children play, socialize with one another, have story time, and are made comfortable by the repetition of their daily routine. This is an important part of their philosophy so that students are not involved in intellectual pursuits before they are ready. Activities include painting, modeling, cooking, sewing, building, making things, learning nursery rhymes and songs in English, French and German. The children also learn eurythmy (an art of movement by Waldorf founder Rudolf Steiner), simple fairy tales, and participate in little plays and seasonal festivals.

The elementary school covers the ages six to fourteen. Each new class (first grade) receives a class teacher who stays with them for the whole eight years. The curriculum includes reading, writing, composition and grammar, math, zoology, California history, mythology and local American geography. Studies include botany, geometry, chemistry, physics, American geography, economics, and ancient and modern history courses. There are specialist teachers in music, art, physical education, Spanish, gardening, crafts, and woodworking. Each year the school hosts an Elves Faire Winter Celebration and the annual eighth grade field trip travels to such places as the Yucatan, Hawaii, Costa Rica and England!

Each morning begins with a main lesson which lasts about two hours. The main lesson is devoted to the main cultural subjects, including mathematics, English, history, geography, science, etc. These are taught in block periods of three or four weeks each. After that the children work with the specialist teachers for the better part of the day.

The children do not use books but create their own books by copying written material from the blackboard. In first grade, they illustrate the books using lots of color. All the illustrations are taken from a rough sketch that the teacher draws on the blackboard. As the years go on, the material is dictated by the teacher after a thorough discussion of the subject matter with the class. Often the main lesson books are beautifully bound, and the covers are designed and decorated by the students. Art is also taught by dictation with the teacher showing an example of the drawing or watercolor painting and the children then copying it. The children's art was everywhere, which gave a great feeling of cheerfulness and color. Unfortunately since all the children painted exactly the same subject, in a rather similar way, no individual drawing stood out in any particular way. The art hanging together in this fashion looks more like a mural than the work of different children.

Here is an excerpt on Waldorf philosophy as taken from the brochure:

> Waldorf teachers utilize a variety of approaches and methods. Central among them is the integration of the arts into all subjects using movement, music, storytelling and rhythm, even in the sciences. Self-expression, self-discipline, and the wholeness of life are among the themes teachers weave into every lesson. Academic excellence is thus pursued in a balanced, supportive, nurturing, non-competitive environment. The result is a well-grounded, culturally literate creative student, curious about the world and eager to explore it.

The Waldorf schools have a unique approach to education that is best experienced through a visit to the campus. Tours are scheduled throughout the year.

HISTORY

The Pasadena Waldorf School was first established in 1979 and is one of 20 Waldorf Schools in California. The curriculum and educational philosophy of the Waldorf Schools was formulated in Germany by Rudolf Steiner, Ph.D., in 1919.

AT A GLANCE

APPLICATION DEADLINE	January 20
OPEN HOUSES	Oct., Nov., Dec., Jan. & March
UNIFORMS	No
BEFORE AND AFTER SCHOOL CARE	Yes
SEE MAP	B on page 255

PILGRIM SCHOOL

540 S. COMMONWEALTH AVE., LOS ANGELES, CA 90020

TEL: 213.385.7351 FAX: 213.385.1060

www.pilgrim-school.org

INTERIM HEAD OF SCHOOL:	PATRICIA KONG
DIRECTOR OF ADMISSIONS	ANGELINA ARRINGTON
TYPE OF SCHOOL:	CO-ED DAY SCHOOL
	BOARDING (9-12)
GRADES:	PRESCHOOL-12
ENROLLMENT: 415	TUITION: $18,500 - 30,750
APPLICATION FEE: $125	NEW STUDENT FEE: $2,000
ACCREDITATION: CAIS/WASC/NAIS	FINANCIAL AID: YES

PILGRIM SCHOOL is a division of the First Congregational Church of Los Angeles. The church and school buildings are impressive structures that blend in with the downtown urban setting. The school has an old-fashioned, sort of Hogwarts feel to it with leaded windowpanes, varnished oak doors and molding, and black and white checkerboard tile floors. Its buttoned-up look belies its progressive attitude toward innovation in education.

Pilgrim School, founded in 1958, is an independent, coeducational, college preparatory, toddler through 12th grade day school with boarding options available in grades 9-12. This is a traditional college-preparatory school with a challenging curriculum. One hundred percent of Pilgrim School graduates go on to higher education, many finding success at Williams College, Columbia, NYU, Stanford, UC Berkeley, UCLA, USC, Cornell, George Washington, Bryn Mawr, Boston University, prestigious art schools including RISD, Parsons, Otis, international schools such as the American University in Paris, Goldsmiths, University of London, as well as smaller liberal arts colleges.

The educators, administrators, and parents I met during my many visits have a great deal of love, dedication, and support for the school. Every holiday season, the Interim Head of School, the lovely and gracious Patricia Kong, rides the bus with all three Kindergarten classes to Chevalier's, the local independent bookstore, where they all read books together and choose a book to recommend to other children. Every Friday afternoon, an emails newsletter is sent to the parents recapping the week's events, various sports triumphs or school field trips, as well as looking ahead to the events of the upcoming week, whether it be a reminder of a visit from an author like Lisa See, Marla Frazee, or Tad Hills, whose visits are sponsored by the Pilgrim School Visiting Writers and Artists Series, or that there is free dress day on Friday at this school.

Pilgrim really is a school community, where everyone is involved, and parents are very active in the life of the school. School "colonies" consisting of students from all grades, along with faculty and staff, gather together throughout the year for various activities. Older students are mentors to younger students and there is a strong sense of community spirit. Families are required to donate thirty volunteer hours a year, but many do much more. Some parent-run activities include the Pilgrim Family Fun Day, the jog-athon ,the Afternoon in the Garden wine tasting and auction in the spring, the Faculty/Staff appreciation luncheons served by parents, and parents can always be found in the elementary school library reading to the younger classes, including junior kindergarten.

Pilgrim has a wonderful ethnic and socioeconomic mix of children in its classrooms reflecting the rich blend of cultures that we have in the city of Los Angeles. Pilgrim has its share of celebrity families, but they are very low key about it. You never get the feeling that they cater to celebrity status at the school.

There are 33 classrooms, two libraries with 12,000 volumes, a gym, a roof-top state of the art Fine Arts Center, two computer labs, (the school is also a one-to-one laptop school and has an iPad program in both Elementary and Secondary school), dance studio, dark room, auditorium/theatre and science labs. They also have an interdisciplinary Fab Lab (one of the four specially-equipped STEM classrooms that exist in Los Angeles).

The campus is very well maintained and functions with the students' different age groups in mind. There is a play yard for the Elementary school and a large outdoor courtyard area where Middle school students can relax at tables under trees or take each other on in ping-pong. A beautiful new sports field was under construction at the time this edition went to press.

Early Education

All activities in the Early Education program are guided by the Reggio-Emilia educational philosophy that encourages learning at the student's own pace, focusing on individual areas of greatest interest, with the teacher acting as the facilitator. The concept of the Outdoor Classroom, which identifies the environment as the "third teacher," along with parents and faculty is also integral to early education at Pilgrim.

There is an Early Education center with a play area with plenty of swings and climbing structures with rubber padding beneath. The playground and lunch area has landscaping that creates a park-like atmosphere with shade trees and tables where preschoolers gather and eat. Planters also provide a hands-on instructional laboratory for students to learn how to grow plants, fruits, and vegetables.

Elementary School

The typical Kindergarten day includes a lesson in phonics, mathematics, computer skills, music, art, snack, playtime, lunch, physical education, playtime, reading and creative writing. Several times a year, the class hosts a "publishing party" for parents when they present books they have written and illustrated, on various themes such as the seasons or friends and family. Hands-on science/engineering instruction begins in Junior Kindergarten. The elementary curriculum includes phonics, reading, arithmetic, English, U.S. History, social studies, and geography. There are specialist teachers in music, art, Spanish, Mandarin Chinese, science and physical education. The elementary arts program involves field trips to local galleries and museums and then incorporating the experience into the students' own work. Second graders study Paul Klee's sculptures and puppets, create their own puppets, write and develop plots, paint and create elaborate scenery, drawing from various exhibits and local museums and galleries. The project culminates in standing room only puppet show performances for parents and other grades. Art and photography students have had unusually creative and unique exhibits both on campus and in galleries throughout Los Angeles.

Outdoor and Experiential Education

Beginning in the fourth grade with Malibu Creek and fifth grade with Astrocamp, each grade has a class field trip. In tenth and eleventh grade, the trip is an alternating East coast/West coast/Midwest college tour, the itinerary worked out each year to encompass the students' interests. The senior year field trip is a community service trip. After Hurricane Katrina, the senior class went to New Orleans to help in the rebuilding. Seniors have worked with Habitat for Humanity to rebuild homes lost in the California fires, and traveled to Hawaii to work at a senior care facility. Secondary Spring Break trips have included visits to China and Japan.

Middle and Upper School

The middle and upper school curriculum includes courses in fine arts (studio art, band, drama, dance, and digital media), English (composition, public speaking, newspaper, and yearbook), Spanish, Mandarin Chinese, math, (algebra, geometry, pre-calculus, calculus, and AP calculus AB), Biology, Chemistry, computer science, engineering, Physics, Anatomy, physical education, social studies, and art history. AP classes are offered in Biology, Chemistry, Physics, Statistics, Spanish, Calculus, English Language and Composition, English Literature, Art History, US Government, and US History.

Electives include Digital Video Production, Game Design, Cryptography, Dance, Jazz and Blues Band, Theater Arts, and production of Ship's In, a student-run video news magazine, to name a few. The school has a terrific student written newspaper, and students also work on the yearbook. A college counseling program is in place for all high school students, with countless hours spent helping each senior find the perfect college for their strengths and interests. SAT and ACT preparation classes are held on-campus by Pilgrim's in-house, college counselor. The student teacher ratio is eleven to one, offering students great, personalized attention and ready access to the faculty.

In 2012, Pilgrim opened the Mayflower House dormitory directly across from the school. It is a warm and comfortable home-like setting where students can study, relax, and connect with the other residents. In 2014-15, Pilgrim boarding students hailed from four different countries - China, Russia, Kazakhstan, and Brazil - as well as the United States. The boarding students enrich all aspects of life at Pilgrim: they expose day students to different cultures, languages, and points of view. In turn, the boarding students benefit from being in a supportive school community, while also having the opportunity to experience the diversity and uniqueness of Los Angeles.

Spiritual Enrichment Opportunities

Pilgrim School prides itself on being a non-denominational educational experience, embracing and encouraging all faiths. An emphasis on ethical behavior and respect for others is intrinsic to the school's program. Each year, Pilgrim picks a theme that is explored on cultural, educational and social levels. "Empathy" for example was one year's theme. At All-School Chapel twice a month, moral and spiritual themes are discussed. During these chapel services, a guest rabbi or imam might visit and discuss different aspects of culture and religion. Holidays such as Yom Kippur and Diwali are observed and taught.

Pilgrim School follows an honor code that all students are introduced to, beginning in age- appropriate ways in kindergarten. All secondary students and faculty sign the code at the beginning of the school year. A student-run Honor Council reviews student issues that might arise during the school year and helps support the honor code in the school community.

Sports

Elementary school team sports begin in grade 4, and include soccer, volleyball and flag football. There is an optional competitive athletic program at the upper school level in football, soccer, basketball, volleyball, baseball, softball, cheer, and cross country. The school has a unique sports policy in that there are no tryouts for teams and a no-cut policy. If a student wants to play on a team, he/she is welcome. Despite this policy, or perhaps because of it, Pilgrim is able to boast 43 championships in various sports. During the 2013/2014 and 2014/2015 school years, Pilgrim's first-ever capital campaign raised funds for construction of the Field of Dreams, a regulation-size sports field over underground parking. Pilgrim students are thrilled to finally be able to have a home field advantage, and in the fall of 2016, they will enjoy an expanded version of the "everybody plays" philosophy at Pilgrim.

All School Events

There are a number of all school events including a holiday concert, spring concert, various dance performances, and poetry readings. This past year there was an all-school (Junior Kindergarten through twelfth grade) production of the musical "Willy Wonka."

The school espouses the 'whole child' educational philosophy, and its motto is "We grow students." The school also grows parents, as it offers parenting classes aimed at solving common childhood issues.

The Pilgrim community is made up of families from Los Feliz, Silver Lake, Echo Park, Downtown, Hancock Park, Pasadena, Hollywood, the Hollywood Hills and as far away as Santa Monica and Pacific Palisades. This is definitely a school worth driving to.

HISTORY

Pilgrim School, founded in 1958, is an independent, co-educational, college prepatory, toddler - 12th grade day school with boarding options available. It offers a challenge curriculum that begins in kindergarten and grows increasingly demanding through the twelve grades. Dr. Mark Brooks led the school for eleven years and made many great changes, specifically his 'Field of Dreams' project and opening up a boarding school. In June 2016 he became the head of C.E.E.

AT A GLANCE

APPLICATION DEADLINE	January 31
OPEN HOUSES	November and January
UNIFORMS	Yes
ISEE TESTING	Yes
BEFORE AND AFTER SCHOOL CARE	Yes
SUMMER CAMP	Yes
SEE MAP	C on page 255

POLYTECHNIC SCHOOL

1030 E. CALIFORNIA BLVD., PASADENA, CA 91106
TEL: 626.396.6300 FAX: 626.796.2249
www.polytechnic.org

HEAD OF SCHOOL:	**JOHN W. BRACKER**
DIRECTOR OF ADMISSIONS:	**SALLY JEANNE MCKENNA**
TYPE OF SCHOOL:	**CO-ED DAY SCHOOL**
GRADES:	**K-12**
ENROLLMENT: 860	TUITION: $25,300 - 33,500
APPLICATION FEE: $100	FINANCIAL AID: YES
ACCREDITATION: WASC	

POLYTECHNIC is a traditional college preparatory school with an outstanding reputation. The campus takes up 15 acres of prime Pasadena real estate and includes two gymnasiums, an athletic field, a performing arts center, a fine arts center, two libraries, a computer lab, science and history buildings, and a media center. The campus is extensive but has more of a residential than a modern feeling to it.

Polytechnic is a private school that offers a great education most notably at the upper school level, but one thing that it doesn't offer is enough spaces for the hundreds of families that apply each year. Even school alumni have trouble getting their children enrolled at Poly.

The school philosophy is the same today as it was years ago, as written by then-principal, Virginia Pease: "The individual, not the class, is the unit of the teacher's interest and the development of the child's power to think and to do, rather than the following of a certain course of instruction, is the direct aim of every teacher and the excuse for every lesson."

The School Credo:

    I. We are committed to honesty, justice, charity, and the pursuit of truth.
    II. We respect the dignity and worth of all human beings – their thoughts, their feelings, and their

    III. We seek to celebrate the joy and love that emanate from the human spirit.
    IV. We strive to be responsible and contributing members of our families, our school community, and

Under the leadership of John W. Bracker, the school is organized into three divisions with separate administrative heads and teaching staffs.

Kindergarten and first grade classes have three sections of 15 students at each grade level with a lead teacher and assistant teacher in each classroom. There are homeroom teachers for each class, supplemented by specialist teachers. Enrollment in the lower school is approximately 300 students. The lower school teachers provide their students with a great deal of individual attention. The daily program includes language arts, mathematics and social studies. Single-subject teachers provide instruction in science, choral and instrumental music, art, Spanish, physical education, and drama. Children regularly use the library, computer facility, and resource center.

Community service is built into the curriculum in the lower and middle schools with additional volunteer opportunities after school. In the upper school, students contribute eight hours in their freshman year and complete a 30-hour project between the sophomore and senior years. Students can select their own projects or work with organizations and schools such as:

Hillsides Home for Children, Willard School, Kidspace, Huntington Memorial Hospital, Special Olympics, and AIDS Service Center.

Middle School - Courses of Study

Grade 6: English, world history; mathematics; science; technology; French, Latin and Spanish; arts and physical education.

Grade 7: English, geography, civics, cultural understanding, math, pre-algebra, geometry, astronomy, marine science, computer keyboarding, word processing; French, Latin, or Spanish, arts electives, physical education

Grade 8: English, U.S. history from 1860, algebra, geometry; French, Latin or Spanish, human biology, computer keyboarding, word processing, desktop publishing, arts electives; physical education.

Upper School Requirements: English, math, history, science, language, fine arts, P.E., outdoor education, community outreach.

All the students at Polytechnic are required to take physical education with an emphasis on cooperation, good sportsmanship, and the development of skills. Seventh and eighth graders are encouraged to select one or more sports of their choice from a list that includes football, volleyball, basketball, soccer, track and field, softball, tennis and baseball. Eighty percent of upper school students earn their required physical education credits by participating in after-school team sports.

The Girls Prep League competes in cross-country, track and field, swimming and diving, volleyball, soccer, tennis, basketball, softball, fencing, dance team, and badminton. The Boys Prep League competes in eight-man football, cross-country, basketball, soccer, tennis, baseball, volleyball, swimming, golf and track and field. Water polo, wrestling, badminton and equestrian teams are coeducational.

Polytechnic's Outdoor Education Program includes hiking, backpacking, mountain climbing, and canoeing. These field trips are structured to expand on the classroom lessons in ecology, botany, geology, and history. They also teach students to work together in the planning and navigating of the trip.

There is a great deal of parent involvement at Polytechnic. Parents drive on field trips, coordinate and promote school functions, serve on committees, and participate in fund raising.

Polytechnic is a prep school that is serious about education and proud of the list of top colleges that accept its seniors each year. The educational background of staff and teachers, is listed in the admission materials. Polytechnic clearly has a fine group of teachers and educators among its ranks.

HISTORY

In 1907, Polytechnic School became the first nonprofit, independent school in Southern California, enrolling 106 students in kindergarten through eight grade. True to its name and to the educational philosophy of the day, Poly's curriculum emphasized both academics and manual arts—from English to math, to sewing and woodworking. The original school buildings were designed by renowned architect Myron Hunt and feature his revolutionary "open air" school design with residential-scale classrooms and adjacent courtyards and playgrounds. These buildings continue to form the heart of the Lower and Middle School campus more than a century later. Fifty years after the school's founding, the decision was made to expand the educational program through the 12th grade. Poly's Upper School campus opened in 1959, and in 1962, the first senior class graduated. Today, Poly remains an ambitious, forward-thinking school community—one devoted not only to scholarship but also to the creative arts, the camaraderie of team sports, the joy of service to others, and the welcoming spirit of friendship—here on our historic campus and around the world.

AT A GLANCE

APPLICATION DEADLINE	December 19
OPEN HOUSE	See website
UNIFORMS	Grades 1-5
AFTER SCHOOL CARE	Yes
SEE MAP	B on page 255

PROVIDENCE HIGH SCHOOL

511 S. BUENA VISTA ST., BURBANK, CA 91505

TEL: 818.846.8141 FAX: 818.843.8421

www.providencehigh.org

HEAD OF SCHOOL:	**JOE SCIUTO**
DIRECTOR OF ADMISSIONS:	**JUDY EGAN UMECK**
TYPE OF SCHOOL:	**CATHOLIC CO-ED DAY SCHOOL**
GRADES:	**9-12**
ENROLLMENT: 480	TUITION: $15,450
APPLICATION FEE: $75	FINANCIAL AID: YES
REGISTRATION FEE: $670	

PROVIDENCE HIGH SCHOOL is a Catholic, college-preparatory school. The school is located in the San Fernando Valley. If you live in Hollywood, you take Barham over the hill and it's near the Burbank Studios and very close to the Equestrian Center. The campus is nestled between a beautiful park and the neighborhood hospital. Over the past four decades, Providence High has flourished to become a recognized outstanding school in the area. Providence attracts students from a wide diversity of economic, cultural and ethnic backgrounds, a diversity which I believe enriches the educational experience of the student body. Children come from all over to attend this Blue Ribbon school.

The school works closely with the parents who are acknowledged as the primary educators of their sons and daughters and are expected to be very involved in their kids' academic lives. This will suit those of us who miss those days of volunteering in our kid's elementary school and feel left out during those middle school years. The Parent Executive Committee at the school allows parents to be involved in the high school life of their children by supporting the school, faculty and staff, and acts as a network with other parents providing a communication link for upcoming events and activities.

The Fritz B. Burns Student Activity Center features a state-of-the-art gymnasium, weight room, exercise room, boys' and girls' locker rooms and conference center. It is a very impressive piece of architecture that is quite eye-catching as one pulls up the driveway. As I parked my car and headed back toward the school building, I spoke to a couple of students who answered my questions with a tremendous amount of enthusiasm. They couldn't wait to tell me about two very unique programs the school has to offer.

The first one is the four-year Health Careers Focus Program, which is offered to about 25 students from an incoming pool of about 40 to 60 freshmen. In their freshmen and sophomore years, students attend weekly rounds at the medical center next door visiting different departments. During their sophomore year, students enroll in honors biology. The Religion Department is involved with the program's second semester of the junior year through their Peace and Justice course. An honors chemistry course is a requirement during this year and students start their hospital internships. They are required to complete 120 hours of internship rotation at a medical facility of their choice. This requirement is continued into their senior year, during which time they are required to complete a minimum of 80 hours for a combined minimum of 200 hours. In their senior year, students must enroll in either AP biology or anatomy-physiology. Graduating students are honored at the Senior Awards assembly for their participation and completed internships after four years of dedication and hard work.

The second is a Media Communications Focus Program. In the first year, the student study important aspects pertaining to the history of media. For instance, the Ethics in Media course deals with questions and dilemmas concerning the role of the media and its moral impact on society. Students learn the basic principles of drawing and filming, explore creative concepts, develop perceptual skills, and learn techniques that will culminate in a major animation project. In the Video Production class they learn first hand what it is like to collaborate on a video project followed by a production oriented course that emphasizes the skills learned in video projection. In this course they will continue to practice advanced editing using AVID and Final Cut Pro software. There's a course of advanced practice in creative writing skills, concentrating on script writing, fiction, drama, and personal essays. Professional writers in film and television are invited into the classroom for special presentations throughout the semester. By the end of the four-year program, student teams will have produced an original commercial, as well as a music video.

Upon completion of the four year media program, these students are uniquely qualified to compete for positions at the best film and media schools in the nation. Your child can then return to the neighborhood and is capable of working for one of the top movie studios in the world!

Mission Statement

> Providence High School's goal is to develop each student to his or her full potential, as a leader, a responsible citizen of the world, who is imbued with a strong set of moral values, a sense of service and a love of learning. We work in collaboration with the parents, who are acknowledged as the primary educators of their sons and daughters. We work with the belief that each student is essentially good and infinitely lovable. Guided by our Catholic tradition, we recognize Jesus Christ as the model of the total person we are seeking to develop. In our mission of education, we strive for academic excellence and the total development of the individual.

Religious women, lay men and women comprise the 32 member full-time teaching faculty. There is a ratio of one faculty member to 19 students. Average class size is 25 students, with a maximum of 30 per class. (43% boys and 57% girls).

Campus Ministry Club

The campus Ministry Club meets to plan liturgies, organize school-wide charity projects and help lead the Days of Recollection. Through these activities, students become ministers to their peers.

Community Service Program

Freshmen are required to fulfill a minimum of ten hours of service, at home, church or school. Sophomores are required to perform 20 hours of service at church or school. Juniors must fulfill a minimum of 30 hours of service for church or community. Seniors are required to do a minimum of 40 hours with service agencies in their local communities.

Kairos Retreat

The Kairos Retreat is a three-day, overnight experience open to all seniors who wish to participate. It is a highly structured program which includes talks by both faculty and student team members, small group sharing sessions, community prayers, celebration of the Eucharist and related activities. Kairos Retreats provide soon-to-be-graduating young adults the opportunity for in-depth and honest self-examination, reflection over the deeper meaning of their relationship with family and friends, and a strengthening of their faith in God. "Kairotics" overwhelmingly affirm the retreat to have been a profound faith experience and a source of personal growth.

College Counseling

The college counselors help students set academic and personal goals to achieve a successful high school experience. Starting in their freshman year, students begin building their own portfolio that they develop through all four years at PHS, which can then be used as a tool for the college application process.

The following, taken from their website, is a very helpful way to show parents how Providence is going to prepare their child for college step by step.

Pioneer Path to College

9th Grade
Take the ACT/EXPLORE for skill assessment
Freshman Study Skills Program
Introduction to course requirements for college
Meet with freshman/sophomore Counselors

10th Grade
Take the PSAT/NMSQT to prepare for junior year
Concentrate on studies and grades
Volunteer for service commitments
Explore college information on internet
Attend college fairs

11th Grade
Take the PSAT/NMSQT
Receive College Handbook
Attend college fairs and begin campus visits
Attend College Case Study Program
Meet with Junior/Senior Counselor
Participate in College internet presentations
Take the SAT I and SAT II in the spring
Continue volunteer work
Visit colleges during spring break and summer

I was impressed with the emphasis on table manners and decorum in the cafeteria. It has always been my belief that being taught good manners early in life gives a young person a foundation that will benefit them throughout their lives. I'm sure they're looking for more girls. So if you have one, take a tour.

HISTORY

Providence High School opened as an all-girls, Catholic High School in Burbank, California in September 1955. Principal Sr. Maria Theresa, Sr. Isabella, and Sr. Esther administrated at the new school which then had its first class of 81 students. By 1960, the number of students swelled to 495. Under the guidance of Sr. Maria Theresa, the staff continued to grow and formed a young, enthusiastic group who worked hard to attain the highest standards, not only in the academic field, but also in games, music and other extracurricular activities. Providence began welcoming young men, as well as women to the school in 1974. The addition of another school building was completed in 1975 to accommodate the growing student population. Sister Lucille Dean became the school's principal in 1986. Providence High School has received recognition throughout its history for its academic achievement and was designated a Blue Ribbon School in 1997.

AT A GLANCE

APPLICATION DEADLINE	January
OPEN HOUSE	November
UNIFORMS	Yes
HSTPT TESTING	Yes
SEE MAP	A on page 255

PS1 PLURALISTIC SCHOOL

1225 BROADWAY, SANTA MONICA, CA 90404
TEL: 310.394.1313 FAX: 310.395.1093
www.psone.org

HEAD OF SCHOOL:	**JOEL M. PELCYGER**
DIRECTOR OF ADMISSIONS:	**BETH KEMP**
TYPE OF SCHOOL:	**CO-ED DAY SCHOOL**
GRADES:	**K-6**
ENROLLMENT: 230	TUITION: $27,275
APPLICATION FEE: $125	FINANCIAL AID: YES
MEMBERSHIPS: CAIS/NAIS/CASE/CAPSO	

PS1 Pluralistic School is located in a business/residential section of Santa Monica. The campus underwent renovations in 1998 and 2012, turning an eclectic group of buildings into a new, state-of-the-art facility for which the school received several architectural awards. The campus extends from Euclid Street to 12th Street where they have two expansive play areas with grass, synthetic soccer field, outdoor stages, rooftop garden, climbing structures, complete with a 100-year-old oak tree and a ball court. All the classrooms are very spacious with special consideration given to air circulation, and natural and reflected lighting.

The 'P' at PS1 stands for 'pluralism.' At PS1 they believe that there is never any one set way to teach a subject. This is a progressive/developmental school where pluralism is stressed, i.e., children are able to experience different approaches to education under one roof. The word 'progressive' indicates an affiliation with the philosophy of scholar and educator John Dewey. The children work with hands-on and project-based activities, are divided into multi-age groups, and there is an emphasis on working together to problem solve. Since it is a pluralistic school, there is an openness to different teaching styles.

As taken from the school brochure:

> A founding value of PS1, pluralism is the belief that a community is enriched when individual differences are respected and welcomed. At PS1, pluralism is a commitment to diversity and inter connectedness in both our community and our curriculum. Combining intellectual and emotional intelligence is paramount to success as a human being and central to PS1's unique pluralistic philosophy.

At PS1 we believe there are three core values in education:

- Competence: What we know.
- Confidence: How we feel about what we know.
- Connection: What we do with what we know.

As stated earlier, the children are divided into both a classroom, and a group of classrooms (called Clusters). There are four Clusters [three Youngers classes (K-1), two Bridge classes (1-2 and 2-3), two Middles classes (3-4), and Olders (5-6)]. Each Cluster shares a retreat workspace. There is plenty of outdoor space used as additional work areas which allows students to take advantage of our wonderful southern Californian climate. There is a two grade equivalent range in all of the classes – (K-1, 1-2, 2-3, 3-4 and so on through Sixth grade) – changing a child's peer group from year to year. In this way, each child has opportunities to be both an older and a younger student within the class at different times through his or her school experience. Problem solving and cooperation are taught through an emphasis on group activity.

The curriculum includes: math, reading, English, grammar, composition, language arts, science, social studies, and service learning. Teachers use the Readers' and Writers' Workshop programs from Columbia University, and Everyday Math from the University of Chicago. There are specialist teachers in Music, P.E., Library, Art, and The Studio (a STEAM workspace). There is no grading system. Goals for the year are discussed with each student at the beginning of the school year at parent/teacher/student meetings. In February they meet again to discuss the student's progress and set new goals for the remainder of the year. Twice a year, detailed progress reports are sent home. Progress is evaluated in comparison to past performance and on a grid of age-appropriate skills with an assessment of each student's growth.

The favorite tradition at PS1 is the annual school camping trip. All the students attend. Children experience sleeping in a tent and cooking outside. To ease any fears, younger children are paired up with an older child. Students in the Youngers Cluster attend just for a day trip. Other school traditions include a holiday gift drive program, PSServes (a community service program), Grandparents and Special Friends Day, Moving Up Day, and Staff Appreciation Day. The after-school clubhouse offers a variety of enrichment classes including various sports, drama, music, art, cooking, gardening, lego robotics, dance, gymnastics, as well as indoor and outdoor play.

There are two things that stand out when touring the school. The first is that there is poetry everywhere, on just about every wall in the school! These poems are all written and recited by the children. It's fantastic to see so many children of all ages that are more literate in poetry than most adults! The study and writing of poetry is part of every child's experience. The second thing is the level of parent participation that goes on in the school. On any given day, parents can be seen volunteering throughout the campus both inside and outside the classrooms. In addition to the Parents Guild, PS1 parents participate in a wide variety of committees, activities and projects. So, if you're one of those parents who loves to be involved then take a closer look at this school. At PS1 there are endless opportunities for involvement!

PS1 graduates have a high acceptance rate at prominent independent schools who value students that bring 'Knowledge plus more' to them. Upon graduation many students go on to attend Archer, Brentwood, Crossroads, Harvard Westlake, Marlborough, New Roads, Wildwood, Windward, public and charter schools, among others.

HISTORY

PS1 was founded in 1971 by current school head Joel Pelcyger and Eleanor Coben in order to provide excellence in academics coupled with joyful learning and a sense of community. The school built an environment that encourages personal reflection and social interaction on a scale comprehensible to young children, and quickly acquired a reputation for producing capable and connected citizens. PS1 chooses to stay small so that all voices are heard and valued, accentuating both the individual as well as the connections that bring people together.

AT A GLANCE

APPLICATION DEADLINE	January, priority status to first 100 received. Applications are available in September for the following year.
ORIENTATION TOURS	October-January
UNIFORMS	Yes
BEFORE AND AFTER SCHOOL CARE	Yes
SUMMER SCHOOL	Yes
SEE MAP	D on page 255

RIBÉT ACADEMY

2911 SAN FERNANDO ROAD, LOS ANGELES, CA 90065
TEL: 323.344.4330 FAX: 323.344.4339
www.ribetacademy.com

PRINCIPAL:	RONALD DAUZAT, ESQ.
DIRECTOR OF ADMISSIONS:	DR. VIVIEN SHI
TYPE OF SCHOOL:	CO-ED DAY SCHOOL
GRADES:	PK-12
ENROLLMENT: 500	TUITION: $9,900 - 14,900
APPLICATION FEE: $100	FINANCIAL AID: YES
ACCREDITATION: WASC	

RIBET ACADEMY is located just off of the Glendale Freeway in the San Fernando Valley. The three-story facility, which was originally a silk factory, also once housed a Catholic school for boys. The building, which can be viewed from the freeway, has something of an institutional appearance, but don't judge this book by its cover.

Inside, the hallways are extra-wide and the classrooms are large and bright. The school administration is constantly working hard to rid the school of the institutional feeling that the facility has had in the past. Having a tuition based budget explains for the slow but sure changes to the campus. The walls have been painted inside and out, there is a gymnasium with bleacher seating for 500+, play areas, tennis courts, football field, and track, and the school has a lovely garden. Other changes include the spacious inaugural marine biology classroom, and the old conversion of the maintenance room to an art studio where students can leave out projects in progress. The chapel has also been converted into a theatre which seats 100 to 120 audience members, and children can learn dramatic arts, lighting, sound, and costume design.

Ribét is a traditional academic school. Character education is also stressed. There is a school cafeteria at the sub-basement level affectionately known as Café Ribét. Here hot lunch is served and it is also used as a meeting site for students and a dance hall. Ribét has a baseball diamond, and three outside basketball courts. In addition to students already attending Ribét, the school hosts about 30 international exchange students each year and has a very active international draw.

The tours are conducted on an individual basis, and everyone that I met at the school was friendly and helpful. Select students often conduct tours, which is one of the many ways they develop their leadership skills. The school curriculum includes history, mathematics, language arts, science, geography, computer, art, and physical education. There are two mobile labs that can go into any classroom in the elementary school. Ribét offers computer instruction beginning in kindergarten. In elementary school, a mobile laptop travels to each classroom for lessons that are incorporated with other curricular areas. There is also an upper school computer lab which is the site for 6 to 12th grade computer classes which include introductory, advanced, web design, and AP. A 23,000 volume library is also used for research.

The school has a chorus, an orchestra, and a drama program. Students learn elementary music, theory, harmony and melody. In fifth grade, all students choose a wind instrument to learn. In sixth grade and up, it becomes more specialized, and there is a jazz ensemble for those students wanting to further develop their musical skills.

Foreign language study (Spanish) is required starting in seventh grade. In the upper school the core curriculum includes English, geography, social studies, science, foreign language, and math. High school electives include psychology, drama, art, business administration, and African-American history. Ribét has won many awards at The LA County Science Fair. No school has ever won as many awards as Ribét in the history of the Fair. The fourth floor courtroom is the impressive home of the Legal Studies Department. This elective course includes Mock Trial in the fall semester and Student Court in the spring. Two administrators each teach the course with a degree in Jurisprudence. Mock Trial is a national program designed to familiarize students with the workings of the American legal system, and schools can compete at the junior high to collegiate level.

Ribét participates in interscholastic sports and has teams (grades 6 to 12) in football, basketball, and baseball for boys, and volleyball, basketball, and softball for girls. Ribét athletic teams have earned other championships in California Interscholastic Federation competition at league, regional, and state levels. The cheer leading squad also took first place at state competition.

Here is an excerpt from the school brochure on the school Mission Statement:

> At Ribét, we focus on three goals: Effective communicating, practical problem solving, and enthusiastic life-long learning. We offer students engaging curriculum, superior instruction and numerous opportunities to practice and to apply learned concepts. At Ribét, students are given the challenge and the chance to excel. We expect all students to become independent, responsible role models in the community.

Accelerated reading groups and math enrichment courses are available in the elementary grades, with an accelerated program for advanced students. There is an after-school program, which offers gymnastics, karate, music, computer and dance. There are twenty available Advanced Placement classes: English language and composition, English literature and composition, French language and composition, environmental science, psychology, statistics, world history, studio art, U.S. history, U.S. politics and government,, biology, chemistry, calculus (AB), European history, Spanish language and composition, music, physics, art history.

Ribét also has a unique program, called The Reduction in Tuition Exchange Program (RITE). They basically feature a barter arrangement, whereby tuition is reduced in exchange for goods or services, time, or skills provided to the school by the family. One family has an awning company, and provided the awning for the outside play area. Another barter re-tiled the girls' bathrooms. Painting, flooring, day-care, computer skills, foreign language classes etc, may be preferred depending on the school's needs, and what you have to offer. Once the application process has been started, a RITE application may be obtained from the admissions office, however, students must be accepted to Ribét before a RITE meeting is scheduled.

HISTORY

Ribét Academy is a privately owned school, founded in 1982 by Jaques Ribét. Mr. Ribét brought years of experience as a high school principal as well as a strong background in traditional education based on the English system to his role as founder of the Academy.

Mr. Ribet specifically employs teachers who harbor a great knowledge and respect for their subjects, who make learning seem like great fun, and who truly love teaching young, talented minds. Ribét started as a small high school in La Cañada and moved to its current site in 1991. It has grown to an enrollment of 500 students from Pre-K to grade 12.

AT A GLANCE

APPLICATION DEADLINE	February, then rolling as space is available
OPEN HOUSES	October and January and April
ISEE	Yes
UNIFORMS	Yes
BEFORE AND AFTER SCHOOL CARE	Yes
SEE MAP	B on page 255

ST. BRENDAN SCHOOL

238 S. MANHATTAN PLACE, LOS ANGELES, CA 90004
TEL: 213.382.7401 FAX: 213.382.8918

HEAD OF SCHOOL:	**SISTER MARTA ANN COTA, C.S.J.**
TYPE OF SCHOOL:	**CO-ED. CATHOLIC ELEMENTARY**
GRADES:	**K-8**
ENROLLMENT: 300	TUITION: $4,150 - 5,200
ACCREDITATION: WASC/NCEA	

ST. BRENDAN SCHOOL is an excellent choice for those considering a Catholic education for their children. It is under the supervision of the Department of Catholic Schools of the Archdiocese of Los Angeles. Their philosophy is to provide an academically challenging Catholic elementary education for the multi-cultural people of the parish. An integral part of the religious program is the monthly school mass which is planned by individual classes and held in the church next door.

I visited the school during the summer break. I dropped in unannounced, which didn't seem to concern the principal in the least. She invited me to look around and was very welcoming. However, the school secretary was not that happy at my unscheduled visit, and seemed a little agitated by my questions and wanted to hurry me along. So off I went on my own to explore.

I noticed a couple of teachers there and when I asked them what they were doing they explained that they wanted to get everything ready for the upcoming semester. The kindergarten teacher proudly showed me her classroom, which was bright and airy and full of brand new computers that had been donated by some of the parents. She explained that children in the kindergarten program were expected to be reading proficiently by the time they entered first grade, and that the curriculum was close to what you would find in any of the higher grades. The students are taught math, language arts, social studies, science, and health. Also included is an art and music program, physical education, and an introduction to the computer. I sure wish I had had a computer instead of struggling with an abacus.

I was introduced to the eighth grade teacher, a delightful woman who had introduced the 'Big Buddies' program to the school over fifteen years ago. At the beginning of a new year, each kindergartner is allocated a Big Buddy (someone in the eighth Grade). During the first week of school, the older kids come down and sing songs and introduce themselves. Over the course of the year, they do many things together. This tradition continues into first grade where they are given to someone in the seventh grade to keep an eye on them. This gives the little ones confidence and teaches the older kids patience and how to care for people younger than themselves.

The two-story facility is located in Hancock Park, on the corner of 3rd and Manhattan on a well-maintained street. It is well protected from the street with high metal gates out front and fences around the perimeter. I looked into the different classrooms which were all large and well-organized, so that any child would feel comfortable there. Since there is only one classroom per grade, each classroom is furnished with ample supplies. I was impressed by their earthquake preparedness guidelines which includes an out of the area telephone number where parents can call in case of an emergency.

There are two enclosed playgrounds. The large one is for grades 1 through 8 and includes basketball and handball courts and is divided into sections. The children are separated by grades and sex and are rotated through different areas during the year. The playground for the kindergarten is smaller, but it is well-equipped with many play structures on thick rubberized mats. Trees provide a shady area for the children to sit down and eat lunch. I noticed that the large playground also had many tables and benches, which were well protected from the sun. There is no kitchen at the school which means that children bring lunch every day, although there is a hot-lunch program which the parents organize once or twice a month.

Educational field trips are a regular part of the instruction. Classes are permitted to have one trip per semester. Students are admitted into St. Brendan School on the basis of availability. Whether the parents support the religious instruction by regular and active participation in parish religious practice and worship is also considered. They are required to participate in St. Brendan's Parent Service Program (30 hours), and help support the school by payment of fees and tuition.

The students are required to give evidence of a Christian attitude and to conform to all school regulations. They are also required to complete the required course of study and related assignments according to their ability. They must also have been baptized. There is a student council in the spring. Students in grades 4 to 7 elect students from next year's fifth through eighth grades as 'commissioners' to serve on a student board. The purpose of the council is to train students in leadership, to encourage a high standard of scholarship, to arouse school spirit, to demonstrate the practical application of democracy, and to advance the welfare of the school and its members. If elected, a student is expected to maintain a 'B' average. All other candidates for the various offices must have at least a 'C' average.

While reading through the Parent Handbook, I noticed a heading 'Mixed Parties' and I quote:
"Mixed parties involving the students of the upper grades, even when they are held at home or at school are strongly discouraged. Parents are asked to cooperate with this regulation, even though, strictly speaking, the matter of parent-sponsored parties is under parental control and not that of the school. The only exception to this regulation would be a school-sponsored graduation party having the approval of the pastor, the principal, and the parents."

You do not have to be a parishioner to be accepted, although I believe that being one would help in the admissions selection. While this school might not be for everyone, it is far more reasonably priced than many other private schools. If you are interested, I recommend visiting the campus.

HISTORY

St. Brendan School was founded in 1912 as a Co-Ed Catholic Elementary School.St. Brendan School is a Catholic elementary school founded to assist parents in their primary responsibility for the Christian education of their children. It is under the supervision of the Department of Catholic Schools of the Archdiocese of Los Angeles and is administered by a Sister of St. Joseph of Carondelet, and dedicated lay teachers.

AT A GLANCE

APPLICATION DEADLINE	First week of February
OPEN HOUSE	January
UNIFORMS	Yes
AFTER SCHOOL CARE	Yes
SEE MAP	C on page 255

ST. FRANCIS HIGH SCHOOL

200 FOOTHILL BLVD, LA CAÑADA, CA 91011
TEL: 818.790.0325 FAX: 818.790.5542
www.sfhs.net

PRINCIPAL:	**THOMAS MORAN**
PRESIDENT:	**FRIAR TONY MARTI**
DIRECTOR OF ADMISSIONS:	**JOE MONARREZ**
TYPE OF SCHOOL:	**ALL BOYS CATHOLIC DAY SCHOOL**
GRADES:	**9-12**

ENROLLMENT: 710

TUITION: $14,400

APPLICATION FEE: $75

FINANCIAL AID: YES

YEARLY REGISTRATION FEE: $650

ST. FRANCIS HIGH SCHOOL is located in La Cañada-Flintridge, off the 210-East Freeway. It has a wonderful view of the San Gabriel Mountains to the north and the Verdugo Mountain range to the south. La Cañada, La Crescenta, and Glendale have become popular places to live if you have teenage children and want them to have the same sort of freedom that most of us did growing up. Friends of ours have moved there, and I can see why. The public schools are among the best in the entire country, and they offer some of the best private school education, too.

My friend took me to see her son's school and we arrived during a break, and the place was teeming with students. The younger ones were outside eating lunch in the gardens surrounding the new performing arts center. The seniors have their own garden, which was very pleasant and well-manicured. They have no kitchen at St. Francis, but what they do have is a mobile kitchen complete with chef, thanks to S&F Catering. The owner worked out an arrangement with the school and parks his truck there all day allowing the children to order freshly prepared food at any time during the school day.

Six friars have been assigned to the school to assure a strong religious presence. They oversee a Christian Service Program requiring 100 hours of service from the students in order to graduate. It was rather heart-warming to see him being asked for some advice by a young student wearing pressed khakis and a polo shirt. Of the present members of the faculty (laymen and laywomen and religious) 14 possess Bachelor Degrees and 22 possess Master Degrees. Two have earned Ph.D. status and 21 are credentialed.

The Fr. Lawrence Caruso Memorial Learning Center is a beautiful library with over 7,000 volumes and mission-style furniture. I met the librarian, Sister Barbarine, a delightful woman who proudly showed me around and made me feel quite sure that my son would be well looked after if he ever needed help finding something. She had strict rules about how many students could be in there at any one time, and how they were to conduct themselves while under her watchful eye. Chairs had to be put back neatly, books returned to the shelves and absolutely no gum chewing allowed. She had never heard of schools allowing children to chew gum in exams to help them concentrate!

Next door to the library is one of two computer labs both fully equipped with up to date hardware and software. The school's website is completely student-maintained with minimal direction from the teachers. Both labs are available to teachers who would like the students to use them for class work. Like many private schools, they also have a 1:1 iPad program.

St. Francis recognized the increasingly important role technology plays in education and the work environment, and so the entire campus has been networked with internet access, and every classroom has a computer station, which is linked to the school network. Additionally, each desk in the biology and chemistry labs is equipped with the same type of computers for research assistance. All teachers have websites with grade books so parents can review progress in real time.

The classrooms, all well laid out and some with amphitheater-style seating, are cantilevered out over the hill with views of both the mountain ranges and overlooking the enormous playing field below. To get anywhere one has to use the myriad of outside stairways zigzagging down the hillside connecting all the various school rooms – not a viable proposition if you are using crutches or in a wheel chair, although after speaking to many of the students, I am sure they would happily carry someone who needed help!

Here is the course work by year:

Freshman Year Studies: Biblical literature, English 9 or honors English 9, geography, Latin I or Spanish I, algebra I or honors algebra or geometry; principles of science or biology; physical education and health.

Sophomore Year Studies: Moral foundation/Christian worship, English 10 or honors English 10, world history or AP, Latin II or Spanish II, geometry or honors geometry, biology or honors biology, physical education; introduction to visual and performing arts.

Junior Year Studies: History of Catholicism, comparative religions, American literature or honors American literature, Latin III or Spanish III or AP Spanish, U.S. history or AP U.S. history, algebra II or honors algebra II/trig., chemistry or AP chemistry.

Senior Year Studies: Christian life; British literature or AP English; U.S. government/economics or AP U.S. government and AP economics, trigonometry/pre-calculus or calculus or AP calculus or AP statistics, AP Latin I, Spanish III or AP Spanish, physics, chemistry and AP biology.

Junior/Senior Electives: Art, constitutional law, criminology, mass media, men's chorus, psychology, sociology, sports medicine, theatre arts.

In addition to the academic requirements for graduation, each student must have:

- A record of good conduct and citizenship.
- Successfully completed a course in religious studies in each semester of his enrollment.
- Attended a retreat during each year of his attendance and completed all required service hours.

Each family is required to give 25 hours of service during the school year, or they may opt to 'buy out' their assistance at the rate of $15 per hour ($375 per year). There is also the Annual Fund Parent Pledge and POSH or Mini-POSH (their annual fundraising event) which enables the school to buy new furniture when needed. Family service hours do not cover your obligations to support these development programs.

The school believes that in order for a young man to become a well-rounded person, who is not only academically developed but graced with an appreciation of the arts, he should be exposed to the influences on the style, techniques, and contributions of master artists in the different fields of the visual and performing arts. The school offers drawing, painting, and sculpture. There are museum trips for reports on specific artists and artistic styles. Students with vocal talents may join the Men's Chorus. The chorus performs in concerts, at choral festivals, for liturgical celebrations, and for numerous school-related functions during the school year. They often perform jointly with local girls' school choruses too. There is a drama course, and the school sponsors at least two productions during the year – a play during the first semester and a musical in the spring. Over the last four years, the Visual and Performing Arts Department has sponsored the Festival of the Arts, a week-long celebration which includes video and drama competitions, choral concerts, drama presentations, an international food fair, a swing night, art exhibits, literary magazine launching, comedy sports, and a battle of student bands.

St. Francis High School's athletic program is steeped in tradition, and the accomplishments of its athletic teams are impressive. The school replaced the grass on their football field with Field Turf, a synthetic turf with a rubber and sand base that is designed to simulate natural grass and dramatically reduce the number of sports related injuries. The drainage engineering allows the field to be used during bad weather. At the varsity and junior varsity levels, football, cross country, basketball, soccer, track, volleyball, and baseball are available to students. Golf and tennis are the other varsity sports. Football, basketball and track are also available on the freshmen/sophomore level. In all, the Golden Knights compete in nine different sports with the Mission League, which is part of the CIF Southern Section.

St Francis school has a variety of extracurricular activities. Among the clubs offered are: Art, Debate, Fishing, Asian-American, Dive, Latin, Astronomy, Drama Guild, Magicians, Comedy, Sports, Thespian Society, Roller Hockey, Computer, Film Workshop, Swing, Cheer, Filipino-American and Tennis.

The College Guidance Center utilizes a collaborative process that includes working closely with students, family, faculty, and administration on all issues relating to the college counseling process which is wonderfully helpful. Definitely worth a visit if you're looking for an all boys education.

A full 99 percent of students attend college immediately following graduation and of those, 84 percent attend a four-year college or university.

HISTORY

St. Francis High School was founded in 1946 by the Capuchin Franciscans. Their tradition is expressed in the ministry of St. Francis High School in regards to the family, church, and society. The Franciscan tenet includes promoting harmony, unity, and love in every special structure, the most fundamental of which is the family. The 'family spirit' is extended from each individual family to encompass the entire 'school family,' that is, administration, faculty, staff, students, and alumni.

AT A GLANCE

APPLICATION DEADLINE	January
OPEN HOUSE	January
TESTING	Only accept HSPT testing
DRESS CODE	Yes
SUMMER SCHOOL	Yes
SEE MAP	B on page 255

SAINT JAMES' SCHOOL

625 S. ST. ANDREW'S PLACE, LOS ANGELES, CA 90005
TEL: 213.382.2315 FAX: 213.382.2436
www.sjsla.org

HEAD OF SCHOOL:	DEBORAH DAVID
DIRECTOR OF ADMISSIONS:	JOAN HESTER
TYPE OF SCHOOL:	CO-ED EPISCOPAL DAY SCHOOL
GRADES:	PRESCHOOL-K

ENROLLMENT: 360
APPLICATION FEE: $125
ACCREDITATION: CAIS/NAES/NAIS/WASC

TUITION: $16,460 - 21,250
FINANCIAL AID: YES

ST. JAMES' SCHOOL is conveniently located between Hancock Park and Koreatown, situated on St. Andrews Place between Wilshire Boulevard and Sixth Street. It is a school at the crossroads of diverse Los Angeles communities and its student body reflects and celebrates that diversity. Every culture Los Angeles has to offer seems to be equally represented. Classrooms have between 20-24 students (two classes per grade level) and are fairly well balanced male to female and ethnically.

The school is under the leadership of Deborah David, a seasoned, enthusiastic, and passionate educator and school leader for many years.

Despite its urban site, the school has a spacious campus that includes a 15,000 square foot grassy field, a basketball court, handball courts, a play structure, and an enclosed rooftop play area. There is also an enclosed shaded courtyard. The school has a large multi-purpose room that is used for school assemblies and events, expanded classroom and learning space, athletics, and various shows and performances.

The Ahmanson Foundation library is truly outstanding, rivaling some university libraries. It is run by a dedicated librarian with the help of parent volunteers. Parents also contribute books regularly to the ever-growing collection.

St. James' has continued to expand and improve its facilities. The Science Lab is state-of-the-art with ceiling-mounted flat screens and a newly planted urban garden just outside the lab (cared for by parent volunteers). Consistent with St. James' curriculum, the garden is used to stimulate learning and provide "hands-on" opportunities for discovery.

A beautiful computer lab boasts brand-new Apple computers and up-to-date, research-based software. Under the direction of an energetic and creative computer instructor, children's time in the computer lab integrates art, language arts, math, and other academic skills. The computer lab also serves as home base for the yearbook team and video yearbook production. It is a lively learning center where students are challenged and inspired. St. James' is ambitiously extending its technology imprint, and additional Smart Boards are acquired annually (via parent fundraising) as are iPads. Technology is something the school takes seriously as an essential learning tool.

There is a wonderful art room. Perched on the second floor with lovely views of treetops and the exquisite church, the art room features an innovative retractable awning, opening the studio to a flood of natural light and fresh air.

The renovated art room will provide additional space for creative learning, an expanded outdoor patio area, and newly acquired tools for computer-generated graphic arts.

A well-conceived PE program with an emphasis on the importance of active and healthy lifestyles challenges students to enjoy sports and games at every age level and to pursue a lifetime of athletic enjoyment and exercise. St. James' is in the process of developing a competitive team sports program.

St. James' is now merged with an attractive pre-school program of the same name featuring a developmentally appropriate program of play, literacy and individualized learning. Situated close to the K-6 facility, the preschool has its own separate site with colorful play equipment, cozy classrooms, a loving and interactive staff, and enthusiastically supportive parents. In recent years, the matriculation of preschoolers to the elementary school (lovingly referred to by the preschoolers as "The Big School") has increased, making the daunting transition from pre-school and kindergarten much easier for St. James' families.

The school has had a reputation of being on the cutting edge of what's happening in education. A strong commitment to leveraging best practices across all grade levels has resulted in dynamic classrooms that are highly engaging and involving for students. In the primary grades, classrooms are organized into learning centers where children are frequently moving from one unit to another so as to create opportunities for learning in various modalities. Even in the upper grades (4, 5, and 6) it is not uncommon to find students working in groups, seated at group tables, and/or working with a teacher outside the classroom's four walls. The school boasts a traditional and academically rigorous program, but it is clear there is also a nurturing and 'whole-child' philosophy at work. A consistent theme of values and character education permeates the environment.

Although the families of St. James represent a wide variety of religious backgrounds, the school is an outreach of the education ministry of St. James' Episcopal Church. The religion program is based on Episcopal values and beliefs, but they have an inclusive approach to spirituality that includes recognition and respect for all faiths. A weekly chapel service for all students and the beloved monthly All School Chapel services warmly welcome parents who wish to join in the communal worship. Religion is taught in class each week, but is ungraded.

A gifted and child-centered playground staff and security team operate a tightly run ship that is safe, stimulating, openly affectionate, and inclusive. St. James' also offers a complete series of after school classes, many of which are taught by the faculty and include courses like sewing, cooking, art, science, chess, athletics, paper mache, ceramics, and more. St. James' robust and vibrant educational program is an exceptional value based on its currently modest tuition. All in all, the ethnically and racially diverse students of St. James' are bound by the school's values of mutual respect and genuine love. They are notably respectful, intellectually curious, and well rounded. Clearly, the growth and development of the individual is as important to the faculty and parents as the remarkable level of academic success the students achieve. With aspirations far beyond that of any "neighborhood" school, St. James' takes pride in the fact that the communities of Hancock Park, Windsor Square, Larchmont, Silverlake, and Korea town have all embraced the school as their own.

St. James' graduates matriculate to some of the finest schools in Los Angeles, including: Harvard-Westlake, Oakwood, Marlborough, Campbell Hall, Polytechnic (in Pasadena), Flintridge Preparatory, and The Brentwood School. The academic curriculum is demanding but the arts, music, science, and creativity are highly prized as well.

HISTORY

St. James' School was founded in 1967 by St. James' Episcopal Church. The original site of the school was on Gramercy Place between Wilshire Blvd. and Sixth Street. The school opened with five students in kindergarten. Additional grades were added as these students were promoted. The first sixth grade graduation class was in June, 1974. The school moved to its new campus on St. Andrew's Place in 1980. There are now two classes in each grade.

AT A GLANCE

APPLICATION DEADLINE	December 4
TOURS AND OPEN HOUSES	During the Fall
UNIFORMS	Yes
BEFORE AND AFTER SCHOOL CARE	Included in the tuition price
SEE MAP	C on page 255

SAINT MARK'S EPISCOPAL SCHOOL

1050 E. ALTADENA DRIVE, ALTADENA, CA 91001
TEL: 626.798.8858 FAX: 626.798.4180
www.saint-marks.org

HEAD OF SCHOOL:	JENN FOLEY TOLBERT
DIRECTOR OF ADMISSIONS:	JOSCELLE SHEN
TYPE OF SCHOOL:	CO-ED EPISCOPAL DAY SCHOOL
GRADES:	PRESCHOOL-6
ENROLLMENT: 340	TUITION: $4,750 - 16,730
APPLICATION FEE: $80	FINANCIAL AID: YES
ACCREDITATION: CAIS/WASC/NAIS	

SAINT MARK'S is a neighborhood school – big in heart and spirit. It is located on a tree-lined, residential street in Altadena. The administrative offices are housed in a quaint old craftsman house on the six-acre property. Head of school, Jenn Foley Tolbert, conducts the parent tour, complete with coffee and a parent-produced video about Saint Mark's for our viewing pleasure.

This place is an undiscovered gem for those looking for a private school education at a (comparatively) low price. The architecture is sixties style. The classrooms have been renovated and science/technology rooms have been refurbished. The art program takes place in the former garage (of the craftsman house), and aside from adding a kiln and lots of supplies, it still looks and feels like a garage. My guess is that much of the work is done on tables outside and considering our fine California climate, it probably suits everyone just fine. There are two playgrounds and several large, grassy recreational fields for the children.

Saint Mark's claims that it is not an academically-oriented school, and I found that to be true at the preschool/ kindergarten level. Children will not be sitting at desks with paper and pencil, and there is plenty of playtime scheduled for the younger students. The goal of the school is to have a happy and inviting atmosphere for a student body made up of children living in the surrounding neighborhood areas. Children are not selected academically. The school feels that testing students is inappropriate. However, by fourth grade students should expect an average of one hour of homework per night, and in sixth grade, two hours. When I asked to which schools the children matriculate I was told Polytechnic, Chandler, High Point Academy, and Westridge. The school appears to be traditionally academic, even though they seem to shun that label.

The school has a student community made up of families from many different ethnic and socio-economic backgrounds. Saint Mark's has a scholarship program that is sponsored by United Way enabling the school to offer a private school education to many children who could otherwise not afford one.

New buildings have been added to the campus providing the much needed space for the doubling of enrollment that has now been completed. One of the buildings provides a multipurpose area for the campus. Also added were two new fifth grade classrooms, one fifth, and a new science lab, a wonderful new building with high ceilings and great natural light. Smartboards have also been installed in classrooms. New early childhood and elementary playfields accompany the new buildings and renovations on campus.

The children take field trips twice a year, and in fourth grade take a two-day boat trip to simulate a pilgrim voyage to America. Before this trip the children learn nautical terms and, while on board the boat, call each other 'Mr. So & So' because they are told "there were no women allowed on ships at that time."

Chapel takes place twice per week in the church next door, and during the service the minister goes over the week's events. The music program focuses on developing a love and appreciation for sacred and secular music.

Here is the school's mission as written in the brochure:

> We believe that children unfold and flourish most effectively in an atmosphere which nurtures self-esteem, cooperation, and respect for original thinking. Our students are encouraged to become self-directed learners in a setting which is enjoyable, stimulating, and challenging.
>
> It is our desire to educate the whole child. We believe that the moral, social, and spiritual development of our students is of equal importance to their intellectual growth. Our programs are built around a respect for individual differences in talent, maturity, motivation, and learning capability.
>
> We strive by example and action to instill not only a joy and respect for learning but moral and ethical responsibility as well. Saint Mark's School encourages its students to become self-confident, direct in purpose, self-reliant in personality, and aware of responsibilities to self, home, school, and the world community.

The kindergarten has its own separate building and play-yard. The room, divided by a partition, is bright and cheerful, and the pitched ceiling gives it a wonderful, open-space feeling. The walls are covered with the children's artwork, and the whole atmosphere is very nurturing.

From Kindergarten to sixth grade, the curriculum includes: language arts, math, social studies, science, Spanish, physical education, and computer. Reading is taught with a blend of phonetic and whole language approaches. The school brochure gives a detailed account of the syllabus studied each grade level, including textbooks used.

HISTORY

Saint Mark's School was founded in 1960 by a group of parents interested in creating a neighborhood school teaching Christian values with a warm, home-like atmosphere and inspirational, nurturing teachers. Saint Mark's School is sponsored by Saint Mark's Church, from which it receives much support and encouragement.

AT A GLANCE

APPLICATION DEADLINE	December
UNIFORMS	Yes
BEFORE AND AFTER SCHOOL CARE	Yes
SUMMER SCHOOL	Yes
SEE MAP	B on page 255

ST. MATTHEW'S PARISH SCHOOL

1031 BIENVENEDA AVE, PACIFIC PALISADES, CA 90272

TEL: 310.454.1350 FAX: 310.573.7423

www.stmatthewsschool.com

HEAD OF SCHOOL:	**STUART WORK**
DIRECTOR OF ADMISSIONS:	**DANA BERLIN**
TYPE OF SCHOOL:	**CO-ED EPISCOPAL DAY**
GRADES:	**PRESCHOOL-8**
ENROLLMENT: 350	TUITION: $15,400 - 30,600
APPLICATION FEE: $100	NEW STUDENT FEE: $1,500
ACCREDITATION: CAIS/NAES/WASC/NAIS	FINANCIAL AID: YES

ST. MATTHEW'S SCHOOL is located one mile from the Pacific Ocean in Pacific Palisades. The thirty-acre campus, formerly The Garland Ranch, has rolling lawns and athletic fields, a swimming pool, tennis court, and old growth trees throughout. The grounds are well maintained and pastoral – not overly manicured.

The facilities are comprised of twenty-six classrooms, which include art and music rooms. In addition to the six classroom buildings, there is an administration building, a 10,000 volume library, and the church which serves as the chapel.

The educational approach is a traditional, academic one, with many of the eighth grade graduates going on to attend area prep schools such as Harvard-Westlake, Marymount, Marlborough, Brentwood, Crossroads, Buckley and Loyola. Saint Matthew's begins with preschool, and if you are seriously interested in enrolling your child, then this is the time to apply, rather than waiting for kindergarten when there are few (1 to 2) or sometimes no spaces available. Because there are so many applicants, this is a very difficult school to get into. Siblings are given priority if their families have demonstrated a significant level of financial support, commitment and participation in school events.

As an Episcopal parish school, the administration will take into consideration families that have joined the church, although you should plan on being members for at least two years before you apply to the school. The preschool uses a developmental approach for its three and four-year-olds and occupies five classrooms, a library, and four spacious play-grounds at the heart of the school's rustic setting. Children improve their skills through exploration of their environment and through hands-on problem solving. The classrooms are carefully prepared to accommodate individual learning styles and levels of development.

The curriculum integrates literature, art, music, movement, cooking, science, gardening, and field trips in activities that promote reading and mathematical literacy. At the kindergarten level the curriculum includes literature-based reading, language arts, a Writers Workshop, hands-on math and science, music, art, social studies, and physical education. There is a brand new science center for Kindergarten to grade 4.

The classes are self-contained and team taught. In grades 2 through 4, there are special subject teachers in art, music, computer, and physical education.

In terms of giving, service learning is a huge part of what they do at St. Matthew's. Students at every grade-level are involved in a variety of community outreach projects as a way to see life beyond their immediate family and school life. Parent involvement and giving can look like a lot of things depending what a family is comfortable giving. Some donate time, whether by serving on Auction or Town Fair Committees. Others give financially, in a wide range of ways. Some gifts are specific to a program (one family has funded a summer program for under served youth from the Neighborhood Youth Association or the Venice Girls and Boys Club to come to campus for a week long science and technology program, taught by a team of their teachers, using 3D printing, maker spaces, science equipment, robotics, etc.)

In grades 5 to 8, all students participate in an Advisory Program where groups of 12 students meet daily with a faculty advisor to plan school-wide activities, form teams for school projects, set goals, and review individual academic progress. There is an intramural sports program, and 7th-8th graders may also join competitive teams in volleyball, basketball, soccer, softball and flag football.

Students receive letter grades beginning in the third trimester of the 5th grade. By sixth grade, the program is completely compartmentalized with classes in English, mathematics, social studies, science, physical education, art, music, and introduction to foreign language. In seventh and eighth grade, students may choose between Latin and Spanish.

Preschoolers attend chapel once a week. All other grades meet twice per week. In addition, the school minister visits classrooms at all grade levels to lead age-appropriate discussions about the Bible and moral/ethical issues within the context of the Judeo-Christian tradition.

Enrichment classes are offered after school each fall or spring, the classes offered vary but have included instrumental music lessons, video animation, foreign language, chess and drama.

Field trips are scheduled twice per year for the sixth to eighth graders. The school puts on a Christmas program (K to 8), a spring play (5 to 8), and hosts a spring fair each May.

Mission Statement:

> St. Matthew's Parish School, an Episcopal day school, is an integral part of the Parish of St. Matthew, serving the children and families of the parish and larger community. The school provides quality education through a challenging, caring, and supportive program, developing intellectual, spiritual, and physical growth. Our purpose is to create an awareness that we are all children of God and to awaken in each student a sense of self as a significant, creative, and responsible member of society.

The school has a guard station as you enter the campus. The have a permanent guard who works for Gates Security and is assigned to St. Matthew's (i.e. same person every day). They have also added a vast network of cameras around campus, all of which the guard and both receptionists in the office monitor. The guard's station is fully equipped with phones, walkie talkies, and internet, so he can check in all visitors and report anything suspicious to Palisades Patrol or the police. Also all teachers/staff members on campus must carry walkie talkies, which enables them to immediately report anything that they might see suspicious on the grounds.

One of the great things about St. Matthew's is that their campus is so far removed from the street, and because paparazzi are not legally allowed on the property, they can't get close enough to take photos. Pickup and drop off occur on the "Loop Road." It's a private school drive that runs off of Bienveneda and up the hill. The Loop road is closed during the day by a gate and is only accessible to parent cars during carpool hours (though they must pass the guard to enter). Parents may either drive up that road to carpool or park in the lower lot and walk up to collect their child by hand.

HISTORY

Saint Matthew's Parish school was founded on May 2, 1949, through the efforts of six women who wanted to create a mission of Saint Matthew's Parish in the Palisades. It was accomplished with the help of The Rev. Kenneth Cary and Mrs. Eleanor Leach. It began as a preschool with 24 students.

In 1950, the school had grown to include grades K to 4 with a total of 105 students.
Shortly after, the school purchased The Garland Ranch, a beautiful 30-acre property which is the present site of the St. Matthew's campus. Today there are approximately 350 students attending.

AT A GLANCE

APPLICATION DEADLINE	December 18
OPEN HOUSE DATES	Preschool: October.; K-8: November.
ISEE TESTING	Requred for 5-8th grade
UNIFORMS	Yes
BEFORE AND AFTER SCHOOL CARE	Yes
SEE MAP	D on page 255

SEQUOYAH SCHOOL

535 S. PASADENA AVE., PASADENA , CA 91105
TEL: 626.795.4351 FAX: 626.795.8773
www.sequoyahschool.org

HEAD OF SCHOOL:	**JOSH BRODY**
DIRECTOR OF ADMISSIONS:	**AZIZI WILLIAMS**
TYPE OF SCHOOL:	**CO-ED DAY SCHOOL**
GRADES:	**K-8**
ENROLLMENT: 250	TUITION: $22,750
APPLICATION FEE: $100	FINANCIAL AID: YES
ACCREDITATION: WASC	

SEQUOYAH is located in Pasadena, at the corner of Pasadena Avenue and California Boulevard, with the 710 Freeway running behind the property. The campus has almost three acres of land with beautiful old pine, oak, and eucalyptus trees throughout.

There are four buildings and a science lab. The main building houses the four lower elementary classrooms, the library, and the administrative offices. Two additional buildings house the upper elementary and junior high classes. The Daycare House is a classic California bungalow, which was formerly a minister's house when the school facility belonged to a church.

The school has an outstanding 21,000 volume library with a vaulted ceiling, huge windows and lots of cozy reading areas (pillows and bean-bag seats) throughout.

The school teaching approach is developmental, based on the philosophies of Jean Piaget and Maria Montessori. Children are guided through their learning years as they are developmentally ready and not before. Emphasis is placed on social skills and working together as a group. When I toured the lower school, I noticed that the children sat on the floor rather than at desks while the teacher taught them. One child was lying in an old-fashioned bath tub filled with pillows reading a book while the lesson went on in the background!

The classrooms are generally on the small side, cluttered with toys, gadgets, manipulative learning tools, and artwork. Today, 250 students are grouped into multi-age classes spanning kindergarten through eighth grade. Sequoyah graduates are recognized for their resourcefulness, initiative and critical thinking, and the school community honors and reflects the ethnic, cultural and economic diversity of Southern California.

The students are clustered into age groupings, which reflect a three-year age span. Whenever possible, students remain in the same classroom for two years, which allows older students to aid and encourage the education of younger children, while demystifying the role of older children for younger students. Sequoyah students are grouped into seven classes. Each class comprises 23 to 26 students whose ages span two to three years. These multi-age groupings allow children to move at their own pace and encourage broader circles of friendship. This peer group enlarges to between 35 and 40 students in the Junior High. Placement is determined by assessing a child's maturity, academic progress and social needs.

The older groups have specialist teachers in science, math, and language arts, and part time teachers for Spanish, art, and music instruction. Every student gets daily exercise as part of the program and computer instruction is introduced starting in the 8 to 10 year old classes.

There are no tests or grades at Sequoyah. This baffled one mother on the tour who kept asking: "You mean my son won't be bringing any papers home?" She was concerned that there would be no way for her to know what and how he was doing in class. This mother was told she would have to put her trust in the system and ask the teacher those questions during the parent-teacher conferences scheduled during the year. This mother didn't look very happy about that – possibly she was not a candidate for developmental education.

Here is a description of the curriculum from the school brochure:

> Sequoyah School is based on an emergent curriculum from which academic skills are utilized by integrating programs and activities that evolve from a child's own interest, from his or her environment, from experiences in the family, and/or from the community at large. Learning is organic and is obtained through the integration of a variety of subjects.

Parent participation is required at Sequoyah. When you enroll your child you automatically become members of the Sequoyah Educational Center, the legal name of the school. The school is a parent-owned, non-profit organization run by an advisory committee of executive officers, elected committee heads, the school staff, and the director. All members of the school community have a vote and are encouraged to participate.

Parents are required to donate 40 hours per year to fundraising and maintenance of the school. Each family is also required to participate in the annual giving fund where tax-deductible contributions are based on yearly income. The standing committees are: Admissions, Finance, Fundraising/Grants, Fundraising/Events, Publicity, Parent Resources, Parent Education, Advance Plans and Maintenance.

Each family must contribute eight hours school maintenance, eight hours fundraising and 24 hours on one of the standing committees. Parents who are unable or unwilling to fulfill their work hours are billed $25 for each hour missed.

At Sequoyah, students learn that most complex and difficult issues are best addressed and resolved by working collaboratively, and often at the intersection of disciplines. Math, literature, art, and science are taught as related subjects. Teachers guide children to see connections, inside and outside the classroom. Activities are chosen to draw on each student's special interests and abilities.

HISTORY

The Sequoyah School is an un-graded, co-educational, humanistic school. Since its founding in 1958 Sequoyah has been committed to education that 'challenges the mind, nurtures the heart, and celebrates human dignity. A model school for open education, The Sequoyah School provides a non-competitive environment where students can learn at their own pace while still meeting solid academic objectives

AT A GLANCE

APPLICATION DEADLINE	January 16
OPEN HOUSES	October through January
SCHOOL TOURS	Most Thursday mornings Oct. through January
UNIFORMS	No
BEFORE AND AFTER SCHOOL CARE	Yes
SEE MAP	B on page 255

SEVEN ARROWS ELEMENTARY SCHOOL

15240 LA CRUZ DRIVE, PACIFIC PALISADES, CA 90272
TEL: 310.230.0257 FAX: 310.230.8859
www.sevenarrows.com

HEAD OF SCHOOL:	**MARGARITA PAGLIAI**
DIRECTOR OF ADMISSIONS:	**OMID KHEILTASH**
TYPE OF SCHOOL:	**INDEPENDENT DAY SCHOOL**
GRADES:	**K-6**
ENROLLMENT: 127	TUITION: $29,350 - 31,650
APPLICATION FEE: $125	FINANCIAL AID: YES
MEMBERSHIPS: CAIS	

SEVEN ARROWS SCHOOL is in Pacific Palisades and as you enter the gates it's as if you are entering into another world: a world of color, shapes, foliage, and laughter. There is an air of excitement about discovering this school.

Seven Arrows is an independent K-6th grade elementary school that offers an engaging curriculum. Their program motivates students, speaks to their broad –ranging curiosities, and encourages creative and critical thinking, as well as collaboration and initiative.

I was treated to a grand tour by several of the administration staff, including the executive director, Margarita Pagliai, and a passionate fifth grade teacher. I was quite impressed with this school, the staff the students, and their philosophy:

> The basic premise of a Seven Arrows Elementary School Education lies in the belief that the most powerful force in education is a love of learning. Our programs instill in each of our students a deep and lasting love of learning, the confidence to achieve one's best, and the knowledge that places one firmly on the road to a life full of purpose, meaning and endless opportunity.

> Our goals go beyond helping our students reach academic excellence. Our diverse, multicultural community of students, teachers and parents values respect for self, others and the environment, honesty, integrity, empathy, and responsibility. We share a deep commitment to promoting positive change in the world through the power of education and the power of our minds.

> The curriculum at Seven Arrows is both academically challenging and developmentally appropriate. They integrate various "pedagogical" styles to best foster the intellectual emotional and social development of the total child. The programs are infused with a multicultural awareness designed to engender a global perspective on learning. The result is a curriculum that speaks to the broad ranging curiosity of children, encourages creative thinking and promotes leadership.

I have seen integrated schools before, but Seven Arrows could be the poster child for this approach in action. For example, when learning about a culture, like ancient Egypt, mathematics, science, reading, writing and the arts are all integrated in the approach. The classrooms are set in motion. Children breathe history by creating pyramids or mummies. They live literature by reading stories and translations of ancient manuscripts or role-playing.

Native foods are eaten and students create art or design a national costume. Studies in history are enriched and reinforced with field trips and presentations by classroom guests who are experts on the target subjects. This culminates in school wide presentations, where they read the most important paragraph about their person in history, and display the costumes designed and co-constructed.

Every Friday morning there is a "Kuyam", a whole school gathering. This is held in the outdoor amphitheater type space, covered with a sail donated to the school by a competitive yacht team. Parents are welcome, and kids can perform. There are student bands. The children become very comfortable with public speaking.

One of the approaches that Seven Arrows uses to facilitate learning in the classroom is based on the theory of multiple intelligences. At the core of this theory is the recognition that each child thinks and learns differently. Therefore the approach is extremely individualized within a subject to make sure children are challenged and have assistance. Parents should ask the school to provide an in-depth explanation.

The arts program is incredible. It is fully integrated into whatever they are studying. Children choose a piece of artwork from the year to represent them in the yearbook. In fact, while studying California History, the fourth grade students were introduced to architect Frank Gehry of Disney Concert Hall fame, and created their own models of unique performance centers. The project finished with a gallery display of their work at the A&D museum, inspired by and dedicated to Gehry's Disney Hall.

A parent of a fourth grader gladly told me about her experience with Seven Arrows. "We were looking for a school that would go beyond worksheets and math fact tests. The kids here do advanced academics, hands-on history projects and art that appears in gallery shows. We've watched our kid blossom into a curious, intelligent thinker thanks to the unique opportunities and enthusiastic guidance."

Sixth graders have a community involvement project every week, and I got to see the spectacular results of their photography project. Each sixth grader also makes their own web page, on PowerPoint. They also make their own graduation video, and do all their own filming and editing.

The specialty classes include karate, music, drama, and of course art. Spanish is taught through emergence five days a week. Spanish is not taught academically because there are so many Spanish speakers. However, because of the ease of language acquisition at a young age, Spanish is intrinsic to math, communication and other studies. The specialty teachers are professionals in their fields, as well as educators.

History and Literature is the core of the curriculum. There are new components to the science curriculum, and brand new science and technology lab. There are computers, flat screens and projectors in the classrooms. The core curriculum for math is everyday math, which complements the spectrum math.

Seven Arrows offers choices within a structure. It is a small, and I mean small, nurturing, and loving school. Parent volunteers assist in for all manner of projects and events. In this way, parents may join their children, not only for the fun, but also for the education!

HISTORY

Colombian born and internationally educated Margarita Pagliai, Founder and Executive Director of Little Dolphins by the Sea Preschool and Seven Arrows Elementary School, opened the elementary school in 1999 both for her own children and because of increasing demand from Little Dolphins parents to create a school that would offer a continuation of the rich philosophy and global curriculum to which they had become accustomed. Margarita assembled a team of educators and students, and together they researched the most innovative and successful elementary schools and curricula from across the nation and around the globe.

What they found, along with the many wonderful programs, was a wealth of evidence highlighting the advantages of a small school environment. With the small school model as its core vision, the team designed the engaging Seven Arrows curriculum focusing on individualized academics and providing a balance between challenging academics and a stimulating arts program.

AT A GLANCE

APPLICATION DEADLINE	January
OPEN HOUSES	Call school to schedule tour
ISEE TESTING	Not required
CAUSAL UNIFORM	Yes
AFTER SCHOOL CARE	Yes
SEE MAP	D on page 255

SIERRA CANYON SCHOOL
LOWER CAMPUS
11052 INDEPENDENCE AVENUE, CHATSWORTH, CA 91311

TEL: 818.882.8121 FAX: 818.882.8218

www.sierracanyon.pvt.k12.ca.us
UPPER CAMPUS
20801 RINALDI STREET, CHATSWORTH, CA 91311

TEL: 818.788.8821 FAX: 818.709.8184

www.sierracanyonschool.org

HEAD OF SCHOOL:	**JAMES SKRUMBIS**
DIRECTOR OF ADMISSIONS:	**AMY CALVERT**
TYPE OF SCHOOL:	**CO-ED DAY SCHOOL**
GRADES:	**EARLY K-12**
ENROLLMENT: 995	TUITION: $13,900 - 33,850
APPLICATION FEE: $150	FINANCIAL AID: YES
ACCREDITATION: WASC/NAIS	

SIERRA CANYON is a private, independent college preparatory day school located on two campuses in the town of Chatsworth. The lower campus is peppered with large pine, oak, and eucalyptus trees, and surrounded by hills and open fields. It feels like you're in the country, instead of minutes away from a bustling valley community. Cofounder Howard Wang took me on a tour of the school, proudly pointing out all the school's facilities. The school has three science labs, library, computer labs, several play areas with climbing equipment, football and soccer fields, two swimming pools, and an outdoor crafts area. There is an outside eating area surrounded by orange trees, and a covered outdoor amphitheater.

Classes are small and individualized, all the teachers are credentialed, and assistant teachers are used throughout the program. The curriculum includes mastery of basic academic skills with children working in small groups at their own levels. There is also Sierra Canyon Television (SCTV), and a broadcast journalism class for grades 1 through 8. Student produced news shows are broadcast weekly via closed circuit television. There are specialist teachers in foreign language, computers, music, science, physical education, and art. Intramural sports include volleyball, softball, flag football, basketball and track.

Themes are introduced at the beginning of the school year and integrated into the lesson plan. For example, one year it might be the Middle Ages. This time period would be explored in history class, social studies, and perhaps the art teacher would design a project that explored the costumes/clothing of that time period.

The school's directors are involved in the school at every level, and it shows. The school referred to the students working together in small groups as 'teams' and noted that, "At Sierra Canyon, we work hard and play hard." The children and teachers that I observed were highly motivated and passionately involved in their work, and there was a team feeling in the classrooms.

Each parent receives a detailed chart at the beginning of the year describing every subject and skill that the children will be taught at every grade level. The curriculum is constantly reviewed and updated to reflect educational tools and methods that are on the cutting edge of the world of education. All teachers meet regularly with the directors to report progress and to make sure that they are on track with the yearly plan.

A student's progress is charted throughout the year on academic profile sheets. Parent-teacher conferences take place twice a year, and report cards are issued three times a year in grades Early Kindergarten to 5 and twice each year in the upper grades.

Sierra Canyon is a Blue Ribbon school and very proud of it. There are blue ribbons and United States Recognized School of Excellence seals on most of the school literature and on the walls of the administration building. The Blue Ribbon Schools Program identifies and gives national recognition to a diverse group of public and private schools that are unusually effective in meeting local, state, and national goals and in educating all of their students. Once nominated by the Council for American Private Education, a panel of educators visits the school and observes for two days, after which they compile extensive reports and make their recommendations to the U.S. Secretary of Education. The decision is based on conditions at the prospective school. These include leadership, student environment, student performance, teaching environment, curriculum and instruction, parent and community support, organizational vitality, student and teacher attendance rates, students' postgraduate goals, and school, staff and student awards.

Here is an excerpt on the school's philosophy and goals as written in the brochure:

> The educational experience at Sierra Canyon promotes the concept that each child is an individual. We respect the uniqueness of each learner. The pace may differ from student to student, the content may be presented at different times and in different ways, but all students will be guided to develop their thinking process to their fullest abilities.

Parents are welcome to volunteer in the classroom on a regular basis but participation in a parent training program is mandatory. Students are invited to participate in a field trip each year. Ski trips for the entire family are also planned several times throughout the school year.

HISTORY

Sierra Canyon School was founded in 1977 by Howard Wang and Mick Horwitz. The school grew out of a continuing desire on the part of the founding directors to provide a program which valued the whole child and in which the children enjoyed learning in a setting of mutual respect.

The school began as a summer camp and later become a day school with an early kindergarten to grade 6 program. Sierra Canyon completed construction on a new middle school building in 1994 and currently offers a college preparatory curriculum for students from early kindergarten through high school.

AT A GLANCE

APPLICATION DEADLINE	February
OPEN HOUSES	Call school for schedule
UNIFORMS	Yes
BEFORE AND AFTER SCHOOL CARE	Yes
SCHOOL NURSE	On duty during regular school hours
ISEE TESTING	Required for 5-12th grade
SEE MAP	A on page 255

STEPHEN S. WISE TEMPLE ELEMENTARY SCHOOL

15500 STEPHEN S. WISE DRIVE, LOS ANGELES, CA 90077
TEL: 310.889.2300 FAX: 310.476.2353
www.wise-school.org

DIRECTOR OF EDUCATION:	**METUKA BENJAMIN**
PRINCIPAL:	**ZAMI WISER**
TYPE OF SCHOOL:	**CO-ED REFORM JEWISH DAY SCHOOL**
GRADES:	**K-6**
ENROLLMENT: 450	TUITION: $10,065 - 24,995
APPLICATION FEE: $150	NEW STUDENT FEE: $1,250
ACCREDITATION: WASC	FINANCIAL AID: YES

STEPHEN S. WISE TEMPLE ELEMENTARY SCHOOL is located in the Bel Air hills near Mulholland and the 405 freeway. The facilities are modern and beautifully laid out on the 10-acre property. The classrooms are well-stocked, clean, and bright, with flowers planted along all the walkways so that the entire campus exudes a deluxe, top-of-the-line feeling.

There are two large playgrounds for physical education and recreational play. These areas have basketball, handball, and tetherball courts, along with special areas for kickball, softball, and soccer. A rooftop play area is available for the kindergarten and first-grade children.

The kindergarten also has special equipment including climbing bars, tumbling mats, and a gymnastic apparatus. The outdoor swimming pool is also available to the Milken Community High School students as part of their physical education program. There are two fully equipped technology labs, a library, art studio, two science labs, a music room and Project Studio. Stephen S. Wise Temple Elementary School integrates technology, art, and science into the social studies curriculum.

Stephen S. Wise offers a challenging, traditional academic program with each class having a credentialed general studies teacher and a Judaica teacher. There are four classes at each grade level with between 18 and 22 students in each class. Subjects are taught thematically.

For example, if children are studying the environment, they might build a mini-jungle to study the effects of the sun and the ozone layer on plants, animals, and organisms dependent upon them for survival. By the time they have completed the project, students will have:

- Used the library and technology to research the topic
- Incorporated math to build their jungle
- Applied biology, and science concepts
- May even have incorporated Hebrew into their work
- Used their artistic abilities

A typical kindergarten day begins with the children socializing and working in various 'centers' such as housekeeping, blocks, books, technology, science, a listening center and art. Then they have a group meeting to locate the date on the room calendar, record the weather conditions, and review the days' activities. Next comes language arts, reading (whole language approach), mathematics, and Judaic studies, where the children begin building their Hebrew vocabulary. In the afternoon, there is instruction in social studies and science. There are specialist teachers in art, music, technology, library, and physical education.

As a synagogue school, the rabbis and cantors are actively involved in the children's lives through classroom visits, Shabbat services, and creative bible programs. Students learn about their Jewish heritage as it is used thematically throughout the program in art, writing, history, and social studies.

The school hosts a Hesed Program to give children the opportunity to become involved in the community. Each grade adopts a community group to care about and to assist. For over ten years, as an example, fifth graders have dedicated their efforts to the St. Joseph Center for the Homeless. The children serve food, stock groceries, and help in the child care center at St. Joseph

The school philosophy:

> Stephen S. Wise Temple Day Schools are Reform Jewish day schools dedicated to the continuity of the Jewish people and to the intellectual, emotional, social, creative, physical, and spiritual growth of each child. As part of a Reform Temple, the schools are committed to individual autonomy in Jewish life, responsibility to the covenant between God and the Jewish people, and tikkun olam (the betterment of the world).

Students applying to the school do not need to be Temple members, however, it is necessary to join before the child is enrolled.

Parents are required to volunteer a fixed number of hours during the school year to support the school. The Temple Parent Association (TPA) is the official school-parent organization, and all parents are encouraged to become members. TPA members organize, supervise, and help at school activities and fund-raisers such as the Book Fair, Junior Olympics, traditional Friday yogurt days, uniform sales, and field trips.

Students at Wise Temple Elementary School continue middle and high school at the Milken Community High School which offers a disciplined academic curriculum in an individualized program. Students in the middle school continue to develop good study habits, critical thinking skills, and cooperative learning. Electives offered are computer science, the arts, and physical education.

At the high school level, courses become more challenging, and the students may participate in advanced placement and honors classes. Academics are supplemented with athletics, Judaism, and the arts. Stephen S. Wise Community High School is a member of the California Interscholastic Federation (CIF), and sports teams compete in a variety of CIF competitions.

HISTORY

Founded in 1977 by world-renowned educator Metuka Benjamin and visionary Rabbi Isaiah Zeldin, their goal was for every child to feel a deep and profound connection to their Judaism as well as the incredible world around them. Today, inspired and challenged by the cutting edge resources and faculty in place, our students are holistically supported to engage in and embody experiences of limitless creativity, depth of learning, and the Wise imperative to make great happen in our lives and our world.

AT A GLANCE

APPLICATION DEADLINE	February
OPEN HOUSES	Call school for dates
UNIFORMS	Yes
BEFORE AND AFTER SCHOOL CARE	Yes
SUMMER CAMP	Yes
SEE MAP	D on page 255

TEMPLE ISRAEL OF HOLLYWOOD

7300 HOLLYWOOD BLVD, LOS ANGELES, CA 90046
TEL: 323.876.8330 ext. 4000 FAX: 323.876.8193
www.tiohdayschool.org

HEAD OF SCHOOL:	**RACHEL LEWIN**
DIRECTOR OF ADMISSIONS:	**GLENDA DRAGIN**
TYPE OF SCHOOL:	**CO-ED DEVELOPMENTAL JEWISH DAY SCHOOL**
GRADES:	**K-6**
ENROLLMENT: 220	TUITION: $19,550
APPLICATION FEE: $150	TEMPLE MEMBERSHIPS: $1,325 - 2,340
ACCREDITATION: BJE/WASC	FINANCIAL AID: YES

TEMPLE ISRAEL is located in a tree-lined section of Hollywood Boulevard, in a neighborhood of well-maintained apartment buildings and old California bungalows. The building is a stone fortress that takes up a whole city block and, although surrounded by large, old trees, a decidedly urban school.

The classrooms are airy, modern and conducive to a calm and creative learning environment. One has the impression of much activity. Children are involved and completely engrossed in the task at hand, whether it be drawing, cutting, pasting, working with manipulative learning tools, or creating a science project. The children seem to be genuinely enjoying themselves and were so engaged in their various activities that they hardly noticed they had a visitor.

In addition to the teacher and aide, there was a parent volunteer. One child had his own helper (hired by his parents) to help him sort out any disputes he might have with the other children. I took it as a very positive sign that the school did not turn away a child that was working out discipline problems, yet required that the family take responsibility to provide extra help in the classroom. The approach at Temple Israel is developmental and the school philosophy is as follows:

> Temple Israel of Hollywood Day School is a private elementary school that provides children in kindergarten through sixth grade with a dynamic developmental education designed to serve the whole child.
>
> Understanding that the world is ever-changing, we cultivate resilient, adaptable students. Knowing that individuals best learn at their own pace, we help students develop the skills to read, write and compute -each at the right time. Awakened to human experience as rich with wonder and awe, we focus on discovery-based learning to develop active contributors and collaborators, engaging every learning style from verbal to musical to visual to kinesthetic. Housed in the heart of a loving and diverse Temple community, we inspire learning and innovation skills, honor and engagement in Jewish heritage and participation as world citizens.

Teaching methods are differentiated and teach to the many modalities of learning, but the curriculum follows the guidelines outlined by the California Department of Education. The school uses the Whole Language approach where children are guided to read for meaning while they learn reading skills. The classrooms are laid out in learning centers where children arc taught math and science with manipulative learning tools, study a community based social studies program, and explore art, music, and dance for appreciation and to learn about other cultures.

Individual expression is encouraged and nurtured. Physical education is taught for enjoyment and self-confidence rather than competitive performance. A love for Judaism and commitment to the Jewish people is developed through an understanding and appreciation of the values of Tikkun Olam (repairing the world), Mitzvot (commandments), Tzedakah (justice), and K'lal Yisrael (the Jewish people). Customs, rituals, and traditions are learned through the celebration of holidays. The Hebrew language is taught as the language for the Jewish people and as a way for expressing prayers. Children learn to read, write and speak Hebrew.

The school is affiliated with the Bureau of Jewish Education, and approved by the Schools Commission of the Western Association of Schools and Colleges.

Temple Israel Day School is growing fast and grades K through sixth grade each have two classes each. This school is going places, and now is the time to be part of this hidden gem before the secret is out and it becomes impossible to gain admission.

HISTORY

Temple Israel Day School was founded in 1989 by a group of dedicated Temple members and educators who were committed to establishing a school within the Reform Jewish Movement that would address the needs of the individual and his/her family. The child would be cared for and educated in a loving, nurturing environment where he can explore, investigate and discover the joy of learning. All this as their souls were being touched by the rabbis and teachers.

AT A GLANCE

APPLICATION DEADLINE	January 31
DAY SCHOOL TOUR DATES	October through December
DAY SCHOOL OPEN HOUSE	February
UNIFORMS	No
AFTER SCHOOL CARE/ENRICHMENT CLASSES	Yes
SUMMER CAMP	Yes
SEE MAP	C on page 255

TURNING POINT SCHOOL

8780 NATIONAL BLVD., CULVER CITY, CA 90232
TEL: 310.841.2505 FAX: 310.841.5420
www.turningpointschool.org

HEAD OF SCHOOL:	**DR. LAURA KONIGSBERG**
DIRECTOR OF ADMISSIONS:	**CHRISTIAN DAVIS**
TYPE OF SCHOOL:	**CO-ED DAY SCHOOL**
GRADES:	**PRESCHOOL-8**
ENROLLMENT: 350	TUITION: $23,821 - 30,579
APPLICATION FEE: $150	FINANCIAL AID: YES
ACCREDITATION: CAIS/WASC/CIS	

TURNING POINT students and teachers are enjoying their beautifully expanded, state-of-the-art campus in Culver City. It is located off the 10 Freeway near Robertson Boulevard. Building 1 is a two-story facility with a Library/Media/Research Center that includes a tiered storytelling room. The structure also houses Primary (preschool) and Elementary classrooms, wet and dry science laboratories, a full-size gymnasium, and an outdoor playground and lawn area. A playing field and outdoor classroom separate the original building and the state-of-the art Building 2. There you will find the Middle School classrooms, music specialists, language labs, and art studios that are enjoyed by students of all ages. The multi-media center comprises two labs; one with Macs, the other with PCs. One of two schools in Southern California, Turning Point also offers a Smart Lab equipped with technology for circuitry, graphic design, robotics, computer simulation, and more. A multi-purpose theater seating nearly 400 people tops off the new campus.

The multi-age Primary Division is a modified Montessori program; the classrooms use traditional Montessori materials and methods, with a focus on independent learning. Teachers determine each child's stage of developmental growth, which tasks have been mastered, and which challenges the child is ready to try. All Primary students visit specialists for music, Spanish, physical education, and library. Students remain with the same teacher during their years in Primary.

The Elementary Division and Middle School continue the focus on the whole child as an individual with experiential, hands-on learning. The two-year K-1 program is designed to aid the transition from Primary to Elementary. Students entering Kindergarten will stay with the same head teacher and assistant teacher for two years, and join Level 1 students for social studies and some study tours. In K-1, students have specialists for art and science in addition to those they enjoyed in Primary. At levels 2 to 5, children are grouped in classes of up to 18 with a head teacher and an assistant teacher. In the Middle School students are placed in small groups with an advisor who takes the place of the homeroom teacher and, in class sizes from 12-18 students, have different teachers for core academic subjects as well as specialist classes.

With a maximum of 18 students in a class, at each level, the curriculum includes reading, language arts, mathematics, and social studies, plus the specialists mentioned above. In Middle School foreign language, Spanish or Latin is a core academic class. Starting in K-1 there are study tours (approximately once a month) to museums, cultural centers, and regions of geographical interest, which the school believes builds on the classroom experience and instills a life-long love of learning. Starting in Level 4, students go on overnight trips. In Middle School extended study tours to the East Coast enhance their studies of history and government. Environmental science and global awareness is taught at all levels, with special emphasis in Level 7.

The School Mission Statement:

Turning Point provides a harmony between structure and freedom to guide each child through the many academic, creative, physical, social, and ethical turning points the school years present. We succeed when our students become responsible, well-balanced adults who are confident, honest, knowledgeable, community-focused, joyful, and well prepared to face a challenging and changing world.

The School Philosophy:

Turning Point believes that children will change, grow, and face the many turning points of life in ways that are different from each other. Because of this, the school has created and will maintain an intimate, focused learning environment committed to individually understanding and respecting each child.

In essential partnership with our students' families, Turning Point balances the many dimensions of a student's life in an integrated curriculum that develops not only the intellectual and physical skills, but also the creative, emotional, and social skills critical to success and active involvement in society.

Classroom instruction is the foundation, rather than the totality of a Turning Point education. Students are immersed in rich learning experiences that foster their innate curiosity and reward their ingenuity. Students are encouraged to embrace challenges as an essential part of growth, leading to the discovery of their own resourcefulness and abilities.

All the teaching staff holds baccalaureate degrees, and 19 members have advanced degrees. There is also an intern program for student teachers to work with the head teacher in each primary and elementary classroom. There is no school nurse; however, all faculty members have received instruction in first aid and CPR.

Turning Point has recently introduced a Toddler Program for children ages 12 - 28 months. This unique program builds upon Turning Point's philosophy of embracing the whole child and respecting diversity, and is facilitated by Babytalk LA, Los Angeles' preeminent Parenting Group program.

HISTORY

Founded in 1970 as a nonprofit institution, the school was originally named "Montessori of West Los Angeles," by a group of educators and business professionals who strongly believed in the education philosophy of Dr. Maria Montessori. In October of 1989, the name was changed to Turning Point to represent the series of turning points that children experience as they grow and mature.

AT A GLANCE

APPLICATION DEADLINE	December 11
OPEN HOUSES	Sept - Dec
BEFORE AND AFTER SCHOOL CARE	Yes
ISEE TESTING	Grades 5-8
SUMMER CAMP	Yes
UNIFORMS	No, dress code
SEE MAP	D on page 255

UCLA LAB SCHOOL

405 HILGARD AVE., LOS ANGELES, CA 90024
TEL: 310.825.1801 FAX: 310.206.4452
www.labschool.ucla.edu

HEAD OF SCHOOL:	**NORMA SILVA**
DIRECTOR OF ADMISSIONS:	**NANCY CHAKRAVARTY**
TYPE OF SCHOOL:	**CO-ED RESEARCH SCHOOL**
GRADES:	**PRESCHOOL-6**
ENROLLMENT: 435	TUITION: $12,476 - 18,715
APPLICATION FEE: $125	FINANCIAL AID: YES
AFFILATION: UCLA	

One of the most difficult things about this school (aside from actually getting in) is deciding on its name. It has been referred to as "SEEDS," "UES," "CORINNE A. SEEDS" and "THE UNIVERSITY ELEMENTARY SCHOOL." If you have heard any of those titles, then know that we are talking about the same place. It's settled, it's now called **UCLA LAB SCHOOL**.

The school is located on nine sylvan acres on the northern UCLA campus. The property is thick with old growth pine, oak, and eucalyptus trees. It has many grassy play areas and a redwood grove. Stone Canyon creek runs through the campus and is used by the students for both pleasure and scientific/environmental research. The red brick buildings, built in 1957, were designed for the school by architect Richard Neutra. There are state of the art classrooms, a beautiful library, community hall, dinosaur yard, playground and research studio.

The LAB SCHOOL is a laboratory of the UCLA Graduate School of Education. The approach is developmental, although being an experimental school, it does not fall neatly into any one category of educational style. Its primary functions are research, experimentation, and inquiry into the process of education. As a center of inquiry, the LAB SCHOOL has the responsibility of exploring and evaluating promising ideas related to education, innovation, and practice.

In this setting, researchers can study all aspects of the learning process, the curriculum, interaction between teachers and students and the effect of home-school relations on education, etc. Researchers use their findings to train teachers and administrators, to develop new programs for the school, and to educate the public at large on emerging educational trends. Since 1955, some research studies have been conducted at the school by UCLA faculty, and graduate students primarily from the School of Education and the Department of Psychology. They offer an Integrated Day Care Program, for the children of faculty-the intent of the program is neither academic enrichment nor baby-sitting.

Children are divided into four multi-age levels to allow each student to work at his/her own developmental pace. There are approximately 50 children at each level. The early childhood division is made up of 4 to 6 year olds, the lower elementary division has 6 to 8 year olds, middle elementary 8 to 10 year olds, and upper elementary 10 to 12 year olds.

The LAB SCHOOL is well known for its 'team teaching' approach to education. Teachers are organized into eight two-and-a-half person teams to encourage the transfer of skills from one teacher to another and to give children access to teachers with a variety of interests and abilities. Each teacher team plans and delivers instruction to approximately 55 students. The teaching teams meet frequently to coordinate curricular activities and schedules for their respective levels. This team approach permits teachers to have planning time, to work with individuals in small groups of children, and explore the interests of the children in an intensive manner.

Discursive Arts: Reading, writing, listening, and speaking are taught in an interrelated way because findings show that skill acquired in one area facilitates skill development in the others. Therefore, teachers at the LAB SCHOOL attend to all four, relating each one to the others, and showing how they work together.

Math: The LAB SCHOOL teaches math first through manipulation of objects, working from concrete to semi-concrete operations and then moving to abstract thinking. Staff believe that this progression is essential to develop a deep understanding of math concepts. The school is equipped with a full computer lab for the teaching of math.

Science: Science education at the LAB SCHOOL includes the three basic fields of physical, earth and life sciences. Science instruction integrates process skills, concepts and attitudes. To accomplish this integration, activities are organized around local environmental concerns. Children explore the natural and man-made world around them, test their ideas and develop the skills and attitudes needed to think scientifically. For instance, students may learn about computers by taking them apart and then putting them back together again.

Social Studies: Social education is viewed as an essential part of the overall education program. Students are provided with the opportunity to acquire the knowledge, abilities, and skills, as well as the beliefs and values that are needed to participate in the social, political, and economic life of their nation and the world. Students become familiar with the meaning and practice of democratic government, its institutions, historic values and requirements.

Visual Arts: Teachers stress the importance of aesthetics, studio art, art history, and art criticism. There is a spacious art studio and numerous field trips to museums, including those at UCLA.

The LAB SCHOOL prides itself on its anti-bias curriculum and for embracing innovations in education. In choosing students for admission, the school is seeking to create a group of children representative of the nation on a number of criteria including race, sex, exceptionality, parental education, occupation, ethnicity and family income. Wishing to include some children with special needs, the school has not yet fully realized this objective.

The school has a unique extended day program which takes into account the needs of each child for a program coordinated with, but not duplicative of, his or her academic experiences. Teachers and the program staff work together so that in the afternoon children have the opportunity to expand projects begun in the morning.

The afternoon program nurtures a strong sense of community, emphasizes values of caring and respect for one another, and encourages appreciation of each child's culture, language and ethnicity. For each group of 20 to 25 children, there are at least three adults, one of whom is the lead teacher. All the adults are highly qualified in terms of training and experience. The Program is entirely funded by parents. Parental involvement is encouraged through the Family School Alliance (FSA), and all parents are automatically members. The school sponsors many fundraising events with the help of the FSA, such as selling grocery scrip, the magazine drive, book fair, Spring silent and live auction, and Spring fair. FSA dues which can be anywhere from $20 to 500, or whatever a family wishes to contribute.

There are many celebrity families at the LAB SCHOOL. As you may have guessed, it is really difficult to get in if you are from a white, middle to upper middle class family. This group is overrepresented in the applicant pool and is flooding the admissions office with "please" and "why not?" It's a gorgeous school with excellent teachers and a comparatively low price tag for a private school education.

HISTORY

The Lab School was founded in 1882 as a training school for teachers at the location of the LA Central Library. In 1919, the school became part of the University of California, Southern Branch (the forerunner of UCLA). Throughout the 1930s until the mid 1940s, UES occupied classrooms on Warner Avenue through a lease with the LA School Board. In 1947, the Lab School moved to its current site at UCLA.

AT A GLANCE

APPLICATION DEADLINE	December 11
UNIFORMS	Yes
BEFORE AND AFTER SCHOOL CARE	Yes
SEE MAP	D on page 255

VIEWPOINT SCHOOL

23620 MULHOLLAND HIGHWAY, CALABASAS, CA 91302
TEL: 323.654.8958 FAX: 323.654.5214
www.fountaindayschool.com

HEAD OF SCHOOL:	**PAUL F. ROSENBAUM**
DIRECTOR OF ADMISSIONS:	**LAUREL BAKER TEW**
TYPE OF SCHOOL:	**CO-ED DAY SCHOOL**
GRADES:	**K-12**
ENROLLMENT: 1,215	TUITION: $28,000 - 34,000
APPLICATION FEE: $125	FINANCIAL AID: YES
ACCREDITATION: CAIS/WASC	

VIEWPOINT SCHOOL is located in the Santa Monica Mountains north of Malibu in Calabasas, and draws students from the San Fernando and Conejo Valleys and nearby coastal communities. After its acquisition of property (The Meadow School), Viewpoint school has grown to 40 acres.

The campus is surrounded by open mountain areas, with no town in sight for miles. The modern facilities include science and computer labs, art and music studios, a beautiful library containing 25,000 volumes, several athletic fields, two regulation-size swimming pools, playgrounds for elementary children, and a basketball pavilion. A 400-seat Performing Arts Center has significantly increased the school's ability to rehearse and to stage dramatic presentations, musicals, dance, and concerts. These facilities offer Viewpoint the room to expand its numerous programs in theater arts, dance, musical performance groups and classes.

It will be interesting to see how Viewpoint does expand its already award winning arts program with this new facility. Viewpoint won the coveted BRAVO award for 2005 in recognition of it's outstanding programs in fine and performing arts. The Music Center of Los Angeles sponsors this annual competition, which honors a school in L.A. with outstanding programs in the arts. This award is open to all pre-collegiate schools, public and private.

There are two Centers of Distinction: The Center for the Arts and The Center for Global Studies. Each center is based on the platforms of going beyond the classroom; advanced and interdisciplinary curricular offerings; project-based learning; and exhibitions and external outreach. A new Primary School was finished in 2015 and centers around Idea Labs, Makerspace, and 21st century learning techniques.

Hugely popular electives at the Middle/Upper level include: filmmaking; robotics; artificial intelligence; video game programming; statistical reasoning in sports; microscopy and biological imaging; biotechnology; behavioral neuroscience; global economics; world archaeology.

4 languages offered: Mandarin, Latin, French, Spanish. Travel/study trips to China; Italy; Greece; UK; France; Spain; Virgin Islands (marine science trip).

Viewpoint's kindergarten and primary school focuses on providing a nurturing environment with a variety of learning experiences to promote growth in all areas: social, emotional, physical, and intellectual.

The core of the Kindergarten through 4 curriculum is made up of language arts, spelling, reading, literature, arithmetic, science, penmanship, and social studies. There are enrichment specialists in French, computer, art, music and physical education.

At the middle school level (grades 6 to 8), teachers and administrators are specialists in education for early adolescents. Academically, the middle school builds upon the skills and knowledge learned in the lower school. There are accelerated math courses in grades 6 to 8 to challenge gifted students and accelerated science courses at the eighth grade level.

Extra curricular and co-curricular electives include photography, ceramics, painting, drawing, creative writing, speech, current affairs, chorus, instrumental music, computer animation, keyboarding, and dance. There is cotillion for the 5th and 6th grades, and there are dances for seventh and eighth grades.

Students put on a musical each fall, and several Shakespearean plays throughout the year. Students in grades 5 to 8 compete in flag football, basketball, baseball, soccer, softball, swimming and volleyball.

The students in middle school go on different overnight trips such as: fifth grade Astrocamp (three days), sixth grade El Camino Pines Outdoor School (three days), seventh grade Catalina Island (four days), and eighth grade the Yosemite Institute (six days).

The upper school core curriculum consists of courses in English, mathematics, social studies, science, and foreign languages. Electives include poetry, oceanography, environmental science, Asian history, computer science, comparative governments, international relations, psychology, economics, and speech.

Arts electives include instrumental music, chorus, music theory, music history, photography, ceramics, filmmaking, video, and drama. In recent years students have won local awards for their films, videos, and artwork.

The upper school offers honors and Advanced Placement courses to able and motivated students. Admission to these courses is by permission of the instructor, department head, and Head of upper school. The school offers the following courses:

Honors: Geometry, Biology, Chemistry, Algebra II/Trigonometry, Pre-Calculus; Advanced Placement: English language, English Literature, Calculus AB, Calculus BC, French language, French literature, Spanish language, Spanish literature, studio art, music history, biology, chemistry, physics, economics, psychology, European history, U.S. history, computer science and music theory.

Seniors may participate in a concurrent program with local colleges (Cal State, Northridge, and Pierce College), and may replace a portion of their regular course work with a special senior project. Past projects have included a study of Einstein's theory of relativity, research on tide pools in Santa Monica Bay, and an apprenticeship with an architect. Students are required to complete at least 45 hours of volunteer work outside the school as part of the Community Service Program. Activities in this program include feeding the homeless, helping children with learning disorders, and doing environmental work.

In the upper school athletic program, boys compete in football, cross-country, basketball, soccer, volleyball, baseball, tennis, swimming, and equestrian events. Girls compete in cross-country, basketball, softball, tennis, soccer, swimming, and equestrian events. There is a total of 20 interscholastic sports teams. Viewpoint's Varsity Boys Tennis and Volleyball teams both won CIF championships in 2005.

The school maintains that numerous debating numerous extracurricular activities develop the ability to work cooperatively with others and teach skills not always offered in the classroom.

These activities include the yearbook, newspaper and literary journal, speech and debating competitions, foreign language presentations, and theatrical and musical productions. Each year, the school hosts a foreign exchange program. High school students have lived for three weeks with families in Russia, Japan, China, France, and Spain.

Make no mistake, this is an academically competitive school. The scores of Viewpoint's students typically exceed the national average. Twenty-one percent of Viewpoint's class of 1999 were National Merit Scholars and the class of 1999s SAT average was 1315. Viewpoint typically achieves 100 percent placement of its graduates in four-year colleges and universities across the country. The information packet Viewpoint sends parents is remarkably comprehensive.

In addition to the normal information, it also contains grade distribution for the most recent graduation class, and the names of colleges to which the graduates have been accepted.

HISTORY

Founded in 1961, Viewpoint is a non-denominational, non-profit, independent day school that provides an enriched college preparatory program. Viewpoint offers a challenging academic program emphasizing excellence and achievement and providing individualized attention.

AT A GLANCE

APPLICATION DEADLINE	December 15
OPEN HOUSE	Oct., Nov., Dec.
BEFORE AND AFTER SCHOOL CARE	Yes
SUMMER CAMP	Yes
UNIFORMS	Yes
SEE MAP	C on page 255

THE VILLAGE SCHOOL

780 SWARTHMORE AVENUE, PACIFIC PALISADES, CA 90272-4355
TEL: 310.459.8411 FAX: 310.459.3285
www.village-school.com

HEAD OF SCHOOL:	**NORA MALONE**
DIRECTOR OF ADMISSIONS:	**ALEX LEE**
TYPE OF SCHOOL:	**CO-ED DAY SCHOOL**
GRADES:	**TK-6**
ENROLLMENT: 290	TUITION: $29,536
APPLICATION FEE: $125	NEW STUDENT FEE: $2,000
ACCREDITATION: CAIS/WASC	FINANCIAL AID: YES

THE VILLAGE SCHOOL is located in the heart of the Palisades Village on two beautiful campuses. The main campus, a three-story building, houses sixteen classrooms, plus Spanish classrooms, a science lab, the library, and several offices.

The Center for the Arts and Athletics, around the corner from the main campus, contains a multi-purpose gym/auditorium, music room with recording studio, visual arts room, and a dance studio. The location also provides children with more grassy areas, although P.E. also regularly uses the local public park.

The Village School has a strong academic curriculum taught in small classes beginning at transitional kindergarten. The approach here is progressive (as opposed to traditional), with children moving to the next stage of learning when they are developmentally ready. The children experience language, math, science, social studies, art, music, and physical education and study the relationships to one another.

Children learn the basics of phonics and language expression through textbooks together with discussion, dictation, drawing, and writing. Students are introduced to a new letter per week, practice rhyming and opposites through whole language activities, and learn to form letters correctly. Reading is taught in small groups when children are ready.

The Village School operates on a trimester system. Report cards are given after each trimester. TK through Second Grade have a checklist of acquired skills and letter grades begin second trimester of Third grade. Conferences between parents and teachers are scheduled at the end of the first two trimesters.

Student activities include: student council, spirit days, and community service projects. Each year the school hosts a Back to School Picnic, Halloween Carnival, Open House, with an Art Show, Science Fair and Sports Day.

The school offers three types of after-school programs. Each trimester, students may sign up for any number of after-school clubs including (but not limited to) drama, dance, cooking, or science. The after-school sports program begins in Fourth grade and the school belongs to a league of other schools, which includes competition in flag football, basketball, volleyball, and soccer.

HISTORY

Village School was founded in 1977 by a group of parents who were committed to building a strong neighborhood school for their children. The school has had several homes in Pacific Palisades over the years before settling in its current location. We celebrate all that we have accomplished and look forward to the future with eager anticipation. Dave Thomsen was one of the original founders of Village. He took out an ad in the Palisadian Post calling for an alternative to public education. In the years since its inception, Village has truly become a neighborhood school and an active participant in the community.

The main Village School building was constructed in 1994. It included TK-6th grade classrooms, a library with over 10,000 books, a technology center and a science lab. In 2007, construction was completed on the new center for the arts and athletics, which includes a gymnasium, visual arts studio, music studio, and performance space as well as a dance studio. The attractive campus is now home to 290 students and supports Village School's vibrant and engaging curriculum and extracurricular opportunities.

AT A GLANCE

APPLICATION DEADLINE	December 1
OPEN HOUSE	October through November
UNIFORMS	No, but dress code is enforced
BEFORE AND AFTER SCHOOL CARE	Yes
SEE MAP	D on page 255

VISTAMAR SCHOOL
737 HAWAII STREET, EL SEGUNDO, CA 90245
TEL: 310.643.7377 FAX: 310.643.7371
www.vistamarschool.org

HEAD OF SCHOOL:	**KAREN ESHOO**
DIRECTOR OF ADMISSIONS:	**PATRICIA GOODEN-BERGER**
TYPE OF SCHOOL:	**CO-ED DAY SCHOOL**
GRADES:	**9-12**
ENROLLMENT: 280	TUITION: $34,900
NEW STUDENT FEE: $1,750	DEPOSIT: $1,500
BOOKS AND MISC: $400 - 700	FINANCIAL AID: YES

VISTAMAR SCHOOL, the first independent co-educational high school in the South Bay area, began as a spark of an idea discussed by a small but ambitious group of women who met in a Manhattan Beach eatery. The location they chose for the school was a good one. Taking up 7,600 square feet of the old Direct TV warehouse in El Segundo offered convenient access to surrounding communities, including Manhattan Beach, Redondo Beach, and Hawthorne, the 405 and 105 freeways and the green Line.

Before you think this is some elitist type school, let me tell you the inaugural class was small. The pioneer class of students (44 in ninth grade and ten in the tenth grade) came from 21 different middle and high schools in 13 different communities. Half are boys and half are girls, and a third represent ethnic minorities. They are looking for students to help shape this community, and build it into something.

Vistamar School empowers students, preparing them to contribute and excel in higher education, and commit to:

- A broad and balanced program that challenges and engages students, building individual skills and inspiring a passion for learning.
- An intimate atmosphere that fosters initiative, responsibility, knowledge of self, and connection to others.
- Diversity of thought and culture that encourages authentic exchange of perspectives, mutual respect, and a mature understanding of the world.

But what about the classes themselves? Here is the academic program overview:

You will notice there is a minimum of three years of a language, and there's language available for 'heritage speakers' that allows students to develop academically in their 'mother tongue' and be fully bilingual. Mathematics is also considered a language instead of a set of procedures. Overall, there is a strong sense of dialogue. In the tenth grade, there is a special course in Forensics, and a class to learn speech writing and public speaking.

Vistamar also recognizes the important link between math and science. Students will study biology, physics, and chemistry for three years starting in tenth grade, having a trimester each. The science lab is one of the most impressive I've seen in a while. There are banks of computers for student use in common areas and a dedicated server ensures parents remote access. Students are able to log on to their teachers web pages for notes, assignments, and links, and an extensive database of journals, reference materials, and text books are also available online.

Also unique to Vistamar are seminars, which students and teachers take together. For example, they may all sit in on a lecture about 'Visual Literacy' and then open a dialogue about the subject . Teachers are also available in the many common areas for help and informal teaching/tutoring in any given subject.

Vistamar requires every student to be physically active, and have a variety of fitness electives. Sports teams include: basketball, baseball, cross-country, golf, soccer, tennis, lacrosse, volleyball, and water polo. However, if they are involved in an after-school fitness activity such as martial arts or dance, this can count towards this requirement. This is an attempt by the school to address an often-overlooked issue, that schools don't really respect a student's time.

There are also high expectations of the teachers. They are expected to spend a lot of time with their students (so they must really like kids!). Diversity is not limited to the student body and the faculty has global experience as well. Vistamar may or may not be right for you, but I highly recommend visiting this school. You will learn a lot about education just from the visit/tour.

HISTORY

Vistamar is an independent, co-educational high school that opened its doors in September of 2005. It offers parents another option in a region where educational choices have failed to keep pace with the gradual rise in the number of families in the South Bay area.

The founding Board of Trustees appointed Jim Buckheit as Head of School in 2004. Prior to Vistamar, Mr. Buckheit served as Head of School at several schools in the U.S. and abroad. As founding Head, Mr. Buckheit played a pivotal role in creating Vistamar's curriculum, combining the best traditions of American independent schools with exemplary practices drawn from other education systems around the world. Mr. Buckheit also set the highest standard for faculty by recruiting only those who demonstrated the highest level of expertise in their curricular fields and in teaching. That tradition has continued and expanded as the faculty has grown to accommodate enrollment.

Today, Vistamar has graduated eight classes, beginning with the class of 2008. Vistamar alumni have been accepted at the nation's best colleges and universities and are making their mark as global citizens on their campuses and in their fields.

Following Jim Buckheit's retirement in 2011, the Board of Trustees unanimously appointed Karen Eshoo as Head of School. Ms. Eshoo, an independent school educator and administrator for over 20 years, most recently served as Assistant Head of School at Lick-Wilmerding High School in San Francisco. In her fifth year as Vistamar's Head of School, her key focus is on enrollment growth and campus expansion while maintaining Vistamar's connected school culture.

AT A GLANCE

APPLICATION DEADLINE	February with rolling admissions
OPEN HOUSES	October
ISEE TESTING	Nov., Dec., Jan. & April
SEE MAP	E on page 255

WALDEN SCHOOL

74 S. SAN GABRIEL BLVD., PASADENA, CA 91107
TEL: 626.792.6166 FAX: 626.792.1335
www.waldenschool.net

HEAD OF SCHOOL	**MATT ALLIO**
DIRECTOR OF ADMISSIONS:	**SARAH LOUGHEED-GILL**
TYPE OF SCHOOL:	**PROGRESSIVE DEVELOPMENTAL**
GRADES:	**K-6**
ENROLLMENT: 118	TUITION: $12,995 - 19,880
APPLICATION FEE: $125	NEW FAMILY FEE: $1,250
REGISTRATION FEE: $150	FINANCIAL AID: YES

WALDEN SCHOOL is located in a self-contained, urban setting in Pasadena. The school purchased an additional building just north of the original in 1999. They now have a library with over 9,000 volumes, a huge dedicated art studio, three new classrooms (one of which includes a science lab), and business and development offices. Walden's learning environment is unique, creative, and enchanting.

The educational approach here is developmental and draws on the philosophies of Henry David Thoreau, Socrates, Jean Piaget, John Holt, Marcy Cook, Carl Rogers, Abraham Maslow, and Maria Montessori. Children are divided into six multi-age groups in class sizes of between 13-22 students as follows:

- Preschool: 3-5 year-olds
- K-1st grade: 5-7 year-olds
- 1-2nd grade: 7-8 year-olds
- 2-3rd grade: 8-9 year-olds
- 4-5th grade: 9-11 year-olds
- 5-6th grade: 12-13 year-olds

In this setting, children are encouraged to learn at their own individual pace through the teacher's guidance and by a collaboration created by the teacher and student.

Walden students select learning materials and activities from a selection provided by the teacher. They then have an agreement to work with what they have chosen. By the elementary grades, Walden students and their teachers agree on the kind and amount of academic work that will be accomplished, and children are responsible for planning their time accordingly.

Walden's approach is based on the concept that even very young children are able to plan and carry out learning activities. Walden teachers support this development of the children. The teacher and students have conferences and outline the appropriate amount of work in each subject each day. When the agreed work for the day is complete the child can then pursue other interests including special projects, extra work in a favorite academic area, library time and other activities, which give the child control of his learning. Thus, the structure of the school day provides its own reward for efficient use of time.

Walden students are also asked to abide by a series of clearly stated agreements, which outline the principles of living and working in a group. From time to time children will forget or disregard the rules and are confronted with the logical consequences of their actions, which are never humiliating or demeaning.

When a Walden child breaks an agreement, he or she is expected to find a way to make restitution. A child who breaks work materials will be expected to help repair it. A child who hurts another will be asked, "What can I do to help you feel better?" A child who drops a piece of trash may be asked to pick it up and another piece as well. In this way, the child's self-esteem remains intact. He learns that when a mistake is made, he can repair the damage.

Each child is responsible to the group, yet is a valuable individual. Walden, while founded on Montessori principles, is not a Montessori school. The learning theories, materials, and strategies of the this approach allow children to select materials from those provided by the teacher and to move at his/her own pace. Specialists teach music, Spanish, art, physical education, sports, dance, yoga, and movement. Walden has a library manager with a resident storyteller as part of their language arts program.

HISTORY

Walden School was founded in 1970 by Marilyn Nikimaa and Ted Calleton as a non-profit, independent, co-educational elementary school with a Montessori base and multi-age classrooms. From 1970 through 1989, located in leased space in the basement of a church in Pasadena, Walden School enrolled approximately 100 students in Pre-Kindergarten through 6th grade. In 1976, Walden was accredited by the California Association of Independent Schools. Additionally, we enjoyed a reputation in the Pasadena area for having a strong developmental emphasis. The "Walden Agreements" were developed during this period to help guide the quality of relationships expected at school.

AT A GLANCE

APPLICATION DEADLINE	January
OPEN HOUSES	October - December
SCHOOL TOURS	Wednesdays in the fall, check website
BEFORE AND AFTER SCHOOL CARE	Yes
SEE MAP	B on page 255

THE WAVERLY SCHOOL

Elementary School
67 W. BELLEVUE DRIVE, PASADENA, CA 91105
TEL: 626.792.5490 FAX: 626.683.5460

Middle School
120 WAVERLY DRIVE, PASADENA, CA 91105
TEL: 626.792.5940 FAX: 626.683.5460

Upper School
108 WAVERLY DRIVE, PASADENA, CA 91105
TEL: 626.792.5940 FAX: 626.584.8531

www.thewaverlyschool.org

HEAD OF SCHOOL:	**HEIDI JOHNSON**
DIRECTOR OF ADMISSIONS:	**JENNIFER DAKAN**
TYPE OF SCHOOL:	**CO-ED DAY SCHOOL**
GRADES:	**JK-12**
ENROLLMENT: 320	TUITION: $13,620 - 27,840
APPLICATION FEE: $75	FINANCIAL AID: YES
ACCREDITATION: WASC/CAIS	

WAVERLY SCHOOL is located on a quiet street in an industrial/business section of Pasadena. The two-story facility looks more like an office building than a school campus, but if you let appearances fool you, you may miss out on one of the best schools in Pasadena. The building has eight classrooms, a library, cooking area, community room, teachers lounge, reception area, and administrative offices. The outside play area (along the side and back of the school) has a basketball court, climbing structure, and swings as well as a shaded lunch area.

Waverly has a staff of some of the most outstanding educators in the greater Los Angeles area. The educational approach at Waverly is a blend of progressive and developmental, employing the philosophies of John Dewey and Jean Piaget. Children are divided into multi-age groups rather than grades. The focus is on working together, cooperating as a group, and being members of a democratic society.

Based on the findings of Jean Piaget and the teachings of John Dewey, Waverly's educational philosophy asserts that students learn best when they are actively involved in their education, when they become responsible for their growth as students, and when their learning is based on life experiences. Waverly expects its students to work at the highest level of which they are capable, and when their learning is based on life experiences, and because children and young adults learn in developmental stages, Waverly aims to have each student satisfactorily complete each stage before moving on.

A Waverly education incorporates all aspects of human development—intellectual, social, physical, aesthetic, and moral—and integrates learning by guiding students to be curious about all that the world has to offer. Waverly students build skills in mathematics, reading, writing, and critical thinking, while developing an appreciation for the arts, humanities, and sciences. Students develop a strong sense of themselves as individuals and as members of a close community.

Waverly is a small community, permitting students and faculty to know one another well. Frequent group work in classes enables students to teach and learn from one another. All students work individually, in small groups, and as a whole class. This close community allows teachers to create developmentally appropriate and interdisciplinary curricula.

The School is committed to the creation and maintenance of a peaceful and secure atmosphere, and to the non-violent resolution of problems and conflicts. Social development issues are addressed as students learn how to get along and be responsible within the school community.

Waverly believes it is essential for students to develop a commitment to the larger community. Through the curriculum and Waverly's community service program, it is their goal that students recognize the importance of their active participation in local, state, national, and global issues. With a rich educational program as a foundation, students can contribute positively to the world in which they live.

The School embraces diversity and values the integrity of the individual. Differences of religion, national origin, race, ethnicity, sexual orientation, socioeconomic status, culture, gender identity, and physical appearance are acknowledged and respected. Everyone strives to behave in a sensitive, tolerant, and respectful manner.

A diverse student body is an essential component of an experiential education. Students are most able to understand, appreciate, and respect differences in a setting that includes these differences. Waverly seeks a diverse community in order to fulfill its mission to provide a strong, humanistic education for all students.

Curriculum Outline

The Primary Grades
The social studies core themes begin with the two smallest units of the society—the individual and the family. Work and play enable the children to explore their personalities, likes and dislikes, and physical appearances.

This exploration expands to a study of the family, neighborhoods, and transportation systems. Mapping becomes an important part of learning. Construction of model neighborhoods and the science of structures joins an examination of the city's transportation system.

During these years, students learn to read and write at their own pace in a language-experience approach, and mathematical concepts move from the manipulative stage to the written record stage. Science begins as a process of discovery and grows into a practice of experimentation. Drama, art and music are integrated into all aspects of the social studies core theme.

Upper Elementary, Grades 1-6
The social studies curriculum expands to explore the study of the cities within our city: food, music, literature, and culture of the many ethnic groups in our area are experienced and enjoyed. Students begin exploring the history of California. Themes such as California Native Americans, the Gold Rush, Westward Expansion and the Urban Explosion, allow students to study primary sources, play simulation games, and write about other time periods.
Reading is literature based with an emphasis on discussion and analysis of quality writing. Mathematical skills continue to develop with equal emphasis on computation and higher level thinking, problem solving, and logic. The arts become more important as students' level of sophistication increase. Scientific skills of conjecture and analysis are added to observation and experimentation to develop better understanding of the scientific method.

The Middle School, Grades 7-8
The humanities is the general theme for these grades. Students explore the human experience on a national and global

scale. Important world history periods, such as the Renaissance, the Roman Empire, and the Industrial Revolution are studied in depth, with constant comparisons made to life today. War, racism, injustice, and freedom are some of the issues examined through the use of literature, film, music, and drama.

Writing and reading skills are developed through intensive analysis of classic literature. Mathematical skills are guided toward preparation for algebra and geometry. Waverly does work to address parent concerns and this year they were able to offer Algebra I through the generous services of a parent mathematician. As beginning scientists, students employ the scientific method to formulate hypotheses, implement experiments, and draw conclusions.

The Upper School, Grades 9-12

The upper school grades 9 through 12, began in 1994 and concentrates on two primary goals namely preparation for the demands and discipline of the college experience, and development of the necessary interpersonal skills for graduates to become active, responsible, thinking, caring members of society. In the high school, the class sizes are small with ten students per grade. With all the extra attention, students have graduated and found their way into top colleges and universities.

The Waverly Farm (at 679 South Pasadena Avenue; walking distance from the school) is an outdoor classroom, not necessarily related to farming. Teachers take their classes to the Farm to write, observe wild life, and conduct science experiments. A plot for each classroom is available if desired by the teacher. The Waverly Organic Farm exists to allow students, their families, their teachers, and the broader community to engage nature on multiple levels. The scope of participation in the life of the Farm is broad, ranging from active cultivation and organic production to inventive play, hands-on learning, and simple appreciation of nature. The Farm also creates opportunities for elementary, middle, and high school students to interact in ways that nurture cross-generational mentoring, leadership skills, and social harmony. The intent is that the Farm be inspirational, experimental, educational, and sustainable.

Children run, climb, dig, poke, observe, and actively explore a variety of existing environments. The essence of the space is that it is complex, protected, and ever evolving, which is valuable in and of itself and raises multiple possibilities, each worthy of pursuit. The Farm continues to develop, grow, and nurture the community, as well as provide new and expansive uses from year to year.

HISTORY

The Tiger Tots Children Center was created as a preschool by Gayle Thompson in 1984. In 1993, it became The Waverly School K-6, and in 1996 expanded to include Young Kindergarten through Grade 12.

AT A GLANCE

APPLICATION DEADLINE	February 1
SCHOOL TOURS	October through January
UNIFORMS	No
BEFORE AND AFTER SCHOOL CARE	Yes
SUMMER CAMP	Yes
SEE MAP	B on page 255

THE WESLEY SCHOOL

4832 TUJUNGA AVE, NORTH HOLLYWOOD, CA 91601

TEL: 818.5084542 FAX: 818.508.4570

www.wesleyschool.org

HEAD OF SCHOOL:	JOHN WALTER
DIRECTOR OF ADMISSIONS:	VERENA DENOVE
TYPE OF SCHOOL:	CO-ED DAY SCHOOL
GRADES:	K-8
ENROLLMENT: 118	TUITION: $22,385 - 25,150
APPLICATION FEE: $125	NEW FAMILY FEE: $1,250
REGISTRATION FEE: $150	FINANCIAL AID: YES

THE WESLEY SCHOOL was founded in 1999 and is located on four acres at the First United Methodist Church of North Hollywood. I have met some Wesley parents who take a lot of pride in their involvement with teachers and administrators in helping the school get up and running. They have created a warm, wholesome environment, and the admissions process is not intimidating. The classrooms are a good size, there is a computer lab, and my favorite, a cedar library. The library reminds me of a woodsy cabin, a place where you would like to sit with a book.

Drama, yearbook, media arts, and mock trial are electives offered in 7th and 8th grades. Spanish is taught beginning in kindergarten and continues through 8th grade.

The middle school is completely departmentalized for seventh and eight grades. To allow for this transition, the sixth grade has two teachers for their academic core subjects with additional teachers for their enrichment classes. In eighth grade, students may elect to participate in a mock trial competition sponsored by the Constitutional Rights Foundation. I had the pleasure of witnessing one of these at an open house and could not have been more impressed. Students can participate in the after-school athletic program beginning in the fourth grade. The students compete in basketball, soccer, volleyball, cross-country, flag football, and golf. Wesley belongs to both the San Fernando Valley league and the Delphic league.

The Chapel program is anchored in the Judeo-Christian tradition and students are encouraged to respect all religions. All students participate in chapel together three days a week. The Chapel program includes non-religious ceremonies and celebrations such as birthdays and academic and athletic accomplishments.

The Parent Association is very active. It is responsible for supporting the faculty and administration in many extra curricular activities including helping in the library, serving hot lunch, putting on both Halloween and winter holiday events, middle school dances and countless other wonderful extras. Every parent is a member, and the school expects every family to participate in the school community. Head of school, John Walter, elaborates about the importance of parent involvement, "Our children watch us--the adults in their lives--very closely. Parents and educators must work together to ensure that we conduct ourselves in ways that provide children with consistent messages and values. The Wesley School prides itself justifiably on parent involvement and communication. Given new technology, our opportunities to increase communication and involvement are immense, but so are the risks of creating distance. We do not take our relationships lightly or for granted, and I see a future in which that bond remains strong and mutually supportive."

I have such warm feelings for this school because when I'm out with my children at sporting events or other activities we always seem to run into students from Wesley, and without fail I find them to be friendly, honest, and unaffected.

HISTORY

The Wesley School was established in 1999 as a successor to St. Michael and All Angels' Parish Day School, which had discontinued operation after nearly 40 years of service to the community. A dedicated group of parents, faculty, and administrators obtained funding and zoning and reunited as The Wesley School.

AT A GLANCE

APPLICATION DEADLINE	Janurary 23
OPEN HOUSES	Oct, Nov, & Jan
UNIFORMS	Yes
BEFORE AND AFTER SCHOOL CARE	Yes
SEE MAP	B on page 255

WESTLAND SCHOOL

16200 MULHOLLAND DRIVE, LOS ANGELES, CA 90049

TEL: 310.472.5544 FAX: 310.472.5807

www.westlandschool.org

HEAD OF SCHOOL:	SCOTT MORAN
DIRECTOR OF ADMISSIONS:	MARCIA CAPPARELA
TYPE OF SCHOOL:	INDEPENDENT DAY SCHOOL
GRADES:	K-6
ENROLLMENT: 130	TUITION: $23,300
APPLICATION FEE: $125	NEW STUDENT FEE: $1,500
ACCREDITATION: CAIS/NAIS/WASC	FINANCIAL AID: YES

Westland School is a progressive elementary school located on Mulholland Drive. The modern, one-story facility sits on nearly two acres and includes large, bright classrooms, a large library, a commercially-equipped kitchen, science lab, woodworking studio, art studio, and an auditorium all grouped around a central patio which serves as a protected work area and a place for informational exchange and community social connections.

The spectacular auditorium has huge windows at the far end that overlook a grove of pine and eucalyptus trees and serves as music room for choral and instrumental work. There are three play yards, a chicken coop, and an edible garden. The upper yard has a basketball court and a large, grassy field for sports. A stream and pond provide for hands-on science experiments and observation.

The school philosophy follows the teachings of John Dewey, who believed that we should make learning more experiential, active rather than passive, in order to educate children for a democratic society. Hands-on, in-depth projects incorporate a variety of skills and themes, making learning relevant, interesting, and accessible. Effort is made to provide a warm, caring, and supportive environment to allow the children to develop and grow at their own pace. The sharing of ideas, collaboration, and group problem solving are an integral part of the system. Children discover that they have an influence on and a responsibility to others and to the world outside. Music, art, drama, and dance contribute to aesthetic development.

Curriculum

Social studies forms the core of the curriculum; examples include Ancient Greece, Westward Expansion, Family Study, and Immigration. The school integrates reading, language arts, science, math, and art into this social studies-based curriculum. By connecting all areas of study with social studies, each subject is placed in a real-world context and learning becomes relevant.

The approach to learning is one of questioning, problem solving, and learning by doing. Younger children may take a field trip to a restaurant and then come back and build and run their own restaurant for a day with parents and other students as customers. They will discuss how the business should be run, assign jobs such as chef, waitress, cashier, manager, and then take turns solving the daily problems that might arise in that particular setting. This way they learn by using their organizational skills, math and problem solving skills, and learn to work together. This gives them a strong connection to the community in which they live.

There is a music specialist who works with each group and who leads a community "Sing" on Friday mornings. Visual arts are stressed at all age levels. Drama, poetry, and creative writing experiences are also important aspects of the Westland curriculum.

There is a deep sense of community at Westland. Every child has a commitment to his/her group and each group has a responsibility to the school, for example, one group takes care of the chickens, one group runs the compost program, one group takes daily attendance, and another group runs the school store.

Parent involvement is central at Westland and parents participate by giving docent tours, working on Friday Hot Lunch, organizing fundraising events, driving on field trips, working in the library, taking part in weekend work groups, and donating time and materials that contribute to the school programs.

HISTORY

Westland School was opened in 1949, during a time of intense political upheaval in the United States – the McCarthy era. The politically active founders of Westland were eager to educate children in an atmosphere of free inquiry. They were inspired by the progressive ideas of John Dewey and the work done by Jean Piaget on the developmental stages of children's learning.

AT A GLANCE

APPLICATION DEADLINE	December 5
UNIFORMS	No
OPEN HOUSES/TOURS	Check Website
BEFORE AND AFTER SCHOOL CARE	Yes
SEE MAP	D on page 255

WESTMARK SCHOOL

5461 LOUISE AVE, ENCINO, CA 91316

TEL: 818.986.5045 FAX: 818.380.1378

www.westmarkschool.org

HEAD OF SCHOOL:	**MUIR MEREDITH**
DIRECTOR OF ADMISSIONS:	**POLLY BROPHY**
TYPE OF SCHOOL:	**CO-ED DAY SCHOOL**
GRADES:	**4-12**
ENROLLMENT: 225	TUITION: $39,720
APPLICATION FEE: $125	NEW STUDENT FEE: $1,500
YEARLY REGISTRATION FEE: $1,500	FINANCIAL AID: YES

WESTMARK SCHOOL is located on almost 5 acres in Encino, California. The school is situated in a quiet neighborhood not far from Ventura Boulevard, where there are an array of restaurants and stores. The school values safety and functions as a closed campus, with one entry and exit point. They have a security guard on duty throughout the school day and once inside you are greeted by Jenny, a fellow English woman whose jolly personality can't help but put you in a good mood.

The tour I went on, along with some other families, was fantastic. I always gauge a tour by how a prospective family behaves. If it's too long, they get irritable (and so do I) and if it's too short, they feel like they haven't been told and shown everything they need to see/hear before making a decision. At the end of it we were all happy and relaxed as could be!

Westmark is a unique school in that it serves children in elementary through high school who have average to above average academic potential, have been diagnosed with learning differences and have not been fully served in other school settings.

In order to be considered for a place at this school, each family must provide a complete psycho-educational diagnostic evaluation which will help the school in determining the student's current abilities and designing a curriculum to fit the child. Not expecting the child to fit the curriculum.

School Mission Statement:

> Westmark School provides a caring environment where motivated students with learning differences discover their unique paths to personal and academic excellence in preparation for a successful college experience.

Westmark helps the families of their students who might have felt a little helpless in the past by asking them to commit to open and full communication with the school. Parents may, for the first time, feel like they are really being heard and that all their concerns are being squarely met. Westmark believes that parents who are actively involved in the school-life of their child will have a profound impact on their child's success. Now I don't think that they expect the parents to know how to do a 11th grade math problem...but perhaps the parent might learn how to do it from their child!

Westmark has 34 classrooms, a Library, a tutorial room, a multi-purpose room/auditorium (with a stage for drama productions), art room, sewing room, kitchen and weight room. The library includes a computer lab with brand new Mac computers. Books are arranged by reading level. Special lighting is used in the library to enhance reading/learning.

The campus has a swimming pool that is used during the warmer months for physical education classes. They have just finished building a brand new state-of-the-art athletic field for football and soccer games. Their woodshop is under construction but will open next year.

Cooking is a very popular elective option for students. Classes utilize a new state-of-the-art kitchen, which was donated by a generous family. Additionally, the kitchen is used for campus events. Other popular electives include sewing, American Sign Language and art.

I love this one: The Westmark News Network (WNN) is a student produced television network and News Show. The program airs daily, produced by the high school students. Lower school students may participate by being featured and/or to make announcements.

The academic building offers:

- A state-of-the-art science lab.
- The WNN/digital media room.
- 2 English classrooms and a math/science room.
- Along with the rest of the campus, each classroom has a flat screen TV for curriculum related purposes, as well as to watch the WNN.
- Along with the rest of the campus, each classroom has an LCD projector.
- All English classes on campus, including those in the new building, can act as computer labs, housing computers for each student.
- Windows that are double-paned to block out sound.
- Chairs that are adjustable and flexible to cater to students who move about in their seats.
- The science/math room has a smart board, as do other classrooms on campus.
- The College Counseling Center.

The school offers comprehensive lower, middle and secondary school programs. Middle and high school students participate in programs tailor made for each student to help them matriculate from Westmark to college or many wonderful career programs. I met Luren Leavitt the college counselor, a wonderfully articulate and energetic woman who told me how she will not only guide students towards a traditional college experience but will offer guidance and information about a variety of career options, technical schools and vocational courses of study that will lead to jobs in media arts, culinary arts, film and TV production and computer technologies. (By the way…all 29 of their seniors are off to college!)

Their whole-child approach to education in a nurturing and traditional environment is definitely working. The kids are brilliant! They genuinely seem happy to be there. As I entered each classroom I was met by happy smiling faces and impromptu offers to look over their work and to hear about what they were studying that day. These kids are not being coached in advance of a school tour, they are left alone and it is in their most relaxed state that you can see how successful this school's approach to learning can be.

HISTORY

In 1983 Landmark School of Massachusetts opened Landmark West, in Culver City as a west coast extension of their school. The Landmark Foundation purchased the Encino campus in 1991. In the fall of 1997 Landmark School was purchased by a non-profit corporation, Learning with a Difference, to provide local control over the development and implementation of the program. These leaders renamed the school Westmark. The basic educational philosophy has remained the same. Use of a multi-sensory approach continues to be effective with students with learning differences. Program changes and modifications continue to occur based on student needs and current research.

AT A GLANCE

APPLICATION DEADLINE	March for the Fall term
OPEN HOUSES	Call Admissions Office to schedule, ext 306
ISEE TEST	No
SEE MAP	B on page 255

WESTRIDGE SCHOOL FOR GIRLS

324 MADELINE DRIVE, PASADENA, CA 91105
TEL: 626.799.1153 FAX: 626.799.7068
www.westridge.org

HEAD OF SCHOOL:	**ELIZABETH MCGREGOR**
DIRECTOR OF ADMISSIONS:	**HELEN HOPPER**
TYPE OF SCHOOL:	**ALL GIRLS DAY SCHOOL**
GRADES:	**4-12**
ENROLLMENT: 510	TUITION: $24,990 - 32,725
APPLICATION FEE: $125	NEW FAMILY FEE: $1,5000
UNIFORMS: $235	FINANCIAL AID: YES

THE WESTRIDGE campus is on a tree-lined residential area off Orange Grove Boulevard in Pasadena. You might even think you were in the country as you survey the surroundings. The campus stretches across an idyllic park-like setting in a quiet residential neighborhood. The trees, lawns, gardens, and pathways are favorite spots for studying, meeting friends, or enjoying solitude and reflection. Through the decades, the school has acquired and maintained contemporary and historic architecture, including Pitcairn House, a craftsman built in 1906 by the influential early 20th Century architects Greene & Greene. In 2010, Westridge completed its most recent construction, the campus' first LEED-certified, environmentally-sustainable facility dedicated to girls studying science and math.

I arrived for one of the open houses, and after walking through some beautifully manicured gardens, was ushered into the auditorium. There we heard the headmistress speak, along with a number of girls who gave very well-rehearsed speeches, letting us know why this school worked for them. These were the same girls that took small groups of us on a tour of the school. They were bright and articulate, and happy to answer all our questions. We visited the Joan Irvine Library, which has over 18,000 books. I asked one girl what was the worst thing about this school, and she said, "No boys." Then I asked her what was the best thing about the school, and she said, "No boys!"

Westridge is keenly aware that in order to become a top-tier school in all areas, it must reflect that in its endowment per student. A lot of careful planning has gone into its capital improvement plan, and they are highly aware of changes that need to be made not only to the school curriculum, but also to the facilities themselves, as competition stiffens and places in universities and colleges become more coveted.

As parents well know, every goal and aspiration articulated in a school's plan has a price, and one may be sure that an ambitious fund-raising campaign for capital gifts will be implemented.

From the school brochure:

> Essential to the school's purpose is the commitment to be a community that reflects and values diversity, respects individual differences, and responds to a changing dynamic world.

> An intellectually engaging and challenging curriculum prepares students to continue their education in college and beyond as discerning, motivated learners who are committed to excellence and goodness in everything they do. The program offers balance among humanities, mathematics and sciences, fine and

performing arts, technology and athletics. A Westridge education offers not only a path to self-discovery and personal fulfillment, but an awareness of the essential interdependence of all peoples, places, and cultures.

Westridge strives to develop young women whose joy in learning, personal integrity, commitment to ethical action, social and environmental responsibility, courage and compassion will lead them to meaningful lives as contributing citizens of the larger world.

Westridge has traditionally provided solid preparation for college through its academic curriculum, but as more is expected of students and teachers, the school is considering extending the calendar and reorganizing the daily schedules to better serve the students' needs.

The school encourages its faculty to be guided by research about how girls learn and incorporate new strategies into their traditional teaching methods. It is hoped that over the next decade, the student experience will become an integrated combination of traditional and experiential settings. They are also committed to developing environmental awareness and to instilling in its students a sense of personal stewardship. Programs that provide hands-on experiences, field learning, and outside experts are incorporated throughout the curriculum.

The school firmly believes that sports, student government, and community service projects provide many opportunities for leadership training. This sense of service goes past graduation. A strong alumnae association keeps everyone informed. Girls can go anywhere in the country or the world and find a 'sister' who will put them up.

In the lower school an integrated language art program focuses on a variety of literary forms. There is significant emphasis on the development of expository and creative writing, in addition to instruction in spelling, grammar, and vocabulary. Mathematics involves a variety of learning experiences designed to balance the acquisition of basic concepts, reasoning and thinking skills, and problem-solving strategies. In science they study physical, life, and earth science. In social studies, girls study California history in grade 4, the Western Hemisphere in grade 5, and ancient civilizations in grade 6.

Grade 4 students begin using computers on a weekly basis and this continues in grades 5 and 6. There is a wonderful performing arts program, and beginning in grade 5, the students study Spanish. They take classes in drawing, painting and mixed media and a semester of ceramics is added in the sixth grade. The lower school enjoys many of its own traditions: the Pet Show, Cirque de Madeline, and the Science Fair. Lower-school girls also participate with middle and upper school students in big-little sister events and their annual Greek and Roman activities. In seventh grade the girls are assigned as Greeks or Romans, all upper schoolers are in friendly competition with each other throughout the year. The middle school program blends a combination of experiential education and community service into the child's academic program. With a student/teacher ratio of 9:1 and an average class size of 15 to 20 there is plenty of individualized attention. Students learn how to do research to weigh evidence, to analyze cause and effect relationships, to synthesize information, solve problems and make concrete applications in an interdisciplinary curriculum, which prepares them for the work ahead of them in the Upper School.

In the Upper School, Westridge offers a 'curriculum planning' course to help each student, in consultation with her advisor and her teachers, create her own program. Requirements for graduation will determine much of the program, but there are many options for consideration that the catalogue helps each student and parents to discover. As your child plans for her freshman year, she should ask herself: are graduation requirements being met? Are special curricular interests and strengths being pursued wherever possible, and do these choices promise both pleasure and genuine interest? Before the final decisions are made, your child should ask herself, how will the days feel? How will my time be spent? The more genuine her choices are, the greater the chances are for success.

Admission and alumnae records show that Westridge students are well-prepared for college and typically 100 percent of graduating seniors are admitted each year to four-year colleges.

Many returning alumnae have said, "Westridge helped me get into a college that was really right for me." Only one alum did not go to college, as she became a soap opera actress! The school holds two open houses each year and schedules classroom visits for prospective students. If you like the idea of an all girls' school education for your daughter, then I recommend you take a look, especially if you live in the greater San Gabriel Valley.

HISTORY

In 1913, a group of parents in southwest Pasadena established Westridge School as a place where girls could pursue a demanding academic program that would prepare them for college. The idea that girls have a right to the best possible education (a very radical idea at the time) remains central to the school's mission and purpose. Westridge School's vision for the beginning of its second century is both a blueprint for preserving the best of an illustrious past and an incentive for the innovation and flexibility that this new century will require.

AT A GLANCE

APPLICATION DEADLINE	February
OPEN HOUSES	Call for school dates
ISEE TEST	Required
UNIFORMS	Yes
BEFORE AND AFTER SCHOOL CARE	Yes
SUMMER SCHOOL	Yes
SEE MAP	C on page 255

WESTSIDE NEIGHBORHOOD SCHOOL

5401 BEETHOVEN STREET, LOS ANGELES, CA 90066
TEL: 310.574.8650 FAX: 310.574.8657
www.wnsk8.com

HEAD OF SCHOOL:	BRAD ZACUTO
DIRECTOR OF ADMISSIONS:	DARLENE FOUNTAINE
TYPE OF SCHOOL:	PRIVATE INDEPENDENT DAY SCHOOL
GRADES:	DK-8
ENROLLMENT: 452	TUITION: $27,025 - 30,450
APPLICATION FEE: $150	FINANCIAL AID: YES
ACCREDITATIONS: CAIS/WASC/NAIS	

WESTSIDE NEIGHBORHOOD SCHOOL is located near Jefferson Boulevard and Playa Vista. It is a 50,000 foot facility that is an architectural wonder—attractive, delightful and functional. There is good planning, excellent financial resources and more importantly you feel the warmth of the 106 teachers and staff. There are cheerful classrooms, a huge play yard, a multi-purpose gym, a library, a technology maker lab, two art labs, and two science labs. The Reggio-inspired DK and K program shares an outdoor classroom/garden center.

WNS's developmental philosophy is like Rousseau's "hold childhood in reverence and do not be in a hurry." New students are tested using the Gesell Developmental Observation to see their level of developmental maturity. This school is looking for the child's welfare in emotional, intellectual and physical growth at all grade levels. Their kindergarten philosophy reminds us that each child has her or her own time line that will lead to academic success.

In keeping with this philosophy, WNS has a developmental kindergarten for children who have outgrown their preschools but need time before starting first grade. This class admits children who turn four and one-half by September 1 of the entering year.

Brad Zacuto, an educator with more than 30 years' experience teaching at and managing private independent schools in Southern California, is in his tenth year as Head of Westside Neighborhood School. For 14 years, Zacuto worked at St. Matthew's Parish School, a PS-8 school in Pacific Palisades, where he oversaw the operation of the middle school as its principal. A lifelong educator, Zacuto has been a classroom teacher in fifth through eighth grades and spent 10 years at Westlake School for Girls. He was also a science teacher and science coordinator at John Thomas Dye School. He is also a past WNS parent and trustee.

With thirteen board members and multiple parent committees this school is a model of community involvement. WNS has a very active Parent Group organization that organizes spirit-building activities, parent support and fundraising for the school. All WNS parents are members, and everyone is encouraged to become involved in the work the Parent Group does for WNS. The school also provides a comprehensive series of parent education events for WNS parents and for the local community. In addition to DK through eighth grade level meetings throughout the year, WNS hosts a series of Speaker Events for WNS parents and the community.

I can honestly say that this is just about a perfect school, with high educational standards, high style and bear hugs!

HISTORY

Entering its twenty-seventh year, WNS is still committed to community, quality education, and a strong sense of collaboration. As the school sets its sights on the road ahead, WNS continues to measure its progress by its ability to help students successfully meet the challenges of a rapidly changing world while maintaining the founding vision of an ideal place to learn.

AT A GLANCE

APPLICATION DEADLINE	January 12
OPEN HOUSE AND TOUR	Check Webiste
BEFORE AND AFTER SCHOOL CARE	Yes
SEE MAP	D on page 255

Wildwood School

Elementary (K-8)
12201 WASHINGTON PLACE, LOS ANGELES, CA 90066
TEL: 310.397.3134 FAX: 310.397.5134

Secondary (6-12)
11811 W. OLYMPIC BLVD., LOS ANGELES, CA 90064
TEL: 310.478.7189 FAX: 310.478.6875

www.wildwood.org

HEAD OF SCHOOL:	**LANDIS GREEN**
ASSISTANT HEAD:	**MICHELLE MEENA**
DIRECTOR OF ADMISSIONS:	**EMMA KATZNELSON**
TYPE OF SCHOOL:	**CO-ED DAY SCHOOL**
GRADES:	**K-12**
ENROLLMENT: K-5: 300, 6-12: 400	TUITION: $31,500 - 37,250
APPLICATION FEE: $125	ENTRANCE FEE: $1,250
ACCREDITATION: CAIS/WASC	FINANCIAL AID: YES

WILDWOOD ELEMENTARY is a developmental Westside school that has wonderful teachers and a state-of-the-art facility. On the first of four visits, I was dazzled by the buildings. These beautiful, modern, two-story structures with clean lines and bright, open spaces were designed by a Wildwood parent/architect. Facilities include a soccer field, running track, tetherball area, science lab, art room, outdoor art yard, auditorium, music room, reading room, and library. The buildings share a common courtyard that is handsomely landscaped with flowers, palm trees, and winding pathways. All the classrooms have connecting doors, a feature that helps facilitate Wildwood's 'team teaching' approach.

There are 'pod' classrooms at the kindergarten through 2nd grade level. This system allows children of different ages to help and encourage each other. Each child stays in the same class for three years and has the opportunity to learn from the older children and to grow with the group. Over the years he will also be able to guide and teach the younger students.

In these mixed-age group classes called "pods," each age group is represented in equal number with a balance of gender. Each pod has a total of 24 children with a head teacher and a full-time teaching assistant. The mixed-age grouping allows for children's development at different rates.

At the third-grade level, children are grouped in single grade classes with a maximum of 18 to 19 students per class. These classes are staffed by a head teacher and a half-time teaching assistant. Specialists work in conjunction with classroom teachers in the areas of science, music, visual-arts, Spanish, physical education, performing arts, and dance. A reading resource specialist and a psychological consultant are available when needed.

The educational philosophy at Wildwood is based on the teachings of cognitive theorist, Jean Piaget, who believed that children construct knowledge from their experiences in a unique, and often, non-linear way and that children should be allowed to work and grow at their own developmental pace. To a lesser degree the progressive approach of John Dewey is also used at the school. It has a social studies core curriculum, encourages block building, and employs cooperative, democratic learning methods. Each classroom is set up in centers, which house materials for children to use. Children know where to find math and writing materials, blocks, books, art, wood-working, and cleaning supplies, and are encouraged to use all of them as well as take projects from one center to another.

Elementary Curriculum

In the primary grades mathematics is taught through the use of concrete (manipulative) materials such as pattern blocks, unifix cubes, geoboards, mirrors, collections of buttons, rocks, etc., as well as a variety of measuring devices for comparing weight, length, and volume.

Over the school year, children work extensively with patterning and problem solving. Estimation, sorting and classifying, graphing, measuring, adding and subtracting, multiplying, dividing, and geometry are other areas that provide a solid understanding of our place value numerical system. Children who are developmentally ready are exposed to symbolic work.

In third to fifth grades children move from concrete math to a program that requires the use of abstract reasoning, problem solving, and computation. Science activities are incorporated within the social studies program and involve exploration, discovery, experimentation, and observation. Children are encouraged to explore aspects of their world that are of particular interest to them. The school's large auditorium is equipped with stage lighting and sound used for music, dance, movement, and performing arts, which are integrated into all aspects of the curriculum. Physical education develops coordination, balance, flexibility, responsibility, cooperation, and teamwork. There is a soccer field for team games and sports.

When homework is assigned at different points throughout the year, it is done in a purposeful and developmentally appropriate way. Pod children do not have traditional homework but are encouraged to play and engage in activities with their families that support their learning. Homework for grades 3 to 5 is assigned for further practice of skills taught in class, to help develop independent learning habits and responsibility, for review, and for research.

Language arts are taught using a variety of methods including 'whole language' as opposed to the point of view of 'skill building,' phonics work, and oral language.

Other components of the program are as follows:

> **Oral Language and Vocabulary**: Vocabulary and oral language skills are developed through plays, story telling, sharing in class, and small group discussions.
> **Sight Word Approach**: Words are learned through visual memorization.
> **Story time**: Books are read to the children daily. Various types of literature and different authors are introduced. Follow-up discussions and projects help to develop comprehension skills.
> **Silent Sustained Reading**: A time is set aside each day when the entire class spends time reading and appreciating books silently.

Reading is seen as a way to convey meaning and not merely the finished product of learning decoding skills. Writing is taught as part of everything children do at the school. Formal writing instruction is taught during the lesson time. Writer's workshop is led by the child's 'inner scribe' and during this time, students write, draw, and dictate.

The visual arts and the performing arts are a vital part of Wildwood's education. Teachers in the visual arts program meet with students regularly in the art studio where they learn painting, drawing, and three-dimensional expression. The performing arts program, which includes music, movement, and drama encourages students to express their unique voices and talents.

Secondary

The secondary campus is located two miles away from the elementary school in a converted TV production studio. It is striking piece of architecture. The spacious loft-like interior of the 50,000 square-foot space features classrooms, an open conference room, gallery, science lab, theater, library, and visual and performing arts studios. The building's high ceilings allow for a soaring mezzanine, used for activities and meetings. A state-of-the-art wireless system and many laptops and tablets allow the students access to technology anywhere on the campus. On the roof of the parking structure there's a large deck that provides an outdoor area for lunch and other activities. Lacking their own playing fields, the school uses several local parks for their athletic programs. Sports teams compete in Westside leagues.

The Wildwood Secondary program is the result of five years of research by parents at the Wildwood Elementary School. They wanted a small middle and high school that would prepare their children for college without subjecting them to the stresses of standardized testing, grading, and hours and hours of homework each night. Parents turned to Theodore R. Sizer, a veteran education reformer who has helped create hundreds of schools where the emphasis is on developing essential life skills rather than memorizing facts.

Wildwood's secondary program has four divisions rather than single grades. Division One is a single year for sixth graders, allowing for a smooth transition from elementary to secondary school. With a student/teacher ratio of 12:1 and 90-minute classes, the students gain a lot of individualized attention. Division Two (grades 7 and 8) make up the middle school. Division Three (grades 9 and 10) and The Senior Institute (grades 11 and 12) span the high school years.

Wildwood's program is built around a series of 'habits,' known as "Habits of Mind and Heart:"

- **Convention**: Meeting accepted standards in any subject in order to be understood and to understand others.
- **Connection**: Looking for patterns and for ways things fit together in order to bring together diverse material into new solutions.
- **Evidence:** Bringing together relevant information, judging the credibility of sources, finding out for oneself.
- **Perspective**: Addressing questions from multiple viewpoints, using a variety of ways to solve problems.
- **Collaboration**: Making the appropriate provisions for accepting and giving assistance.
- **Ethical behavior**: An awareness of how personal habits influence behavior and a set of principles by which to guide one's life.
- **Service to the common good**: Demonstrating awareness of the effects of one's actions and the desire to make the community a better place for all.

These 'habits' are used by the student in every subject to set a standard that they can apply to every class, helping them to create their portfolios. The academic curriculum is structured around a series of questions and generative themes that pull together content from the core subject areas of humanities, science, math, foreign language, and visual and performing arts.

Therefore in math and science, students might use physics and geometry to design and build a model of a bridge structure. To progress from one division to the next, students must fulfill a set of portfolio requirements in these areas, as well as community involvement, personal reflections, and goals for the future.

Wildwood believes that detailed narrative assessments give students and their families a clearer idea of the student's progress. Therefore this school uses narrative assessments instead of grades to inform students and their parents of how students are progressing. This also helps the school assess whether students are mastering the work given to them. These assessments are part of each student's permanent file and provide the basis for college transcripts.

However, if a college or university requires a grade point average, Wildwood will convert their narrative assessments to grades, which pleased those parents who were worried about the 'no grading' approach. It should also be noted that Wildwood courses meet the criteria for the University of California system, as well as public and private colleges and universities around the country.

While founded on the idea that massive nightly homework can be counterproductive, the school believes in homework for the reinforcement of current work, review of skills, research projects, reading, and reflection. While the amount of homework will vary with the particular assignments and interests of each student, homework is a significant component of the program.

They believe that properly guided athletics and competition makes students well-rounded individuals. There is a no-cut policy for the middle school sports program. Once in Division three and the Senior Institute, students can earn team positions based on athletic skill, desire and commitment. Boys' Team Sports include cross-country, flag football, basketball, soccer, baseball, golf, track & field, and tennis. Girls' Team Sports include cross country, flag football, basketball, soccer, softball, volleyball, track & field, and tennis.

Wildwood's Advisory Program allows small groups of students to meet with their advisors on a daily basis to help guide their academic programs and social-emotional development. Advisors also act as mentors, monitoring each student's growth and meeting with the student's family during the year to review narrative assessments that provide parents with an in-depth look at each student's progress.

Once in the Senior Institute in eleventh and twelfth grades, Wildwood's internship program gives students the opportunity to connect what they learn at school with real-life practical experiences. Students may experience several different professions, expanding their interests by 'trying out' various career paths. Internships enrich students' educational experiences by connecting what they learn in the classroom with the professional skills they will need.

HISTORY

When Wildwood opened its middle and upper campus in 2000, our Board of Trustees had a parallel vision: To create a center devoted to supporting public and independent schools across the country in their efforts to create small, learner-centered schools. That vision crystallized in 2001 when the Wildwood Outreach Center was awarded a multi-year grant from the Bill & Melinda Gates Foundation. Since it opened, nearly 1,000 teachers and administrators from over 300 schools in 20 different states and 6 foreign countries have benefitted from Wildwood Outreach Center programs. Today, the Center continues to advance Wildwood's status as a hub of educational best practice through a broad menu of professional development workshops, school visits, summer institutes, and mentorship opportunities.

AT A GLANCE

APPLICATION DEADLINE	Grades 6-12: Dec., Kindergarten: Oct.
UNIFORMS	No
BEFORE AND AFTER SCHOOL CARE	Yes
PARENT INVOLVEMENT IS EXPECTED	
SEE MAP	D on page 255

THE WILLOWS COMMUNITY SCHOOL

8509 HIGUERA STREET, CULVER CITY, CA 90232
TEL: 310.815.0411 FAX: 310.815.0425
www.thewillows.org

HEAD OF SCHOOL:	LISA ROSENSTEIN
DIRECTOR OF ADMISSIONS:	KIM FELDMAN
TYPE OF SCHOOL:	CO-ED DAY SCHOOL
GRADES:	DK-8
ENROLLMENT: 442	TUITION: $27,900 - 31,700
APPLICATION FEE: $125	FINANCIAL AID: YES
ACCREDITATION: CAIS/WASC	

Take a determined group of wealthy parents, a number of teachers that have achieved 'star' status among the educational community, a swarm of architects, planners, and facilitators, an empty warehouse in a now-defunct industrial section of Culver City, give them all a seven month deadline, and...voila! A private school is born.

One must admire the spirit and determination of **THE WILLOWS COMMUNITY SCHOOL**. The school's '94/'95 brochure was the size of a small newspaper and featured a two-page story of the struggle to open the doors in seven-month's time. The founders had to convince parents to enroll their children in a school that did not have an actual address and to schedule visits for them to the present site before the lease was signed. The glue on the floor installation was barely dry when the founding parents, new parents, and grandparents converged on the school to organize the classrooms, library, and art room.

In three months time, builders transformed this once-dilapidated 11,000 square foot warehouse into an air-conditioned, hip, modern schoolhouse with exposed wood beams, skylights, and large bright classrooms. The huge, open hallway/common areas have white walls covered with some of the most wonderful children's artwork.

The atmosphere at The Willows is very informal, with first names on office doors, and casually dressed children scooting to and from their classroom activities. The day I visited, the tour group was besieged by a group of children running by in stocking feet and faces painted blue preparing to shoot a video.

The school has a huge library, a large outdoor playground with climbing equipment, and a cement play area for basketball. The children take buses to a nearby park for additional recreation. The school also purchased two more buildings, one behind and one to the side, to provide room for the seventh and eighth grades. One building includes a rooftop P.E. facility, complete with basketball courts. A new full-size gym and a 200-seat theater have been added as well.

The grades start at developmental kindergarten in which there is a group of four to five-year olds who are preparing for kindergarten but are not quite developmentally ready. Last year in DK, the curriculum included: exploring the five senses, the study of seeds (the cycle of food from seed to table), the study of penguins and their young, exploring the properties of ice, and a unit on transportation.

The curriculum at the school is integrated and focuses on children learning to work together as a group. Integration means that each subject relates to another whenever possible. For example, if children are studying tsunami waves, they might integrate that science unit with a field trip to the Los Angeles County Museum of Art to view Hokusai's woodblock print, "The Great Wave." Field trips, block building, and experiential learning are all important aspects of the program. This is definitely a school for the art-oriented family. The program is outstanding. Art is integrated into 'units' with mathematics, language, science, and history, not as a tool to teach or illustrate these subjects, but as a partner with these disciplines and a discipline in itself.

When the third grade studied caterpillars, along with research of the scientific facts, they made technical illustrations and scale drawings. In studying the artistic tradition of scientific drawing, these students learned that even the most technical drawing contains expressive and evocative elements in addition to functional and scientific ones.

This integration of art into units ensures that art is valued not just as an adjunct skill but also because it helps develop young observation skills and provides a vehicle for abstract thought and expression.

Here is a brief paragraph from the school's brochure:

> The Willows Community School is committed to a strong, progressive education, rooted in academic excellence and social values. Its developmentally structured curriculum is founded on the principles of experiential learning and thematic instruction. The students learn to think, to have mutual respect and tolerance, and to understand the value of cooperation. The school strives to provide an environment where children, like the trees for which The Willows is named, bend gracefully in the wind but do not break.

There is a maximum of 23 students per class with two credentialed teachers in each class. There are two classes at each grade level from DK to grade seven and one eighth grade class. The admissions staff will visit your child at his present school for an evaluation, but they do not require testing for applicants.

Major construction of the first phase of The Willows Master Plan began during the summer of 2013 and continued through January 2014, with the Dedication of the New Campus held on January 26, 2014. The Willows campus now has new, flexible learning spaces, a warm and welcoming entrance, dedicated outdoor athletic courts, enhanced security, a S.T.E.A.M. (science, technology, engineering, art and math) educational lab, and a total updating of The Lower Elementary Building. The Library/Media Center, which has been moved to the heart of our campus, has been redesigned as a fluid, dynamic space conducive to interdisciplinary learning, the sharing of knowledge, intellectual discourse, and individual growth. The transformation of their campus exterior areas continued in 2014 resulting in beautiful landscaped areas with the addition of shade trees; an expanded organic garden; a new, interactive playground with a slate wall and sand and water play areas; a Kindergarten Yard; play areas devoted to both active and imaginative, quiet play, and community gathering spaces; and a Middle School Alley. Completion of this phase of their Master Plan is a true reflection of The Willows' spirit and culture.

HISTORY

The Willows Community School was opened in September of 1994 by a group of parents with the common belief that education should be an exciting, hands-on experience that allows the curious mind freedom of expression and enjoyment of learning. In an amazing 20 years, the school's student body has increased from 106 to 445 students, grades developmental kindergarten through eighth. During this time The Willows has achieved a reputation as one of the pre-eminent independent schools in Los Angeles, known for its highly regarded technology program and educational innovations. Several leading national educators have recently spent time at The Willows, unanimous in their praise of the school's creative and stimulating learning environment and its engaged, involved students. The Willows received the 2014 and 2015 Culver City Private School Award for Excellence.

AT A GLANCE

APPLICATION DEADLINE	December 19
OPEN HOUSES	RSVP on Website
SCHOOL TOURS	Sept - Dec
UNIFORMS	Yes
ISEE TESTING	Required Grades 6-8
BEFORE AND AFTER SCHOOL CARE	Yes
SEE MAP	D on page 255

WILSHIRE SCHOOL

4900 WILSHIRE BOULEVARD, LOS ANGELES, CA 90010
TEL: 323.939.3800 FAX: 323.937.0013
www.wilshireprivateschool.org

HEAD OF SCHOOL:	**EDWARD SHIN**
TYPE OF SCHOOL:	**CO-ED DAY SCHOOL**
GRADES:	**JK-6**
ENROLLMENT: 100	TUITION: $6,500 - 7,500
APPLICATION FEE: $150	FINANCIAL AID: YES
ACCREDITATION: WASC	

WILSHIRE SCHOOL is an interesting smaller school, in my very own neighborhood, a Junior Kindergarten through 6th grade oasis at Wilshire and Highland. The school sits right across the street from our local public middle school, John Burroughs, and occupies a healthy piece of real estate in this Hancock Park neighborhood.

Wilshire School's Philosophy:

> Wilshire School welcomes students of all cultures in grades JK through 6. Our unique learning community flourishes in an atmosphere of safety, nurturing and academic challenge. Small class size and individualized attention are the hallmarks of a Wilshire education. Students, faculty, and staff come together to model respect, tolerance, and the democratic process. The core curriculum is infused with opportunities to grow in the areas of music, technology, foreign language acquisition, and service learning. To round out the program, teachers incorporate art, drama, dance, and field experiences into their activities.

I arrived unannounced one morning and made my way to the main office. There I met the old head of school, Raquel Kislinger, who also happened to be arriving. She was very enthusiastic and couldn't wait to show me around. As we toured the school she told me that her own experience of the school system was at Polytechnic, where for almost 16 years her two daughters enjoyed their JK through 12 years. She was both a teacher and lower school Head at the school during that time. She told me that she had read my book and resonated with my comments about the importance of finding the right school for an individual child.

The school opened under the umbrella organization of The Korean Institute of Southern California. While the majority of students are Korean-American, the school is open to the entire community and they are definitely wishing to attract a more diverse student population.

Raquel Kislinger went on to say:

> Here at Wilshire School, community-building is an ongoing theme. As we spell out the word 'community' the letters 'U-N-I' are particularly striking. How better to express the idea of collaboration, alliance, camaraderie, and cooperation? 'You and I' is the heart of community. School communities must embrace, empower, challenge, and protect the children and adults within them. There is no magic wand to encourage connectedness, foster responsibility or create universal safety. But the 'You's' and 'I's' of the world, working together, can make a difference.

Edward Shin, Head of School, in conjunction with the input of the Faculty Team, believes strongly in addressing the needs of worthy students and challenging them to reach their potential through a variety of educational approaches that work best for the individual student. No one philosophy or program is forced on a student group as a whole, but instead, with small class sizes, WPS teachers are able to effectively meet the needs of a wide variety of student skills and personalities. However, no one school is ever right for all students, and it remains necessary for the Faculty Team to recognize when a student's needs exceed that which WPS can address and therefore direct that family towards a more appropriate setting.

We continued on the tour. The school is well laid out and the classrooms are generously stocked and clean. This is a small school with no big grassy fields or inside gymnasium, but there is a nice sized outside playground with plenty of climbing equipment for the kids. They cook for the kids every day and the cafeteria is pleasant and welcoming. I asked about the curriculum and here is an overview of the classes offered.

Language Arts

From the earliest grades, a love of reading is fostered. Students are encouraged to read widely, learning that literature bridges the richness of all cultures and ways of thinking. As early readers become more proficient, they begin to develop writing skills. They quickly regard themselves as young authors and their writing grows in sophistication each year. By the upper grades, writing is clear and confident.

Mathematics

Students use hands-on activities to explore different areas of mathematical study, beginning with basic operations and progressing to logic, geometry, and pre-algebra. Gradually, that learning is translated to the abstract symbols we use with paper, pencils, and calculators. Games, software, and homework solidify new problem solving processes.

Science

Students combine in-class learning with hands-on laboratory activities. Through observing, investigating, measuring, predicting, and comparing/contrasting data, students gain firsthand information about the natural world. They are encouraged to think independently, while gaining a respect for nature.

Social Studies

Beginning in kindergarten, children learn about societal relationships through the study of their own communities. In time, they see the interrelatedness of subjects such as art, music, math, science, and literature as they explore a wide range of ancient to modern cultures. The social studies curriculum encourages an appreciation of and respect for similarities and differences among the worlds' peoples. Students learn to ask analytical questions, read maps, use a globe, take notes, do basic research, write reports, create and read tables and graphs, and give effective oral presentations.

Foreign Languages

All students in grades JK through 6 have the choice of studying either Korean or Spanish. Both programs meet five days a week, offering language instruction, as well as cultural enrichment. Academic classes are taught in English, but for students needing English language support, an ESL teacher provides assistance.

Technology

Students progress from keyboarding to word processing, researching, illustrating, and using presentation tools.

A well-equipped computer lab offers a variety of programs that give students the ability to extend and explore a wealth of curricular topics.

Music and Art

An outstanding music program provides opportunities to join a chorus, play hand chimes, study an instrument, be part of an orchestra and participate in musical theater. Classroom teachers use a variety of tools, techniques, and materials to explore the visual arts, and dance/movement.

Community, Leadership and Service

The entire school community joins together weekly to sing, brainstorm ideas, celebrate success, discover ways to mediate conflicts, and enjoy mutual support and encouragement. The Student Council is composed of representatives from each grade level. Meetings provide an arena for the exchange of ideas, the development of leadership skills and an understanding of representative government. Service learning is a way for students to experience the joy and necessity of giving back to their communities. Whether it is through organizing a canned food drive, marching in the Korean Community Parade, or pooling resources to help those less fortunate, Wilshire students regularly participate to benefit others.

Physical Education

Students of all ages work on coordination, ball handling and agility, through the use of obstacle courses, tumbling exercises, relays and scrimmages. Gymnastics, hockey, volleyball and basketball form the core of sports instruction, with an emphasis on the value and importance of teamwork.

Parents are encouraged to participate in the school's Parent/Teacher Association (PTA). As it is well-known, the PTA can be a powerful tool to help the school grow and prosper. Because tuition often does not cover the cost of educating your child, the school relies on families to help raise additional operating funds. This is a great way for you as a parent to test the waters and find out if you have a future in professional fund-raising!

If you are looking for a school where you can be involved, look no further! The school welcomes parent participation at many levels. Helping out in the classroom, being a room parent, chaperoning field trips, joining the school at Community Meetings, and volunteering for school-wide events are all ways that families can show their support for this unique learning community. If it sounds like The Wilshire Private School might be a good fit for you and your child, do go to one of community meetings.

HISTORY

Wilshire Private School was founded in 1985 by the Korean Institute of Southern California for the express purpose of offering a K-6 quality academic education enhanced with courses in the arts. Wilshire Private School was not only founded to serve the Korean Community, but all communities and as such, we welcome students of any cultural background. Our learning community flourishes in a well-located and safe environment conducive to well-rounded educational achievement. Small class size and individualized attention contribute strongly to positive growth among our students. Wilshire Private School has the strong positive support of faculty and parents. Finally, and most importantly, Wilshire Private School has a strong professional administration dedicated to the successes of the Wilshire Private School Community.

AT A GLANCE

APPLICATION DEADLINE	Rolling admissions
OPEN HOUSES	RSVP on website
UNIFORMS	Yes
SUMMER SCHOOL	Yes
AFTER SCHOOL PROGRAM	Yes
SEE MAP	C on page 255

WINDWARD SCHOOL

11350 PALMS BLVD, LOS ANGELES, CA 90066

TEL: 310.391.7127 FAX: 310.397.5655

www.windwardschool.org

HEAD OF SCHOOL:	**THOMAS W. GILDER**
DIRECTOR OF ADMISSIONS:	**SHARON PEARLINE**
TYPE OF SCHOOL:	**CO-ED DAY SCHOOL**
GRADES:	**7-12**
ENROLLMENT: 550	TUITION: $35,543
APPLICATION FEE: $125	FINANCIAL AID: YES
ACCREDITATION: CAIS/NAIS/WASC	

WINDWARD SCHOOL is located in West Los Angeles across the street from the Mar Vista Park, close to the freeway on a nine-acre spread. A man-made river runs through the entire length of the school grounds and divides the tree-lined campus. The Leichtman-Levine Bridge takes you to the heart of the campus - a group of modern classroom buildings that reminded me of the MOCA complex downtown with its sleek roof lines, pathways and striking colorful umbrellas dotted outside the school restaurant.

While I was visiting the school, I joined a group of students who were being given a tour of the school by a very enthusiastic member of staff. As he passed by the school store, which resembled a mini-Gap, he told the students, "All you have to do is sign your name for things you want because your parents automatically get an account here when you join the school."

That brought smiles to their faces, so be warned, your young students could be adding to your already high tuition costs! A new Science/Math Center and Center for Teaching and Learning is under construction. There is also a green-screen studio for production and a Mac Lab.

Mission Statement

1. Creating a balanced college-preparatory program within a caring environment.

2. Complementing strong academic preparation with the development of ethics, character and well-developed people skills.

3. Maintaining small classes and an accessible faculty, creating a positive atmosphere for learning.

4. Communicating effectively with parents, students, faculty, alumni and friends to promote a strong sense of community.

5. Developing innovative programs, challenging course work, and dynamic co-curricular activities that meet the needs of students.

6. Having faculty and staff well trained, supervised, highly motivated, and committed to Windward's vision.

7. Creating a welcoming community that embraces diversity and encourages students to develop a sophisticated understanding of the world they will inherit.

8. Providing facilities and resources to create the strongest educational setting for optimal student learning.

The Center for Teaching and Learning (CTL) contains extensive traditional and technological resources for information gathering. Additionally, the three-floor CTL contains multimedia production facilities, custom-built spaces for collaboration, and breakout rooms for group brainstorming and studying.

The 13,000-square-foot Lewis Jackson Memorial Sports Center contains two indoor basketball courts, training facilities, and an exercise and fitness center. In the fall of 2000, there was a complete, professional renovation of the athletic fields, which seem to stretch out as far as the eye can see. The fields are home to the Winward baseball, softball, soccer, football and lacrosse teams. Physical Education is required of all students through grade 10 and students may participate in football, volleyball, basketball, soccer, lacrosse, baseball, softball and dance. The Littlefield Plaza and Student Pavilion, gives students and faculty a place to get together and eat lunch, and a dedicated conference center to host club meetings and community projects. The Pavilion provides a venue for a natural unforced interaction between students, faculty, coaches, counselors and advisors. The athletic fields completed additional renovations in Fall of 2013, with a wider field (facilitating regulation play for sports such as 11-man football) and a new baseball diamond. Additional facilities for spectators were part of the project and provide comfortable seating for outdoor sporting events.

There is a state-of-the-art Arts Center, a spacious environment containing studios for classes in computer graphics, drawing, painting, printmaking, sculpture, photography and ceramics. Their arts program offers students a truly multi-media experience.

The Irene Kleinberg Theater offers a very sophisticated and intimate environment for performing arts and a spectacular venue for choral and dance performances. Separate dance and rehearsal halls are next door. There is a wide variety of disciplines, ranging from beginning instrumental instruction to studies in film and television, and from photography to Advanced-Placement Studio Art.

The dance and theater programs begin in middle school and form the foundation for the fall play and the spring musical. Students may audition for these productions and may also participate behind the scenes as stage manager, house manager, set crew member, artist or publicity manager. In recent years, the Madrigal Singers and Chamber Orchestra have received gold medals at the prestigious Heritage Festival.

A new design center was built in 2015 to prepare a new generation of designers and artists. This space provides students with the type of creative thinking and working space that Windward has seen modeled within great universities such as Stanford and Harvard. This studio's open, flexible layout allows for the integration of two and three dimensional design and an innovative approach toward creativity.

Windward's Global Scholars Program offers preparation to engage with the 21st century global community through cultural immersion, intensive language study, and global leadership experiences.

The students can take advantage of classes through the Global Online Academy, a consortium of the world's leading independent schools. The courses offered by the GOA focus on global issues and allow our students to work directly with peers throughout the world through interactive web-based technologies.

Their STEAM Scholars Program challenges students to bridge real-world applications, out-of-class experiences, and academic studies in order to enhance their abilities to succeed in the 21st century. Through an approved course of study, students in 9th through 12th grades may follow an interdisciplinary series of science, technology, engineering, design arts, and mathematics courses.

Entrepreneurship at Windward prepares students for the ever-changing world and our new, global economy by giving them the experiences and skills to be resourceful, flexible, creative, and problem-solving leaders. Our world is comprised of social entrepreneurs, political entrepreneurs, artistic entrepreneurs, and economic entrepreneurs. At Windward, entrepreneurship is a process that results in creativity, innovation and growth and is fully integrated throughout the 7-12th grade curriculum. Their hope is to instill an entrepreneurial spirit so that students embrace the worldview of possibility in their life after Windward.

The Windward Studio for Writing and Rhetoric sparks curricular innovation across departments and forms a critical part of the acadmic support system. This inter-disciplinary, faculty-supervised, and student-led space provides resources to those who would like additional support with their papers, digital media projects, and oral presentations. It is staffed by teams of peer tutors who have been trained to bring a college writing model to Windward.

Shaped in partnership with experts from Northwestern University, Windward's Academic Integrity Initiative researches best practices for building on their commitment to help students mature into well prepared and ethical individuals. An Academic Integrity Advisory Board (AIAB), comprised both of faculty and students, educates and spreads awareness about the importance of academic integrity in the Windward community.

The Windward Institute brings faculty, parents, students, alumni and the educational community together to engage in the exploration of and dialogue about groundbreaking ideas. The primary mission of the Institute is ongoing educational research and the generation of transformative ideas and practices, achieved through partnerships forged with universities and thought leaders around the world. Recently, the Institute has brought speakers to the Windward community such as: Dr. Craig Barrett (Former CEO, Intel Corporation), Governor Michael Dukakis (1988 Democratic Presidential Nominee), David Levinson (Founder, Big Sunday), and Dr. Laurie Leshin (NASA Scientist and Mars Rover Project Leader).

The Service Learning/Community Service Program is a big part of the Windward experience. The school believes that learning through being involved in the community and caring for the environment is every bit as important as preparation and success in academic subjects.

Students are encouraged to engage in hands-on service projects through which they learn they can make a difference in their community.

There is also the opportunity to participate in a variety of extracurricular activities, such as The International Thespian Society, The Madrigal Singers, Jazz Ensemble, Chamber Players, the yearbook, the student newspaper, Robotics, and speech and debate.

Entry to this school is very competitive and openings occur traditionally at the seventh- and ninth-grade levels, although students may apply for eighth and tenth grades with permission of the admissions office. As part of the application, each student is required to submit a two-to-three-page autobiography. The interview, at which one or both parents must be present, cannot be scheduled until the school receives the application and autobiography.

HISTORY

Windward School is a not-for-profit, co-educational, college-preparatory day school founded in 1971 through the determined efforts of Shirley Windward, a well-known educator and writer.

AT A GLANCE

APPLICATION DEADLINE	December 11
OPEN HOUSES	October, December, February
BEFORE AND AFTER SCHOOL CARE	No
ISEE TESTING	Required for Applicants
UNIFORMS	No
SUMMER SCHOOL	No
SEE MAP	D on page 255

PUBLIC SCHOOL: ALTERNATIVE PROGRAMS

Families who want to use the Los Angeles Public School System but want a higher quality education, i.e. schools with smaller classses, special teacing appraoches, and subject-specific programs often choose one of the following:

CHARTER SCHOOLS

Charter Schools represent the opportunity to examine practices and develop structures that can help solve the many challenges facing schools in the Los Angeles Unified School District and the greater educational community.

Mission Statement from Los Angeles Unified School District:

The Los Angeles Unified School District view charter schools as part of the District's family and as an asset from which we can learn. Therefore, the Los Angeles Unified School District will encourage and nurture the development and continuation of charter schools that are accountable for improved student learning and that can:

Provide possible solutions to urban school challenges through practices that can:

- Ease the shortage of school facilities and seat space.
- Narrow the achievement gap among students of various backgrounds.
- Increase responsible parent and student involvement in learning.
- Improve teacher quality and performance evaluation systems.
- Provide data to help identify and evaluate issues that affect quality educational programs and student learning and achievement.
- Serve as laboratories to test, demonstrate and disseminate ideas that can promote better educational practices.
- Provide an additional educational option for parents.

Charter Schools are public schools that have received charters from local Boards of Education. In our case, The Los Angeles School District (LAUSD) Board of Education. The school district guides each charter, but the school is free from the rules and regulations that govern standard public schools. In plain English, Charter schools can be started by anyone-outsiders with a vision, parents, teachers, anyone who can win approval from the local school board, and given the demographic trends, the LAUSD will feel pressured to approve lots of new charter proposals. If some of you parents banded together and decided to open one, I bet you could!

That was the case with one of the first charter schools in California, The Los Angeles Open Charter School. It was opened in 1993 by a group of parents and teachers who wanted an alternative to the 'back to basics' approach that dominated the district at that time. They wanted to model their school on the principals of Jerome Bruner and the practices of the English elementary schools. By applying these principals, the school has become the premier charter school in the Los Angeles area. Getting in is tough, there are far more applications than spaces.

Charter schools are still very much in their infancy. The first charter school opened 26 years ago in St. Paul, Minn. There are now more than 400 charter schools in California and nearly 2,700 nationwide. They are required to participate in the statewide assessment test, called the STAR (Standardized Testing and Reporting) program. The law also requires that a public charter school be nonsectarian in its programs, admissions policies, employment practices, and all other operations. Each of these schools has a special focus like the arts, multiculturalism, military discipline or just good old rigid academics.

Social Justice is the focus of the most recently opened charter school in the mid-Wilshire district-The Leadership Academy. The school rents space at the Immanuel Presbyterian Church near the old Ambassador Hotel on Wilshire Boulevard. This year-old school is the vision of the school's founders, Roger Lowenstein, a 60-year old former attorney-turned TV writer, and Susanne Coie, a 33-year old teacher. Lowenstein built an impressive network of backers. Among them are Steve Tish and his wife, who have pledged $250,000 over five years and Lowenstein, who put $200,000 of his own money in.

The mid-Wilshire district is a very densely populated area where the public middle schools bulge with as many as 3,400 students. The high school has about 5,500 students, which is among the nations largest. Because of over-crowding, 900 high school students and 1,500 middle school students are bused from the area to the western San Fernando Valley. The good news is that the LAUSD plans to build 79 new schools and expand 80 others during the next six years. In addition to these regular public schools, the district expects to add at least 100, possibly 200, more charter schools to the 51 already operating. If you have a newborn or are just thinking about starting a family, this is the time to get involved-hell, even if you're single and still in high school! It's never too early to begin laying the foundations for your child's education.

We were there at the outset, one of our first families to show our support by turning up at every meeting. Because of that, I got my name down near the top of the list and was as good as guaranteed a place. If you're interested in a charter school for your child, I reccomend that you participate early on. Show your enthusiasm, put your hand up, and ask questions. They want parents like that involved. But I also caution you to do your homework and find out what your teachers' credentials are. Several teachers at The Leadership Academy were teaching subjects they had never taught before. I don't know about you, but I don't want my child being used as a guinea pig while they iron out those sort of problems!

However, what a charter school does offer is educational niche marketing, in the form of a specialty that might appeal to you and your child. So if you're interested, you can attend one of the monthly development meetings to find out more about starting your own charter school.

The Charter Schools Office will continue to hold monthly orientation meetings for potential Charter School Developers. The meetings are held at:

333 South Beaudry Avenue, 25th Floor, Room 102, Los Angeles, California 90017

For more Information call (213) 241-4625 or visit their website at: www.LAUSD.net/charterschools

All it takes is a determined group of parents and educators to open a Charter School, and that is what happened with the Larchmont Charter. The school opened in 2005 with 100 children in grades K-2nd. Larchmont Charter now goes all the way through middle school, and is operating on three separate campuses.

All three schools have modeled themselves after the Open Charter School, one of the most acclaimed public elementary schools in California. So grab your 'Choices' catalog and look for these schools. You can visit all three schools through the www.LAUSD.net/charterschools website.

Here are some Charter Schools I would recommend taking a closer look at. You can find out more by visiting:

www.ccsa.org

Camino Nuevo Charter Academy

Burlington site, Los Angeles• Opened August 2000 • Grades K-5 • Enrollment 280

Camino Nuevo Charter Academy

Town House site, Los Angeles • Opened August 2000 • Grades K-5 • Enrollment 130

Camino Nuevo Charter Middle Academy

Harvard site, Los Angeles • Opened August 2001

CHIME Charter School

Woodland Hills • Opened 2001 • Grades K-5 • Enrollment 110

Kenter Canyon LEARN/Charter School

Los Angeles • Opened 1993 • Grades K-5 • Enrollment 435

Larchmont Charter

Hollywood • Opened 2005 • Grades K-8 • Enrollment 500

Los Angeles Leadership Academy

Los Angeles • Opened 2002 • Grades 6-7 • Enrollment 130

Marquez Charter School

Pacific Palisades • Opened 1993 • Grades K-5 • Enrollment 663

The Open Charter Magnet School

Los Angeles • Opened 1993 • Grades K-5 • Enrollment 364

Paul Revere Charter Middle School

Los Angeles • Opened 1995 • Grades 6-8 • Enrollment 1982

Tom Bradley Environmental Science & Humanities Magnet: Crenshaw/Dorsey

Los Angeles • Opened 1999 • Grades K-5 • Enrollment 694

Westwood Charter School

Los Angeles • Opened 1993 • Grades K-5 • Enrollment 750

Westwood Charter School

Westwood • Opened 2001 • Grades K-12 • Enrollment 400

Santa Monica Boulevard Community Charter School

Hollywood • Opened 2002 • Grades K-5 • Enrollment 1,299

MAGNET SCHOOLS

You can pick up a Magnet School Directory (known as the 'Choices' catalog) at any public school office, local district offices, and 73 branches of the Los Angeles Public Library. They are usually available by the beginning of November, with a deadline in the middle of December. Alternatively, you can visit **eChoices.lausd.net** and apply online. Here is a brief description of how the program works:

Magnet schools are set up for integration purposes and are governed by the Los Angeles Unified School District (LAUSD). These programs are special learning centers for students living within LAUSD. There are two types of magnets. One type centers on a particular subject specialty such as math, science, performing arts, or business. The other type uses a special teaching approach such as alternative, gifted or fundamental.

Some magnets involve the entire school, so everyone attending is part of the magnet program. In others, the magnet program is a school within a school, and exists separately within a normal Los Angeles Public school. There are magnet programs for gifted/high ability children, and these require special testing before a child may apply. There are also Highly Gifted Magnets which require students to meet the criteria of 95 percent on an intellectual assessment administered by the LAUSD Psychological Services branch.

Magnets have smaller classes, and they receive additional funds for special activities, facilities, and labs. Many magnet programs work hand-in-hand with local universities and businesses.

There are 155 magnet programs located all over Los Angeles. You apply by submitting an application, but this is not to say that magnets are easy to get into. A computer picks from the applicant pool looking for a balanced ethnic mix, equally represented socio-economic backgrounds and geographic locations so you can put your letters of recommendation away.

Here is how the computer processes the application. Once all the information on the application is verified, the computer automatically assigns each applicant a priority, according to the following criteria:

a) (12 points) Students who are eligible to matriculate (graduate) from one magnet program to another.
b) (4 points) Students whose resident LAUSD schools are designated as overcrowded schools.
c) (4 points) Students whose resident LAUDS schools are designated predominantly Hispanic, Black, Asian or Other Non-Anglo.
d) (4 points each year) Students on magnet waiting lists for the current and/or last two years. Priority credit is given for each of these three years a student has been on an official magnet waiting list.
e) (3 points) Students with a brother or sister continuing at the same magnet.

Applications are selected at random; yours will receive priority depending on how many points you have, the number of openings at your school of choice, and the number of applicants for that grade and race/ethnicity category.

Here's a trick-if you currently have a child in a private school but want to look at a magnet for the future, you can begin 'earning' points by applying every year. Choose a school where you are unlikely to get in (i.e., loads of applicants and not nearly enough spaces). This way, in a couple of years when you're ready to move your child, you will have:

a) Enough points, and
b) Carefully chosen a school that you have a good chance to get into.

For more information about magnet programs, call the Office of Student Integration Services in Los Angeles at:

(213) 625-4177 or (213) 625-6572

For information on Gifted and Talented Education program (G.A.T.E.) call:

Los Angeles (213) 625-6500
San Fernando Valley (818) 782-2306

ACCREDITATION/MEMBERSHIP CODES*

AEGUS	Association for Educating Gifted Underachieving Students
AMS	American Montessori Society
AWSNA	American Waldorf Schools of North America
BJE	Bureau of Jewish Education
CAGC	The California Association of Gifted Children
CAIS	The California Association of Independent Schools
CASE	The Council for the Advancement of Support in Education
CHADD	Children & Adults with Attention Deficit/Hyperactivity Disorder
CEEB	College Entrance Examination Board
CIF	California Interscholastic Federation
CLS	Cum Laude Society
CRIS	The Council for Religion in Independent Schools
CSF	California Scholarship Federation
ERB	Educational Records Bureau
FCE	Friends Council on Education
ISAMA	Independent School Alliance for Schools Minority Affairs
ISM	Independent School Management
LABJE	The L.A. Bureau of Jewish Education
LACS	Los Angeles Commission on Schools
LACSS	Los Angeles Consortium of Secondary Schools
LAD	Learning Disabilities Association
NACAC	The National Association of College Admissions Counselors
NAES	The National Association of Episcopal Schools
NAEYC	The National Association for the Education of Young Children
NAGC	The National Association of Gifted Children
NAIS	The National Association of Independent Schools
NAPSG	The National Association of Principles of Schools for Girls
NCGS	The National Coalition of Girl's Schools
NIPSA	The National Independent Private School Association
SCCC	Studio City Chamber of Commerce
SKWLD	Smart Kids With Learning Disabilities
SSDSA	Solomon Schechter Day School Association
WASC	The Western Association of Schools and Colleges

*Please note:
The author has made every effort to list the acronyms used by the schools in this guide; on occasion, for the sake of space, we have made up acronyms for organizations.

TABLE OF SCHOOLS BY PHILOSOPHY

TRADITIONAL

Archer School for Girls
Berkeley Hall
Brawerman
Brentwood
Buckley
Campbell Hall
Carlthorp
Calvary Christian
Chadwick
Chandler
Chaminade
Christ the King
Clairbourn
Crespi
Crestview
Crossroads
Curtis
Flintridge Prep
Flintridge Sacred Heart Academy

Immaculate Heart
John Thomas Dye
Laurence School
LILA (French School)
Loyola High School
Le Lycee Francais
Marlborough
Marymount
Mayfield
Milken
Mirman
Notre Dame
Notre Dame H.S.
Oakwood
Pacific Hills
Page School
Pilgrim
Polytechnic
Providence

Ribet Academy
Sierra Canyon
St. Brendan
St. Francis
St. James Episcopal
St Mark's Episcopal
St. Matthew's Parish
Steven S. Wise
Turning Point
Viewpoint
Village School
Westridge
Wildwood
Wilshire
Windward

DEVELOPMENTAL

Adat Ari El
Brentwood
Center for Early Education
Country School
Crossroads
Echo Horizon
ESLA
Friends Western

Hollywood Schoolhosue
The Oaks
Oakwood
Pacific Oaks
Sequoyah
Seven Arrows
Temple Israel
UCLA Lab School

Vistamar
Walden
Waverly
Westmark
Westside Neighborhood School
Wildwood

PROGRESSIVE

Bridges
Children's Community School
ESLA

New Roads
PS 1 Elementary
Westland

Willows Community School

WALDORF

Pasadena Waldorf

CARDEN

Highpoint Academy

MONTESSORI

Glendale Montessori

Glendale Montessori Elementary

CPSIA information can be obtained
at www.ICGtesting.com
Printed in the USA
LVOW03s0335250117

522097LV00007B/209/P